Forrest Reid

FORREST REID IN 1935

FORREST REID;

A Portrait and a Study

by

Russell Burlingham

With an introduction by

Walter de la Mare

FABER AND FABER

24 Russell Square

London

First published in mcmliii
by Faber and Faber Limited
24 Russell Square London W.C.1
Printed in Great Britain by
Western Printing Services Limited, Bristol

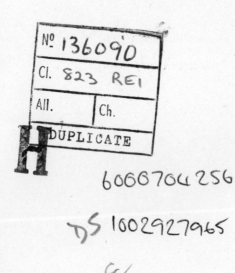

Contents

Illustrations

Introduction
by Walter de la Mare

As any reader of this book will at once discover there was not the least need for any word in it by way of an introduction. This, however, does not make it any less of the special pleasure it is to me to have the opportunity of saying how sure I feel that Forrest Reid would himself have greatly valued and delighted in it. And how could that be otherwise? It has qualities not only after his own heart but such as he abundantly shared—insight, understanding, sagacity, courage, candour, enthusiasm and a true affection. And every page of it is clearly the outcome of a most scrupulous care. Nor does this in the least strain Mr. Burlingham's own declaration on page 18 that Forrest Reid could 'never be roped in, no lasso was ever long enough'! I see again, as I read these words, that slow, familiar, mischievous smile stealing over his face—the long upper lip, the restless eyebrows, the slanting glance from those greenish, scrutinizing, unfaltering eyes.

He was in everything that he cared for most (and he cared for much) an unflagging devotee—from old woodcuts to Championship croquet, to street cricket, bull-dogs, story-technique, and, via Wagner, to Italian Opera. He exulted in the rigour of the game, whether it was Bridge or prosody. In the work of others, as, within its chosen range, of his own, he was a zealot—an eager and therefore exacting zealot. He loved this earthly life, and no less fully and fervently that of the imagination and the spirit. All this is explored and made clear in the pages that follow. And, no less, how devotedly he loved his friends, and they him; and

9

how honestly and openly he detested—what he detested. That
many of them should have recently expressed their affection
and admiration 'over the air' would have delighted him. That
Mr. Burlingham has still, in Time, so far to journey, and, in
ink, will then so much achieve, before even middle-age comes
within view, would have been no less a joy to him. For 'F. R.'
that battered abstraction, 'the younger generation', cast no shadow
of disquietude; nor, I am sure, had he any relish for the philan-
thropic phrase, 'juvenile delinquent'. You had to take him or
leave him as he was in himself; he could no other. Endlessly
active, he was yet a Dreamer; unflinchingly matter-of-fact, he
had drunk 'the milk of Paradise'; and the Greek Anthology was
in his bones. The belief he blessed most was the belief in goodness; and nothing could be more sovranly typical of his most
generous simplicity than the last few words of the first letter,
clean out of the bluest blue, that, on June 1, 1912, he wrote to
me, mentioning that he had reviewed one of my books:

'I do not suppose you take much interest in such things, but
if you should gather from them that I wish you well . . . that
is all I desire.'

And so it always was, throughout an unbroken friendship of half
my long lifetime: an inexhaustible patience (sadly needed); wise
counsel; life-giving encouragement; a selfless sharing of all he cared
for most. As for labour for love; for years and years we 'took in'
one another's proofs: his a model, mine a sort of literary mince-
meat. He never spared *any* pains, his counsel was beyond price.[1]

No wonder, then, this book rejoices me beyond words. No
longer will Edwin Muir's recent tribute and lament *both* hold
good concerning this 'true artist'—that 'his genius has never
been adequately examined'. And once discerned and established
in the minds of those possessing even a grain of it themselves,
the roots of genius pierce deep, and its fruit never fails.

[1] Concerning a certain Miss M., her old friend Mrs. Bowater, and their
evening pastimes, he declared emphatically, "You *can't* have Dummy Old
Maid. . . . I've played bridge myself with two Dummies, but Dummy Old
Maid is inconceivable. After all, Miss M. is intelligent. . . ." That delicious
"After all"!

Preface

I have not found this study an easy one to write. The analysis of works of art, of whatever kind, can never be a simple process, and in the case of Forrest Reid, where the art reaches a singular perfection, the task is less easy still.

Fish, newly landed, gleam for a few brief moments with all the hues of the rainbow. Soon after their struggles have ceased, the prismatic colours fade away. I have, all along, been only too conscious that my fish may have lost their radiance in the catching, and that (to vary the simile) what should have been an album of carefully chosen, carefully developed photographs may prove, in the outcome, to have been no more than a clumsy shuffling together of faded snapshots. Nevertheless, faded and ill-contrived as the views in many of these pages may appear, the book has been written in accordance with a belief (however inadequate) as to the proper functions of criticism. Briefly, this approach suggests that the choice of three possible tasks awaits the critic of literature, and that two only of them can possess validity. These three tasks are Illumination, Interpretation, and Interpenetration. By Interpenetration I mean, firstly, that process by which a critic endeavours to relate the subject of his writing to current topics of wide general concern far removed from the literary ones with which he is preoccupied; and secondly, the parallel pursuit by the critic, in the same enterprise, of equally impertinent but less generally shared concerns of his own. Between the upper and the nether millstones of these two conceptions of criticism the individual identity and the individual flavour of many persons and periods engaging the attention of our modern critics, are crushed into an unrecognizable mass. Each critic, having placed his subject between these millstones, proudly extricates for the inspection of his dispirited public a product which is, in essence, indistinguishable from his neighbours'. For the millstones have this virtue: everything offered to them they obligingly grind into an approximate but involuntary uniformity.

Against the fashionable but debilitating critical code of today—faintly political, faintly authoritarian, faintly philosophic, and barely at all literary—we may set the confession of faith made by a great critic of the recent past. 'Enthusiastic appreciation of letters', declared George Saintsbury, 'is the highest function of criticism.' To turn the pages of our critical weeklies, or to grapple with the more considered manifestoes and theorizings proffered by the reigning literary journalists and academes in their printed works, is to realize how far we have travelled since that statement was made a quarter of a century ago. Cleverness is up: and if ever any one thing were more certain than the evanescence of all mere cleverness, that something is its popularity today. Opinion in matters literary is fast ceasing to be thought of as a hand-made product: its place is taken by the slick and unappetizing, manufactured, austerity object turned out from the courts of Cambridge, the wireless studios of Portland Place, and the unnumbered seminars of the United States of America.

All this was foreseen by Saintsbury many years ago: quick to sense the change in temperature, he was no less apt in his analysis of the resulting climate; we were, he saw, in for a bad time, and that bad time is with us still. He looked out on the literary scene, and what met his eyes then—' . . . the pose of naughtiness . . . the pose of violence . . . the pose of distorted form; the pose of attempted mixture of science and literature; the pose of cosmopolitanism . . .'—meets ours today with undiminished vividness.

Saintsbury penetrated to the root of the trouble: style, he recognized, was 'essentially an aristocratic thing; . . . the spirit of today . . . is essentially democratic.'[1] Now the growth of an extreme democracy, which we are witnessing, has two effects on literature,

[1] *Collected Essays*, vol. iii, p. 73.

both clearly discernible in current criticism: firstly, it transforms the popularizers perforce into vulgarians; and after that it frightens the honest critic of letters, tumbling him into an attitude of proud and esoteric obscurantism. The broad view of letters falls into disrepute; the authority of scholars is (*pace* Dr. Leavis) inflated beyond all desert; and a horde of literary jerrybuilders run up their semi-detached erections on any site available and for whatever price they can command. In literature, no less than in wider spheres, 'things fall apart'; as Yeats prophesied, 'the centre cannot hold'. That is the predicament with which we are faced today.

Forrest Reid, the subject of this literary study, has been called 'the first Ulster novelist of European status'; and while the phrase is a true one it could also prove a misleading one to those unfamiliar with his work. For surely no novelist of comparable power and originality ever took as his chosen material experience drawn from so limited a field. There is very little of the European and scarcely more of the specifically Ulster in Forrest Reid's writing. Even in his own province, in his own city, Belfast, he himself was little more than a vaguely apprehended 'name'. He didn't climb, he never pushed, and he carefully avoided the company of all those empty, busy persons Newman once stigmatized as 'viewy men'. 'Forrest Reid', wrote one of his Irish friends after his death, 'was most brave. He went through difficult times, he was ignored, sometimes actively disliked, by the philistines who were numerous in the city where he lived. He wasn't bitter, he stayed quiet ... the philistines ... were left out of account; he did not mention them; *except* to say that he rather liked the general run of them.' He steered an even course.

> *Though fast youth's glorious fable flies,*
> *View not the world with worldling's eyes;*
> *Nor turn with weather of the time.*

To Swinburne all artists were 'bad, or mad, or sick' but none of these adjectives ever applied to Forrest Reid. Melville's precept represented his own attitude. Yet his temperament, though buoyant and ironical, was equally never a sanguine one. His writings are shot through with a poetic melancholy, the whole cast of his mind was essentially poetic, and the books are informed with a spirit which is lyrical, elegiac, rhythmic, even though their form was cast in the 'other harmony' of prose.

I have in this study carefully eschewed any concessions to that cant psychological approach which, once so widely applauded, counts perhaps less practitioners today than it did even a decade ago. Few men can have understood themselves better than Forrest Reid—*Apostate* and *Private Road* make that sufficiently clear—and there is small evidence, either in his books or in the reports of his friends, that an interpretation of his character in the light of Freudian or Jungian theories would produce any useful or significant additions to those facts which he already knew and admitted: the influence of his nurse Emma and the 'King Charles's head' among them. Human character and human motivation are continually revealing a richness and depth, an inconsistency and an unexpectedness, greater than is ever dreamt of in the psychologists' philosophy.

Youth was the constant subject of Forrest Reid's writing and thought, and the understanding of youth—sympathetic, ironical, and uncannily intuitive—the key to his achievement. Over all his best work there floats a golden mist of beauty; and just as Chardin transmuted with his brush the sober, commonplace domestic events which his paintings depict into studies of quietly unforgettable depth and plangency, so Forrest Reid possessed the same ability of investing *his* subject 'with the glamour of the moment in which his imagination was stirred'.[1]

And behind the acute sense of beauty there lay a visionary streak. 'My work'— Forrest Reid might have used these words of Morris's—'my work is the embodiment of dreams, to bring before men's eyes the image of the thing my heart is filled with.' Like Narcissus—for by far the greater part of his fiction took shape as the re-creation of his own experiences—he gazed and gazed at the reflection which met his eyes in the mirror of the

[1] Ernest Boyd.

past over which he pondered so deeply. To his work there clings a paradoxical quality: his themes were restricted, but they were never shallow ones; his outlook was limited, but without narrowness; his responses selective, yet not exclusive, unexpected but never incongruous. He brought to literature something new, creating a world unlike any world that has been created before, a vision and a perception of beauty previously unexpressed. He was a true member of that numerically inconsiderable band of rare spirits, a handful in the brightest generation, who quietly and almost unnoticed enrich the lives and imaginations of others through the uncovering of fresh aspects of truth and of moral and ideal beauty.

In making my acknowledgements my first and greatest debt is to Mr. Stephen Gilbert, Forrest Reid's friend and literary executor. By his kindness I have been enabled to examine the unpublished papers and notebooks left by Forrest Reid, and a great deal of the correspondence which he received. Mr. Gilbert's unfailing hospitality made my visit to Ireland as enjoyable as it was memorable.

My obligations to Mr. S. Knox Cunningham and to Mr. J. N. Hart are twofold. Not only did they, with rare candour, allow me ready access to all the many letters received by both of them from Forrest Reid,[1] but they also supplemented many personal kindnesses by vivid recollections of his personality and activities. The information I have gained from them has been of the very greatest help to me in attempting to give some picture of Forrest Reid as he appeared to his friends, and without their co-operation this little study would have been sadly incomplete. Mr. Hart is in addition the owner of a nobly bound collection of Forrest Reid's later manuscripts, and it is through his kindness that the facsimiles on pages 168-9 are included. In addition, Mr. Gilbert, Mr. Hart, and Mr. Knox Cunningham have each read my book in typescript. Their patience, thoroughness, and attention to detail have saved me from many errors, and I have been glad (while

---

[1] It is greatly to be hoped that the project of a selection from Forrest Reid's letters—with an accompanying personal memoir—will reach fruition.

retaining responsibility for all the opinions expressed) to adopt a large number of improvements which they have suggested. To each of them I should like to take this opportunity of expressing my very grateful and very sincere thanks for the ungrudging help and encouragement they have extended to me while I have been writing this book.

I have also to thank many of Forrest Reid's friends in Ireland, including Mr. R. J. Wright, of Newtownards, who drew on a large stock of memories extending over many years, to my great advantage; Mr. Robin Perry, of Bangor, Co. Down; Mrs. Lowry, of Lennoxvale, Belfast; Mr. G. Moorehead Fitzpatrick, of Dublin; and others.

I must also acknowledge my gratitude to Mr. John Sparrow for his kindness in allowing me to see the script of the broadcast talk he gave shortly after Forrest Reid's death; to Mr. George Buchanan, of Limavady, for a similar kindness, and for reading my book in typescript; to Miss Doreen Sheridan, for her patience and care in reading the proofs of this, as of Forrest Reid's own later books; to Mr. Donald G. Brien, of Ardmore, Pennsylvania, who has given me much enthusiastic help, and particularly in connexion with bibliographical points relating to the American editions of Forrest Reid's books, which are listed in the Appendix; to Dr. W. G. Frackleton, of Belfast, for his kindness and care in supplying details about Forrest Reid's health and the course of his final illness; and to Mrs. Apps, of the Croquet Association, for a similar service in connexion with Forrest Reid's achievements as a croquet player. Mr. Norman Douglas kindly allowed me to make use of the extract from a letter to Forrest Reid, quoted on p. 218. I am also grateful to my friend Mr. Patrick Gardiner for several useful suggestions as to presentation and arrangement, which I have adopted, and for stimulating criticisms and discussion.

Acknowledgements are also due to Messrs. Edward Arnold and Co., Messrs. Collins, Sons and Co., Ltd., Messrs. Martin Secker and Warburg, Ltd., and Messrs. Faber and Faber, Ltd., for permission to quote from those books by Forrest Reid which respectively they published.

I

Forrest Reid

*O that I might have my request; and that God would grant me
the thing that I long for!*

JOB

'The last thing one settles in writing a book', says Pascal in his *Pensées*, 'is what one should put in first.' A remark from this somewhat unexpected quarter suggests itself while turning over in one's mind some prefatory words for a book about Forrest Reid; for the man was as unusual, as idiosyncratic, as his books.

About his life it is difficult to speak briefly. Though he passed the greater part of it in Northern Ireland, shunning the literary coteries, he was never out of touch, and enjoyed the friendship, indeed devotion, of an ever-widening circle of very dissimilar friends. Perhaps it was just because most of these friends were not literary that, among the gossiping, he gained the reputation of being a recluse: modish literary circles are quick to take their revenge on the nonconformists who live out of their earshot. For in fact nothing could have been further from the truth. But the virtues that counted with him were the private virtues. 'To those who knew and loved him,' wrote one of his oldest friends after his death, 'he was more than a creator of books.' 'No man', declared another, 'ever gave more or set a higher value on friendship, and when he gave his it was lasting.'

It was his misfortune that so much of his work had to be written at a time when to place emphasis on those virtues was to court neglect. Other voices—loud, assertive, strident—held the stage, and he had to be content with a place in the wings. Not that he was really disappointed at being crowded out; because it was really the wings that all along he preferred—you saw so much more of the play. But his belief in individuals and scepticism about 'movements', coupled with his utterly uncompromising independence of outlook, explain his relation to the literary life of his time. 'Whether Ireland is to have a literature or not,' he declared in his book on Yeats (written when the Irish revival was still at its height), 'depends upon whether she can evolve an artistic conscience,—at present she has only a political one.' He was always quick to taste the pill beneath the jam: 'a spirit of patriotism', he pointed out, 'is but a blind guide in questions of aesthetics.' Cliques, politics, regionalism—activities which sooner or later attract most writers, and so often spoil their work—all these left him coldly suspicious, he could never be roped in, no lasso was ever long enough. Internationalism, committee work, 'progressives', organizers—that sort of thing left him bored and distrustful. The braying and self-contradictions of imperfectly educated politicians, the facile patter of those ever accustomed to prescribing fresh patent medicines for the body politic —these apparently permanent characteristics of modern society he viewed with the irony and detachment befitting any sensitive and thoughtful human being.

But to his many friends the representation of him as a hermit was simply grotesque. He was the most sociable of men, relying on his friends to an extent which they sometimes failed to realize. He could be 'difficult'—desperately difficult—and, never far beneath the surface, there lurked a kind of urchin mischievousness which sometimes disconcerted the unwary. But though he was not awed by reputations, he never showed truculence, nor egoism save of the most innocent description. His croquet companions, countless boys of all ages and outlooks, old friends in Ireland he had known for the greater part of his life—these formed a wide outer circle of acquaintance. Rather closer in, there was a much smaller circle of devoted and much-loved intimates. Some of these—such as Mrs. Workman or Arthur Greeves, or, later, Robin Perry—had their homes in Ireland. A few, like Knox Cunningham, George Buchanan or J. N. Bryson, were Ulster born

yet usually lived and worked elsewhere. But his oldest and closest
friends were for the most part in England. It was his custom to
come over from Ireland once or twice a year, and a tour would
then ensue, during which he would stay at Taplow with Walter
de la Mare, near Potters Bar with J. N. Hart, and with E. M.
Forster at the foot of the North Downs, at Abinger.

To these small progresses he looked forward dearly, but
although attempts were often enough made—attempts in which
de la Mare was usually the prime mover—to persuade him to
settle in England, these were never successful. His friends' most
characteristic memories are of him at his own home in Ireland,
'sitting in the firelight, a book on his knee, talking with enthusiasm on some favourite subject, pausing now and again to knock
out his pipe and driving home his more subtle points with that
curious Puck-like twitch of his eyebrows.' He stuck to Belfast.
There were his roots, there, or thereabouts, the sources of his
inspiration, and these things, as he well knew, a creative writer
neglects at his peril.

Forrest Reid was of middle height and rather stockily built,
his movements emphatic rather than graceful. But it was his face
which attracted your attention: not handsome indeed, even perhaps rather ugly, but ugly in a friendly, blunt-featured, attractive
fashion. Square high forehead, kindly, ironical eyes, the nose
rather broad, and the Ulsterman's long sardonic upper lip—these
were the characteristics which first struck those who met him.
In middle life it was his habit to wear pince-nez and, before he
started using the normal horn-rimmed glasses, this gave him an
aspect careful and almost professorial, belying the great natural
force in his features. His clothes were a little old-fashioned, and
for the most part he wore the familiar, narrow, rather short blue
suit with baggy pockets and something of the air of outworn
schooldays about it.

For many years before his death Forrest Reid lived in a small
house in Ormiston Crescent, on the outskirts of Belfast. Ormiston
Crescent isn't really a crescent at all, just a modest street of semi-

detached houses, with small strips of garden, adjoining the road which runs out to Newtownards. Here he lived quite alone, doing his own domestic work for the most part, with occasional help; living a very simple and frugal but absolutely independent life of his own, a life centring round his writing, his friends, his books, and confined within the limits of two small bedrooms, a study, a kitchen and a bathroom.

He liked usually to do his writing in the mornings, and after lunch he would walk into the country, which was never far away, or perhaps stroll up to visit his friend Mrs. Workman who lived nearby at The Moat, a large walled house with extensive grounds. In the evening he would write again, or read, or perhaps play over some of his big collection of gramophone records. Friends would call, he would call on friends. Occasionally youthful writers would come by appointment, in search of advice or help. Even more youthful stamp-collectors, cricketers, and other inhabitants of the district would arrive, without appointment, armed with pressing invitations to participate in some impending event of excessively local significance. He played bridge; he played croquet. There were the trips to England, fewer as time went on, and summer holidays on the coast in Donegal or County Down alone or with some chosen friend. Small things such as these made up his life, and in this fashion its even tenor continued. One of his last and keenest pleasures was the publication of *The Landslide*, Stephen Gilbert's first novel, in which he had taken a close interest. This delicate and beautiful fantasy, dedicated to himself from 'his friend and pupil', delighted him. In the summer of 1946, when he was in his seventy-first year, he began to suffer from a complaint (taking the form of an inflammation of the bowel) which had not troubled him since childhood. He spoke in *Apostate* of the sharp bout of illness he then experienced: it seems that this attack had been tubercular in origin and now, long latent, it had struck again.[1] There was discomfort and, as he grew

---

[1] Dr. Frackleton, his physician, writes: '. . . the possible diagnoses [of the early attack] are either an acute appendix or an acute inflammation of tuberculous glands. . . .

weaker, pain, but few of his friends realized how close the end
was, and when, in the following December, it became apparent
that he had a short time to live, it was too late. He died at Warren-
point, on the coast of County Down near Newcastle and close to
the scene of so much of his writing, in the house belonging to the
widow of his old friend James Rutherford, on 4th January 1947.
Above his grave, on high ground in the Dundonald cemetery
close outside Belfast, stands a headstone bearing the simple
inscription 'Forrest Reid, 1875–1947'.

It is chiefly through his letters that we catch glimpses of his
way of life in these later years. He was a delightful letter-writer,
and his beautifully clear hand, open and regular and unhurried
(for all his life he wrote with the old-fashioned dipping pen),
made the letters as easy to read as they were pleasant to receive.[1]
One of his chief enjoyments was keeping his friends posted
with humorous, half-cryptic little details about the novels he
was writing. To Knox Cunningham, who had inquired about
the progress of *Young Tom*, he sent a long and delightful letter
about Tom, whimsically couched in the present tense. And J. N.
Hart was similarly made acquainted with the earlier Tom book,
The Retreat. This correspondent had evidently been perplexed by

---

'[In] May 1946 . . . he began to have attacks of abdominal pain and sickness.
Examination . . . revealed a tender swelling on the right side of the abdomen,
and X-ray examination proved this to be a mass of calcified glands. Calcified
glands are generally accepted as being tuberculous in origin.

'From this time on he deteriorated steadily in health. . . . His final illness was
almost certainly an exacerbation of a latent tuberculosis leading to a tuberculous peritonitis. . . .

'From a medical standpoint'—Dr. Frackleton adds—'his illness is of interest.
Many men of genius have, of course, suffered from tuberculosis—one thinks
off-hand of Keats, Sir Walter Scott and R.L.S. It has been suggested that all
through life these geniuses were stimulated mentally by the mild toxaemia and
slight rises of temperature due to the toxins of tuberculosis.'

[1] Henry James, in his first letter (20 December, 1900), made gratified reference to 'a legibility so exquisite and admirable.' As James himself acknowledged, this was a compliment difficult to reciprocate.

an earlier report of the novel's title, for 'I expect you thought it was one of my usual War books'—Forrest Reid explained on a postcard—

'But the full title is

The Retreat
or The Machinations of Henry.

'The "Retreat" is Vaughan's (see Anthologies), and Henry is a cat. Does that sound more like it?'

He had the born letter-writer's gift of putting himself directly down on the paper in front of him; so that what his friends received was not a letter from Forrest, but an extension *of* Forrest, part of his personality in an envelope. Thackeray's test—that the reader of the letter must be able to hear the voice of its writer —he passed triumphantly. Intimacy was always successfully achieved, here even more, perhaps, than in the novels. Some of the touches are altogether characteristic. 'Did I ever tell you of the wonderful bathes I used to have in the Lido?' he wrote to one of his friends:

'Last night . . . I renewed this experience. The water was delightfully warm, and I swam slowly and gracefully to and fro under the soft blue Venetian skies, basking in a lazy *dolce far niente*. (Keeping up my Italian, as you see.) But, as the poet Aeschylos has truly said, "Alas for mortal matters! Happy-for-tuned—why any shade would twin them"; and on awaking I discovered that I was indeed afloat on warm waters, the stopper of my indiarubber bag . . . having betrayed me. . . . All today I have fancied a rheumatic chill to be hanging about me; at any rate I don't feel in the least Venetian, but very much the inhabitant of a "northern shore".'

Sometimes it is a snatch of autobiography which provides the occasion for some unexpected comment or speculation:

' . . . what must have been either my first or very nearly my first novel was called *Tom Vere*, and was an adventure yarn, the scene laid in the tropics, and the main incident a fight to the death between the hero and an army of venomous spiders—tarantulas. I was about eleven when I wrote this book, and was bitterly disappointed because I couldn't spin out the adventures even to fill an ordinary exercise book. And there were illustrations too, or perhaps only one illustration, a full-page portrait of the dauntless youth. If one could possibly collect the material, a most enthralling essay might be written on the subject of these lost books, or ghosts of books. I don't mean *Tom Vere*, but more mature efforts, such as the novel of which Byron wrote the first chapter and then chucked it, or Pater's novel of modern life, though in Pater's case he published the solitary chapter as *The Child in the House*. And there must be tons of others. . . .'

Often it is no more than sheer good spirits, as in the following little anecdote in one of his letters:

'It is Sunday morning, bright and uncommonly cold.

Unbroken silence:
Save now and then, from very far away
The barking of a dog.

'They are the only lines I remember from my Cambridge Prize Poem on *Edward the Second*; and "when I crumble" even that last glimmer will have vanished. So perish masterpieces, and so are "inglorious Miltons" blighted, and take to writing prose chronicles of the adventures of small boys. When is a prize poem not a prize poem? When it doesn't get a prize, I suppose, which was the fate of mine. It was unprized even by its author, and the only copy was never returned by the judges. All the same, I never hear the distant barking of a dog without those lines floating back into memory, so that, considering all I have forgotten of Homer, Shakespeare, Milton and every poet since, something of their quality may be divined. . . .'

The incident itself is nothing; everything depends on the charm, the gaiety, and the spontaneity with which the trifle is recounted.

The multitude of chance contacts which filled up the corners of his life were treated with the same ironical tolerance that is such an integral part of the novels:

'"Why should Eton be picked out for bombing?" someone had demanded one afternoon. The partner with whom I was playing bridge this afternoon explained to us that it was because the last war was said to have been won on the playing fields of Eton. . . . These Saturday bridgings I enjoy. The conversation is not usually so high-brow as the example quoted, nor is the play of a standard that need daunt the neophyte. Still the atmosphere is friendly and homely and pleasant.'

Another pastime, a very simple one of which he never grew tired, was jigsaws. The ingenuity, and the gradually increasing excitement of seeing the picture form itself piece by piece, appealed to the child in him that was never far beneath the surface. 'The jig is a great one and frightfully hard. I must have put in twelve hours at it, yet have only done a bit of the sky . . . it really is a corker.'

This childlike immediacy of response made him able to enjoy trifles like these with a sort of self-forgetful glee. He loved fires. Readers of *The Retreat* will remember the wonderful fire towards the end of that novel, made by Tom and Pascoe, and the havoc it caused. Here is another:

'This afternoon I spent . . . with three woodcutters, three little boys, three little girls, and the mother of some of them . . . We had an enormous and glorious bonfire, the crackle and flame of which was what first drew me to the scene, as moths are drawn by lighted lamps. The fire, about eight feet high and more than that in circumference, blazed continuously, and we cut down a fine big tree and lopped the branches of others, and sheltered when a shower of hail came on, and emerged again with the returning sun. . . .'

Late in life, when he was over fifty, he suddenly started to collect stamps. This was to provide an endless source of pleasure, for just as when he had begun to collect 'Sixties woodcuts 'practically everything is a "find"'. He threw himself into the new activity, and soon was writing proudly to J. N. Hart: 'I've got 6,421 stamps. I'm afraid it's rather childish to have ascertained the exact number, but there it is.' Amusing contretemps often arose: 'I have been exchanging what he calls "doublets" with a German named Rotter who lives in Berlin,' he writes in 1938. 'His name is quite suitable. He began very well by sending me some quite good stamps, but has steadily been deteriorating, and the last lot were full of holes, torn perforations, corners off, etc. . . . I've written to tell Rotter I don't collect fragments. . . .'

One of the great advantages of stamp-collecting was the opportunity it gave him of meeting small boys on equal terms. 'I had a visit from a very youthful philatelist the other morning, who in the course of showing me his album asked me, if Germany was a British colony? I replied "Not yet. . . ."' J. N. Hart remembers a fête in the grounds of his house, in preparation for which Forrest Reid spent the previous afternoon happily absorbed in filling small envelopes with stamps as prizes for the children.

The war came as a shock, but he soon accustomed himself to regarding the conditions imposed by war-time as more of a challenge than the threats of the actual enemy. He hated the black-out —for he didn't see easily in the dark—and he hated the idea of air-raids. 'We had an air-raid warning the other morning, which, as it was announced beforehand in the newspapers [which he never read], took in nobody but myself. And I did nothing but stare out of the window though I knew all the precautions that ought to be taken. I hoped it would be gas and not a noise—that was all.' As the years passed he began to be apprehensive and decided to take belated safety measures: 'Stephen [Gilbert] and I' —he wrote in 1942—'spent a couple of evenings rigging up a . . . shelter in the kitchen—no light work, though Stephen did most of it. I've even a few books there, so if I perish my remains will be found among first editions and "association copies". The latter, in fact, ought to acquire an additional "associational" value. . . .'

The war stopped his reviewing, and this with later publishing difficulties meant a good deal of enforced idleness. The gap he filled by a voracious course of reading. 'I am reading more than I have read since I was a boy' he wrote in October 1940, '—entirely old stuff—writing nothing.' Many old favourites were pulled down again, their appearance reviving nostalgic thoughts. These re-readings led to the idea of the Youth Shelf. He announced his plan in a letter to Knox Cunningham early in the war: 'I'm going to make a special shelf of books dealing with youth. To this end I've been re-reading all those I possess, school stories and others. The unworthy I shall weed out and have already rejected half a dozen. Hitler or no Hitler,' he ends, 'I'm going to lead my own life in my own way till it ends.' On this note of defiant individualism he turned his back on the war and immersed himself in these attractive schemes.

There were many other shelves besides the Youth Shelf, and books all over the house—books on the stairs, books in the bedrooms, even books in the kitchen; books everywhere, in fact, except the bathroom. His collection reflected his own tastes and no one else's, but it managed to be a remarkably comprehensive one as well. He loved the excitement of tracking down scarce books, and when he was in England he spent a good deal of his time hunting round the second-hand shops in search of rarities. 'Why does nobody write a novel about a book-collector?' he demanded one day. 'Here is an unhackneyed theme presenting considerable dramatic possibilities. Think of the tense excitement of the great sales, the suspense, the despairs, the triumphs; the wolf-like prowling among second-hand stalls and shops (old furniture shops should not be neglected), the stealthy smuggling home of treasures so that domestic criticism—always adverse—may not be aroused. Recklessness, envy, duplicity, pertinacity, the true collector knows them all—to say nothing of temptations to downright dishonesty. Every passion may be his except the one that novelists eternally harp upon. . . . I shall not get what I want; nor anything nearer to it, I suspect, than such a tale as *The Spoils of Poynton*. . . .' He had himself all the true collector's love of the mere physical aspect of books and the memories they stirred, as well as of their contents; writing to thank J. N. Hart for a gift of some novels by the now forgotten Victorian author W. E. Norris, of whom he was fond, he exclaimed: 'The sight of those fat green Bentley bindings recalled the days of my youth and filled me with joy. Nothing will ever alter my affection for that particular format—not outstandingly beautiful perhaps, but teeming with memories.'

He possessed a great deal of French literature, and a large collection of the classics, especially the Greek ones. These he seemed to prefer in French translations, which he thought rendered the conciseness of the originals more neatly than most English versions. But the real glories were the Henry James, the Yeats, and the de la Mare collections. Henry James and Forrest Reid never met, but the younger man always retained a kind of hero-worship for the older, an admiration for his artistry and courage that never flagged. 'Henry' (he was always 'Henry', *tout court*, to Forrest Reid) wrote enormously, and Forrest Reid's claim was to have read, not once only but three separate times, every line from that inexhaustible pen. This in itself was astonishing proof of his devotion and piety, but it was not all; for of this immense body of work he must himself have possessed very nearly a complete run, and among James's monumental output this included one item that had unique value. He refers to this item in *Private Road*:

'*Rejected Stories*, by Henry James, is a good-sized volume, and I imagine only one copy of it exists. These tales, buried in the files of extinct American periodicals, were not easy to acquire, but I acquired them, eighteen of them. The earliest tale, *The Story of a Year*, is dated March 1865. "In early May, two years ago, a young couple I wot of strolled homeward from an evening walk, a long ramble among the peaceful hills which inclosed their rustic home." The manner . . . is not precisely that of *The Golden Bowl*. Nevertheless, the tale is Henry's.'

(*Private Road*, p. 31.)

27

The Yeats and the de la Mare books had an added value because most of them were signed or presentation copies. Then, too, his 'Sixties books formed probably as complete a collection as one man can acquire single-handed. It included several very rare books: 'I searched for many years for a copy of George Mac-Donald's *Dealings with the Fairies*, illustrated by Arthur Hughes, and advertised for it more than once without getting a reply; but in the end, in a shop in Eastbourne, [it must have been during a croquet tournament] dumped on the floor among a heap of Sunday school prizes, I came upon a perfect copy which cost me ninepence.' (*Illustrators of the Sixties*, p. 7.)

Judged from the point of view of the strict collector, nurtured on 'points', first issues, and the other mysteries of strict bibliography, Forrest Reid's books were doubtless often imperfect. He did not make a fetish of details like these, and—which is perhaps more surprising—he did not insist on his books being in perfect condition. Many, in fact, were in a woebegone state. But, and in this unlike many greater collectors, he did know his books, and it is unlikely that any among them remained unread.

Boys often made appearances in the letters. He used to enjoy the casual contacts he made with youngsters in the neighbourhood. Often he joined in the impromptu games of cricket in Ormiston Crescent. 'Fred', he writes in answer to a correspondent's inquiry, 'is Fred McGivney, age about thirteen. . . . He looks as if he had Spanish blood in him—with that colouring, a broad brow, the nose perhaps a little coarse, the mouth perfect, and dark eyes gleaming with friendliness and the joy of animal life. In summer he runs about half-naked, with an open shirt and a pair of crumpled shorts.' With Desmond Montgomery he struck up another and a singularly pleasant relationship. Desmond, grandson of his old friend Mrs. Montgomery of Ballyhackamore House, was 'just the kind of boy I liked—toughish, self-reliant, fond of animals, and the best of pals—'. With him too Forrest Reid used to play cricket, and together they built and ignited the memorable bonfire described in *The Retreat*.

FORREST REID WITH DESMOND MONTGOMERY

Someone sent him a photograph which delighted him:

'The photograph of the little winter-bound boy is lovely—
don't lose the negative. Arthur[1] thinks you should have taken it
from much nearer at hand, but he is wrong. It is the surrounding
waste that gives him his isolation and the picture its atmosphere.
The soft black tree too helps. The thing is not only charming but
beautiful, and every time I look at it, it awakens faint sounds and
stirrings that must be the wings of the Muses, though they haven't
yet whispered a direct message.'

Lewis Carroll used to declare, 'I am fond of children, except
boys', but Forrest Reid was as amused by some little girls as he
was by their brothers. Such a child he once met while on holiday:

'I have played several games of clock golf with a little girl who
always expects to win the ninth hole because her age is nine. She
is a loquacious conversationalist and collects seagulls' eggs. I was
interested in this collection and it was some time before I discovered that she hadn't yet found any eggs, owing to the amazing
habit gulls have of building in inaccessible places. It is a Platonic
collection, existing in the idea only, and therefore perfect, but
on the other hand invisible. With two still smaller boys I dig in
the sands.'

The picture of himself which his letters paint is the same as that
produced by a reading of the books: ironical, independent, pre-
judiced, loyal, eccentric. Even in his small eccentricities he contrived to be unusual; he described his hatred of small shiny objects
—buttons, new coins—in *Apostate*; another curious trait was his
inability to sleep with a clock in the room. At one house where
he was a frequent guest the offending object would be found in
the morning placed neatly by his shoes outside the bedroom door.
He had also a taste for small practical jokes of a literary nature. In
Mr. Hart's copy of the special (and very scarce) offprint of *Minor
Fiction in the Eighties* Forrest Reid added a line from Beaumont
and Fletcher. 'O rare . . . rare' ran this apposite quotation; but,

[1] His friend Arthur Greeves. The 'little winter-bound boy' is the statue to
Charles Lamb in the Inner Temple Garden.

alas, it must be taken from an edition of the dramatists' own works which is even rarer, for the words occur in no known printed version. Another and even more successful ruse was the sentence he prefixed to *Brian Westby*. The author of this study himself has to admit somewhat ruefully that he conducted not a little research into the identity of the mysterious Yakovnin, to whom this quotation is attributed; and only the revelation of a chance remark brought that inquiry to an abrupt conclusion. The quotation, nevertheless, *is* impressive and provides, in fact, an important clue to the meaning of the novel; and having composed it Forrest Reid felt no compunction, indeed probably he experienced a stealthy joy, in placing it at the head of his book. Such quiet pieces of leg-pulling, especially when they could be accomplished with a grave face, he found very pleasant to perpetrate.

Forrest Reid had wide interests, and each was pursued with the enthusiasm whose particular quality of infectiousness only his friends knew about. He was, for instance, an energetic and life-long collector. He collected everything, insatiably; at first they were humble enough: short-lived hoards of matches, wallpapers, posters—even a natural-history museum which, left untended by its curator, disclosed a distressing tendency to spontaneous parturition. . . . But these early experiments developed later into more ambitious interests: first editions, 'Sixties woodcuts (on which he was a leading authority), old-master prints, gramophone records, even, later on, stamps. Of this acquisitive instinct, so strongly developed, some of his friends mildly disapproved. E. M. Forster, in a note accompanying a special copy of *A Passage to India*, ironically declared that he was pandering to the basest of his passions. Forrest Reid, in fact, was cut to no ordinary pattern; 'I enjoyed bridge, dog shows, playing in tournaments, book-hunting, print-collecting'; he had always, he declared, 'had a foot firmly planted in the Philistine world', had 'even been extremely happy at school, when, like Shelley and everybody else,' he 'ought to have been miserable.'

And, of course, many of the enthusiasms found their way into the novels. One was opera. He had gone to his first London opera

when he was still in the tea-trade. At this time he would have been
about nineteen.[1] Each summer, when he came over to England,
he and his friend J. N. Hart would usually be found in the gallery
at Covent Garden. At first it was German opera, but later his
taste veered: 'What about Italian ops?' he asks before the 1937
visit. '*Otello* and *Turandot* in particular.' And so, in *Following
Darkness*, it is natural that Peter should describe his first visit. It
was Gounod's *Faust*:

'With the end of the overture the lights were turned down. . . .
The sugary sweetness of the music had an almost hypnotic effect
upon me . . . and the ecstatic sensuality of the duet rapt me into
a world of love, where everything else was forgotten. It was all
utterly new to me; it thrilled me; it drowned me in erotic dreams
that swept me onward like the waves of the sea; and through all,
subconsciously, as I listened and watched, I was carrying on
another love-making of my own, with which Faust and Margaret
had nothing to do.

'. . . I resolved that I would go to the opera every night that
week . . . Between the acts I had eagerly studied my programme,
and the delightful, unfamiliar, romantic names, "Tannhäuser",
"Il Trovatore", "Aida", "Lohengrin", were like syrens singing
to me through the darkness, with an irresistible and passionate
sweetness.'

(*Following Darkness*, pp. 168–70.)

Another source of pleasure he found in the enjoyment of
painting. Though not a collector, he had always been interested
in pictures, and he showed in his writing a painter's eye for the
detail as well as for the broad effect of any natural scene. 'He told
me,' recalls J. N. Hart (with whom he used to visit the Academy
and the National Gallery), 'pictures had almost the same effect
on him as poetry.' His response to art, though determined by the
same instinctive sense of quality which pervaded his judgement of

[1] Throughout that first visit to London his only conversation (he related,
years after) was with the waiter in his hotel. This conjures up a picture reminis-
cent of David Copperfield's experience at Yarmouth.

books, was made largely from a literary standpoint that is discredited today; nevertheless the judgements rested on aesthetic premises, and though they might make concessions to sentiment, none was ever made to sentimentality. He set out his attitude towards this vexed topic in the introduction to *Illustrators of the Sixties*. It was sensible and unequivocal:

'The fact [he declared] that a picture may be devoid of aesthetic value and yet, because of some story or sentiment in it, give pleasure to those indifferent to form and colour, means nothing. If the sentiment is false or cheap it is bad, that is all. Take Ghirlandajo's famous portrait of the bottle-nosed old man and his grandson:— does not much of its charm lie in the relation of trust and affection that obviously exists between the old man and the child; lie, that is to say, in its sentiment? It is certainly there, the dreaded quality, yet, being the expression of an emotion that is true and fine, it becomes a part of the picture's beauty; in other words, possesses a definitely aesthetic value.'

(*Illustrators of the Sixties*, p. 2.)

Common sense, humanity, sensitiveness—these are the characteristics which distinguish his art criticism. And that his standing was not at one time altogether an amateur one is evidenced by the review—one of his earliest pieces to be published—of the Royal Hibernian Exhibition at Belfast in 1905.[1] He took this occasion to launch a severe condemnation of the facile yet moribund academic art of the day, with its ever-recurring motifs: 'the draped model who is sitting beside a well, and who is called Solitude, or Melancholy; the undraped model who is standing with her arms uplifted, and who is called Dawn, or Morning, or Innocence; the two models who are embracing each other in a room paved with marble, and who are called Hector and Andromache'; and he went on to administer some further strictures on the work of Sargent, then, of course, much admired in conventional artistic circles:

'There is a kind of hardness about most of Sargent's portraits.

[1] See Bibliography.

32

. . . They are clever, and American, and sometimes striking, but they are never very much deeper than the paint itself, and one can always smell the varnish.'

At Cambridge he had used his vacations to travel on the Continent, and among his papers there still exist copious notes—scribbled on the floridly embossed hotel notepaper—of his impressions in the galleries of Berlin, Prague, Wurzburg or Florence. He was fond of writing thumbnail sketches either on the spot or soon afterwards of paintings which attracted him. This practice early accustomed him to the necessity of seeking precise expression for his feelings, and also provided a useful literary exercise.

Another product of his leisure were the translations which he made from the Greek Anthology. The original title for these was to have been *Youth*, *Gods*, *Beasts*, *Earth*, and in that stage the book comprised renderings of many of the pieces in the Anthology. It was not until later that he decided to publish a selection only from the original book. He got a great deal of pleasure—craftsman's pleasure—out of this work:

'Could you look in on me at this moment you would find me surrounded by Greek texts and Latin texts and French texts, from which I try to hammer out an English text. It is work of the idlest kind, but no idler than playing the piano and more harmless than collecting butterflies. These little poems are indeed very like butterflies, brilliant, lovely, and only too perishable when one lays a coarse finger upon them. It is strange to think that not even Porson really knew how Greek words sounded. He could count the syllables, but how by the Greeks themselves the words were pronounced he could only guess. But we know the sound of English and it is amusing—in a jigsaw kind of way—to try to satisfy one's ear while keeping as far as possible to the literal meaning.'

Descending the scale, he was also a formidable croquet-player. The croquet world is an intimate one, a world where sooner or later everyone gets to know everybody else: there is no professionalism, and the players find themselves meeting each other again and again at succeeding tournaments. At this normally tranquil pastime he was, indeed, a lion, among the champions, and in that close and friendly fraternity Forrest Reid was acknowledged to be one of the leading players. The 'billiard eye and the chess brain' which the game demands were both his. The infrequent visits to England usually took the form of whirlwind tours, in impressive motor-cars belonging to his friends, the Frank Workmans, of the chief croquet tournaments. Nearly every summer in the twenties he would come over and several months would then be devoted to travelling from tournament to tournament: from Oxford to Winchester, Harrogate or Buxton to Cheltenham, Norwich or Brighton—preceded usually by the matches in Ireland earlier in the season. And more often than not a cup would await him at the end of an event, for he was nearly always up among the finalists and not infrequently the winner. 'Mr. Forrest Reid' remarked the correspondent of the *Croquet Gazette*, commenting on his victory at Winchester in 1926, 'gave a particularly convincing exhibition of croquet.'

So, as a complete contrast, here is a glimpse from that delightful early book *The Spring Song*. Here, it will be noted, the croquet is *not* so convincing:

'Grif wandered out on to the croquet-lawn, where the others were knocking balls against hoops in a desultory fashion, all playing at once, and arguing at the tops of their voices.

'"Where have *you* been?" asked Jim, trying to stand on the winning-peg, which at once sank over sideways, levering up a portion of the ground.

'" . . . I've been choosing my room," answered Grif.

'"What room?" With the handle of his mallet passed under his armpit and projecting well above his shoulder—for it was nearly as tall as himself—Jim took aim at a ball. "Shaved it! Shaved it!"

'Ann was indignant. "No you didn't, Jim; you never touched it."

"'I did. I shaved it.'"

"'You can't see it from here,' Grif went on. "And there's a swallow's nest under the window-sill.'"

(*The Spring Song*, pp. 19-20.)

Finally there was the love of animals. Chiefly domestic ones, but he did not insist on this. He recalled how, in far-off childhood days, he used to sally out for walks with his nurse to feed the stone lions in University Square. The lions have long since vanished from their proud position, have been relegated to an ungrateful obscurity,[1] but the humanizing impulse which prompted that act of Forrest Reid's remained with him all his life; for, like the Greeks, he extended this feeling of community even to the humblest creatures of the earth. Tom (in *Uncle Stephen*), scurrying along in the dusk on his first arrival at Kilbarron, keeps his eyes on the ground lest inadvertently he crush the snails in his pathway. This curiously touching idea was very typical of Forrest Reid, as it makes us love Tom at once, and love his creator for it also. So catholic was his taste that he even became—for an unexpectedly short period—the owner of a monkey. But it was dogs that he liked particularly. He enjoyed going to dog shows; he was the owner of, among others, two bulldogs, Pan and Remus; and many of the dogs he owned or with whom he struck up acquaintance went, suitably disguised, into the novels.[2]

'I've got a dog,' he writes to Knox Cunningham, 'a young Irish terrier called Joey, who comes for walks with me and back for tea. The acquaintance is only three days old, so I can't say yet how it will turn out. I don't even know where he lives. But I don't think he'll be a second Roger, though he's very anxious to please. Of course he's much younger than Roger—only an adolescent. I put

[1] They now stand in the small front-garden of a private house—169, Upper Newtownards Road.

[2] Pan appeared in *Following Darkness* as Tony (in *Peter Waring* this was changed to Remus), and Remus himself came into *The Spring Song* as Pouncer. Roger the sheepdog, mentioned in *Private Road*, belonged to a neighbour. Barker (see *Young Tom*) was introduced by Stephen Gilbert, and Micky (in *Brian Westby*) was actually owned by the Gilberts.

the finding out of his name in the hands of the wolf-cubs, but it was a small girl who actually brought me the information. I don't like the name Joey, but I suppose it would confuse him if I changed it.'

In these creatures he found some of the qualities he admired, but too rarely found in human beings—'qualities that I happen to place very, very high'—trust, loyalty, unswerving affection, even communication:

'I talked a lot to Pan, and later to Remus, another bulldog, and later still to Roger, who was a sheepdog. I remember, one day, when I was unhappy, Roger very nearly talked to me. . . . I am inclined to believe that these canine friendships were more successful, and certainly far less disappointing ultimately, than any human relationships I have ever achieved. They were not perfect; there was no discussion of ideas; on the other hand there was no failure, no change.'

(*Private Road*, p. 108.)

This gives, better than could any words of mine, some idea of the enormously high, the supreme value he set upon the affections. 'Happiness is only made by affection. Nothing else in the long run matters'; the theme is implicit in all the novels. Significantly, writing about W. H. Hudson in *Retrospective Adventures*, he picked on the phrase—

'But the Dwarf answered: No; something human is dearer to me than the wealth of all the world'

—as characteristic of the chief quality in Hudson's writing. It was this 'something human' which, more than anything else, illumined his own world. He was, in fact, a humanist in the most literal sense, for him human beings were infinitely the most important things in the world, and their relationships the most important thing in the novels.

Forrest Reid was born on the 24th of June 1875 at 20 Mount

Charles, Belfast.[1] In that city he was brought up; and there he continued to live and write his books for the rest of his life. The Belfast of his childhood was in many ways a different place from the great commercial and manufacturing centre of today, 'spiritually closer' to the sad, lyrical countryside that impinged on its bustle with such a strange incongruousness. But in essentials it is the same city Forrest Reid knew in his childhood. E. M. Forster, in his essay, has given as vivid an impression of it as one could wish; and it is by his kindness that I reproduce it here:

'One slides up to it at dawn [begins Mr. Forster] through mists and past the clangor of shipyards. Unreal yet squalid, its streets lack either picturesqueness or plan, and manage to exclude all prospect of the mountains that neighbour them.[2] A clammy ooze clings to the pavements, to the dark red bricks, the air is full of the rawness though not of the freshness of the sea, and the numerous Protestant places of worship stand sentinel over huddled slums and over dour little residences whose staircases are covered with linoleum and whose windows seem always to face the east . . . one could scarcely find a city which stood nonsense less. And yet she is haunted by a ghost, by some exile from the realms of the ideal who has slipped into her commonsense, much as the sea and the dispossessed fields, avenging nature, have re-emerged as dampness and as weeds in her streets.'

(E. M. Forster, *Abinger Harvest*: 'Forrest Reid', p. 75.)

[1] In the reference books Forrest Reid always gave the date of his birth as 24th June 1876. This curious error was first pointed out to me by Mr. Stephen Gilbert. A copy of the original Certificate of Birth, obtained from the General Register Office in Dublin by Mr. Knox Cunningham, has now put the matter beyond doubt. The birth was registered at Belfast (on 9th August 1875), and is stated in the document to have occurred on the previous June 24th. Mr. Knox Cunningham writes: 'The mystery of the year of Forrest [Reid]'s birth only came to light after his death. I always accepted the date in the reference books and I doubt if he knew about it himself. I don't think it would have mattered one way or the other to him. He was very casual about things he thought did not count. You remember how vaguely it is put in *Apostate*.'

[2] This last is perhaps a debatable statement. 'In nearly any Belfast street,' Mr. Gilbert points out, 'you can see the hills.'

The intransigent Protestantism is no doubt less in evidence,[1] but the flax mills and the great dark warehouses, the high teas and the whisky and the drummings, the political inflammability and the perfervid loyalty are the same today as they were sixty years ago. And still for backcloth, now as then, the grey curtain of a continual, unremitting drizzle.

Forrest Reid was the youngest of a family of twelve, only six of whom survived. His schooling he received at the Royal Academical Institution, whose pleasant, old-fashioned front, looking down Wellington Place into Donegall Square, still remains. He has drawn a picture of the school in his story *Pirates of the Spring*. His father, Robert Reid, an Irish merchant of middle-class Presbyterian stock, died when the boy was only five or six years old. In earlier life a shipowner, he had come to grief financially in an attempt to run the blockade during the American Civil War. Of him Forrest retained no more than a few shreds of memory. One of his uncles was Professor of Medicine at the Queen's College in Belfast, and another relative on his father's side of the family had been Professor of Ecclesiastical History at Glasgow.[2] The name of Forrest had come into the family through a previous marriage. His mother (his father's second wife) was English, an aristocrat, a Parr from Shropshire. For her he had 'a very real admiration, queer and detached as the word may sound in expression of the emotion of a young boy'; and among his papers there still exists, as proof of his pride of ancestry, an elaborate family tree which he drew up, tracing his mother's collateral descent from Henry VIII's only fortunate queen. But on certain subjects he and his mother did not see eye to eye. There was, for instance, the matter of his choice of companions:

'As for her estimation of my friends, I dismissed it as mere prejudice. I had plenty of prejudices myself, but they were not of a kind to prevent me from making friends with an errand boy if I

---

[1] 'Only one real novel remained off the list of the Puritanical *Index Expurgatorius*, this was *John Halifax, Gentleman*.' That was before 1914. (F. Frankfort Moore, *The Truth About Ulster*, pp. 163–4.)

[2] On the latter, see Robert Allen, *James Seaton Reid* (Belfast: Mullan, 1952). Reid died in 1851.

happened to like him, as was quite often the case. With my mother this class-feeling was innate, half-unconscious, and inexorable. For her there were no degrees; the possession or the absence of talents or virtues did not affect the issue in the least; you were either within the pale or you were not; and, if you were not, no careful training, no discreet burial of compromising ancestors, no manner acquired at Eton and at Oxford, could deceive her. She knew. And when she knew, her sweetness was redoubled—but she talked to you about the weather.'

(*Apostate* [1926], p. 44.)

After this it is only fair to add that there is not wanting evidence which shows that perhaps he and his mother were not so far estranged in their attitude towards the social niceties as it pleased Forrest Reid to make out. There is, for instance, that passage (cut out from the book) in the typescript version of *Apostate* referring to his attendance at some shorthand lessons where, with innocent snobbishness, the youthful scion of the Parrs discovered to his chagrin that 'the class of people I met . . . seemed to me impossible, and, having put down my name, I never returned.' Possibly this latent fastidiousness was exacerbated by the circumstances of home life; for, after the shipping disaster, the large household must have had to undergo a humiliating retrenchment.

But neither his father nor his mother exerted an influence in any way comparable to that of Emma. Emma was his nurse, and about her he has written beautifully and with affection in his autobiography, *Apostate*. She came from Bootle—'a town I privately decided to be unattractive'—and although she left the family when Forrest was six, the impression she made on him was not effaced. In her wisdom she captured the small boy's affection in a way his parents were never able to do. 'Her deep desire was that one should be good, but her still deeper desire was that one should be happy.' It is to be feared that the youthful Forrest was not destined, by Emma's simple lights, to achieve that life of 'goodness' for which she had designed him. The boy was a natural rebel, a rebel with the vehemence which, paradoxically, only the shy and introspective child can command.

Especially did he hate the narrow religious atmosphere in which he was brought up at home. This dislike, in a modified form, he retained to the end of his life. Believing, as he did, that the letter killeth, he found a literal religion chilling, instinctively sensing that it would be hostile to the free life of the imagination. Emma, he confessed in *Apostate*, was 'the only deeply religious person I have met with whom I have been able to feel quite happy and at my ease.' But after she had gone, this antagonism concentrated itself on more immediate objects. 'I hated Sunday, I hated church, I hated Sunday School, I hated Bible stories, I hated everybody mentioned in both the Old and the New Testaments, except perhaps the impenitent thief, Eve's snake, and a few similar characters.' Sunday at Mount Charles became 'a veritable nightmare, casting its baleful shadow even over the last hours of Saturday. . . . Everything seemed to live a natural life on Sundays except people. Cows, birds, cats, dogs, all lived exactly as cows, birds, cats and dogs had lived from the beginning of the world. It was only people who made difficulties. . . .' Incidents, in this inflammable atmosphere, were pretty frequent. There had been, for instance, the occasion when Mr. Farrington the curate had imposed upon a temporary sick-bed immobility to the extent of proffering the sick one a copy of *Daily Light*; with deplorable consequences. . . . There had been the fiasco of Confirmation, which was in itself an interesting ceremony enough; but 'the moment he [the bishop] had removed his hands from my head my interest in the scene died, and what had been designed as the beginning of my religious life proved to be the end of it.' The very next Sunday the confirmee refused to go to church, 'pointblank'. And so, peppered with alarums and excursions like these, the day of rest was transformed, each week, into one of 'storm and battle from dawn till sunset'—until, at last, the young warrior's determination was rewarded, and he gained his freedom.

In these not wholly congenial surroundings his childhood and adolescence went by. He was a sensitive boy, but he was no timid onlooker at life, for ever standing a-shiver on the brink of experience; outwardly this 'broad-nosed . . . wide-mouthed youngster, of a distinct and somewhat Socratic ugliness' led the normal existence of normal boys of his age and position—games, school friendships, fights, collecting: all the rough-and-tumble of an ordinary boyhood in a large family.

Only in his head did he lead a different—and most *un*ordinary —existence. There were, he recollected long afterwards, two lives—'one the external life of . . . games, collections, and the rest of it; the other a private life haunted by visions of beauty and the longing for an ideal companion . . . and it never occurred to me to ask myself whether one were less real than the other.'

In the second of these two worlds—the world of his imagination—there was growing up a life of intense activity, unique and vivid. This life, filled with dream and reverie, he has described in *Apostate*: its colour and atmosphere were extraordinarily luminous and actual. He tells how Emma, reading aloud an improving story from one of those Sabbath magazines in which an earlier age proliferated, unwittingly opened for him the doors of this world. The commonplace, probably sanctimonious little tale became for him

'thirteen years before I saw [it], simply Watteau's *Embarquement pour Cythère*. The scene was there before me, strangely familiar, as if I were retracing my own footmarks in the sand. Not that it was described in the actual tale. It was only that I saw—saw while Emma read—the dark summer sea widening out and out till it melted into a golden haze that hid yet suggested an enchanted land beyond. The light turned to bright burnished gold where it caught the top of a remote mountain, but here, close at hand, in the rich deep drowsy afternoon, was a smooth green lawn dropping down gently to a white sandy bay where dark waves toppled over in foam and music. Here was a bright delicate company, young, beautiful, gay, yet "sad with the whole of pleasure". Here were the brown faces, the pouting lips, and naked unspoiled bodies, the slim Pan pipes, the shadowed grass. . . . "My world! My world!" I could have shouted. . . . It was the only heaven I wanted, or ever was to want. Fleeting glimpses I have had of it, and lost them: and from the flame of that vision I have awakened desolate and sick with longing.'

Night after night he 'awoke' to this same world, a world where 'it was always summer, always a little after noon, and always the sun was shining.' It was a consistent and perfectly real world in which he found himself; the description he has given of it is far too vivid for it to have been anything else.

'The place [he explained] was a kind of garden. . . . Always when I first awakened I was in broad sunlight, on a low grassy hill that was no more than a gentle incline, sloping down to the shore. A summer sea stretched out below me, blue and calm. No white sail ever drifted across the horizon; no footsteps ever marked the unbroken crescent of the sandy beach. . . . But I did not feel lonely . . . I was waiting for someone who had never failed me—my friend in this place, who was infinitely dearer to me than any friend I had on earth. And presently, out from the leafy shadow he bounded into the sunlight . . . a boy of about my own age, with eager parted lips and bright eyes. But he was more beautiful than anything else in the whole world, or in my imagination . . . from the moment I found myself on that hill-side I was happy.'

(*Apostate* [1926], pp. 73-4.)

The sense of exile from a terrestrial paradise, the longing to visit those

Summer isles of Eden lying in dark-purple spheres of sea

is perhaps not an uncommon emotion in the minds and hearts of sensitive artists: what is unusual here is the all-embracing nature of this emotion. Forrest Reid's motive for such a search was different from Tennyson's; he had no reason, no desire to flee from the 'malady of thought'; but the impulse was none the less powerful for not being an impulse of escape. Coleridge spoke of a 'predominant passion', or mood, which gave to a poem its unity of effect. This acute sense of exclusion is the 'predominant passion' which is diffused throughout Forrest Reid's books, diffused through nearly everything he ever wrote. It is what gives the whole of his work—whether critical or creative—its underlying unity of tone and sentiment, what in a sense draws together all his writings into a single work of art.

> *Ever before my face there went*
> *Betwixt earth's buds and me*
> *A beauty beyond earth's content,*
> *A hope—half memory. . . .*

The dreams continued, with diminishing frequency, until he was sixteen or seventeen. Then they faded away, scarcely ever to return. Their warmth and prismatic beauty made the life of everyday seem, by comparison, pale, thin, starved of colour. Only in poetry could he find a waking world which bore any relation in its pure intensity of feeling to the world of his dreams.

Life, however, was more than dreaming; a career had to be considered; and the romantic had perforce to be a realist as well. The environment of his boyhood makes it likely that this transition to reality was not as abrupt as it might appear. The dreams and half-articulate longings of adolescence were lived out amid the noise and bustle, the squalor and harshness of a great city. 'My world'—the world, he means, of Belfast, with its docks and factories, its trams and fogs—'was narrow and provincial on one side, and extending unto the eighth sphere on the other.'

This distinction between the realist and the romantic in his character is mirrored in his work. He was, as an early critic[1] pointed out, both a Celt and a Greek. The contrast well expresses the two parallel lines of development in his books. On the one hand, there is the interest in the mysterious, in dreams, the strange borderland where the magical and the everyday commingle and 'where the lights from two worlds meet and struggle for mastery'—though to call this strain a Celtic one is possibly misleading; some of his earliest work had, it is true, appeared in *Ulad* (the nearest Ulster approach to Yeats's *Samhain*, which was the organ of the Irish Renaissance in the south), but strictly literary

[1] S. M. Ellis, in *Mainly Victorian* (Hutchinson, 1924), p. 344.

influences usually passed him by and his debt to this phase of the Irish revival was indirect, perhaps amounted to nothing more than the stimulation of an already inherent tendency.

But alongside lay something quite different. This something was the note of directness.[1] Developing steadily in his work, until it finally ousted everything else, was the Greek passion for the concrete, for life seen by the clear steady light of noon, the feeling for nature sensuous yet unsentimental, for all young growing things, and for the sadness and transience of their beauty.

> *You remember, perhaps you remember, when I spoke to you that sacred verse: ' Springtime is loveliest; springtime is fleetest; not the swiftest bird in the sky can overtake spring.'*
>
> *Now, look!—all your blossom lies scattered on the ground.*
>
> (*Poems from the Greek Anthology*, p. 57.)

The sense of directness, born of his love for the Greek ideal, was part of the rigid self-discipline which prevented the appearance of any trace of sentimentality, of anything mawkish or falsely stressed, in his own writing.

But this is to run ahead. At present, the disagreeable necessity of earning a livelihood had to be faced. Forrest's idea of a career had been simple. He wanted to work in a library, to go to London. But his mother, distrusting the capital and what she conceived to be its temptations, overrode this project. Probably she was right in doing so. It is highly doubtful whether he would himself have greatly enjoyed the reality. The following passage from *At the Door of the Gate*, which is clearly autobiographical, shows what his feelings were when eventually he *did* visit the place:

'Once he went for a holiday to London. He went alone, and it is significant that the most vivid impression stamped upon his mind during this visit was perhaps that of the stony masks presented by the wonderful ladies he had seen coming out from the opera. He hated them, yet they fascinated him. . . . He marvelled

[1] The phrase is Sir Richard Livingstone's. (*The Greek Genius and its Meaning to Us.*)

at their lack of individual expression. There had been two or three who had looked, as they sat staring straight past him, or through him, like painted idols. . . . The whole monstrous city gave him an impression of desolation. The life was the swarming noisome life of a corpse, out of which gleamed the white bones of death. Death leered in the smile of a painted girl who stared into his face with hard bright eyes. . . . He felt it most keenly at the end of one hot interminable day when, instead of going to a theatre or a concert, he wandered about in the open air. . . . The moon shone down softly between the trees, and the dim strange light through which he moved seemed to isolate him from the world that discouraged and bewildered him. The darkness deepened rapidly, and the embraces of neighbouring lovers ceased to be obtrusive, became dim, remote. . . . The tall lamps, haloed by a hovering swarm of winged insects, cast broad pools of purplish light upon the worn, faded grass; and through the delicate grey-ness of the trees came the flash of endless vehicles. . . .

'He passed out through the gates, walking slowly, almost at random, by tall, brilliantly-lighted windows that were opened wide to the night, and presently he found himself in Leicester Square. . . . The very aspect of unreality and futility that glittered over the surface of things seemed to mock at him with the elusive and meaningless horror of a dream. He leaned against the railings and closed his eyes. By an effort of will he called up a scene that was most opposed to all that now glared and flared upon his senses—a bare hill-side under the moon, with dark woods below, stretching down to a lonely sea. As he called to it it responded staightway, rising within his mind again, just as it had been—the faint rustle of wind, the smell of heather, the black curved vault of the open sky, vast and infinitely still—bringing him back to sanity and peace.'

(*At the Door of the Gate*, pp. 141-3.)

But if he would have disliked living in London he would have been even more unhappy in business. For commerce as a career, 'I confess,' he said, 'I had little esteem. Smartness, and the kind

45

of geniality that blossoms into dirty stories, seemed the most valuable assets there; intelligence was a negligible quantity, and integrity a drawback.' (*Private Road*, p. 19.)

Eventually he was apprenticed to the tea-trade, in Belfast. Of his experiences at Musgrave's he has written in *Apostate* and, in a thinly disguised form, in the early novel *At the Door of the Gate*. He did not dislike his new life and indeed found the easygoing routine of an old-fashioned commercial firm in many ways a pleasant one. He struck up friendships—of a sort—with the other apprentices and was in turn befriended by a 'white-haired, white-bearded man', one of the firm's oldest employees, who constructed the great wooden boxes into which the tea was packed. There is a pleasant portrait of old James Quigley in *Apostate*.

But with one of the apprentices, who joined the firm as a junior some months after his own arrival, he formed a friendship that was something more. The name of this apprentice was Andrew Rutherford. For him he developed an affection, the deeper for being unexpressed, which transformed his life. 'When I was with this boy I was happy, and I could conceive of no greater happiness than to be with him always. He was an odd enough youngster in his ways, not a bit like any other boy I had known; but he was extraordinarily lovable. Sometimes, indeed, the sunshine, filled with little dancing golden dust specks, touching his hair or his cheek, would set me dreaming of him as a kind of angel who had strayed into this world by chance, or perhaps not quite by chance. . . . Life in this humdrum old warehouse, amid its simple daily tasks . . . became a wonderful voyage of discovery to be undertaken no longer alone.'

Eventually they were to drift apart under the pressure of incompatibility of outlook, but that lay in the future. For the present, he had his happiness. The future 'lay before us like a wide green plain. There were plans and day-dreams. . . . I got him to read poetry, to listen to music; I poured out all my enthusiasms, and in return became absorbed in his.'

To Forrest Reid this friendship seemed to have been, when

ong afterwards recollected in tranquillity, crucial for his development. Writing thirty years later he saw it as the culmination of
his youth. The pages of *Apostate* embrace, as he recognized, a
definite period, a period which 'began in dreamland' and ended
with the morning—the 'cold bright winter morning'—when for
the first time he met Andrew.

'Or perhaps' he adds, 'I should say that it ends on an evening
some five or six months later.'

Forrest Reid had been keeping a sort of journal, into which he
poured out his thoughts and feelings, and the emotions that this
new friendship had brought him. He wanted desperately to take
his friend into his confidence, and yet he could not bring himself
to do it. *Apostate* ends by describing how he took this plunge:

'Yet now I wanted him to read it. I knew it contained pages
he might find bewildering, extravagant, and perhaps distasteful:
but I also knew that if I looked back over it with a view to tearing
out such pages I should never show it at all.

'And the desire to take him completely into my confidence
had begun to haunt me. It was what filled my mind as we walked
home together one day some five or six months after our first
meeting, and what kept me silent when, later on, we went out for
a ramble through the fields and woods by the Lagan. Yet, though
I was silent, I was intensely excited, for I had made up my mind
to conquer my cowardice. Already I had had an opportunity to
do so, and had put it off by coming out here. I would put it off
no longer.

'"There is something I have at home which I want to show
you—something I have written. Do you mind turning back?"

'Without questioning me he did what I asked.

'And when once more we had reached the house in Mount
Charles I took him upstairs to the room I now used as a study,
and where I knew we should not be disturbed. It was growing
dusk, but I welcomed the minutes I could employ on busying
myself with the lamp, and fumbled longer than was necessary as I
unlocked the desk where was my manuscript book. I gave him

the book, moved the lamp nearer to an arm-chair, and myself sat down at the table, some distance off, and facing the window. For the first time I had admitted someone to my secret world, to my innermost thoughts. . . .

'Already he must have crossed the threshold. In the quiet of the room I could hear no sound but now and then the rustle of a page when he turned it. For an instant I glanced at him. His face was a little flushed, his dark hair tumbled down over his forehead. But I turned away quickly and did not look back. I sat waiting, trying now to shut out every thought from my mind. . . .

'The time slowly drew on: half an hour, nearly an hour must have gone by. The window grew darker and darker, and presently I knew that in a little, a very little while, the reading must come to an end. Then the silence seemed all at once to grow so intense that I felt nothing could ever again break it.'

(Apostate [1926], pp. 232, 233, 234-5.)

It was, of course, first love; first love
> *Tender as dawn's first hill-fire, and intense*
> *As instantaneous penetrating sense,*
> *In Spring's birth-hour, of other Springs gone by.*

That love which in the uniqueness of its kind and the intensity of its degree comes only once in any lifetime.

The visionary gleam never vanished, that was part of the charm and what struck so many of his friends throughout his life, but something, nevertheless, did perish. It was the end of youth. His faith in human beings had received its first check, and in the ensuing disappointment many of the untried hopes and untarnished illusions so deeply cherished in boyhood and youth faded into the light of common day.

At this point *Apostate* ends. The King Charles's head had been severed, the author stands, poised, on the verge of maturity. There is, I think, only one book with which *Apostate* can be compared: and that is Edmund Gosse's *Father and Son*. But Gosse's book is less of a work of art than *Apostate*, and Forrest Reid never had to submit to a religious domination so absolute, so utterly exacting, as that exercised by Philip Gosse; nor did he go through the stage of undeniably priggish acquiescence which preceded the young Gosse's final rebellion. Indeed, it is very hard to imagine Forrest Reid submitting, without the sternest struggle, to the horrifying ceremonial of that baptism by total immersion, still less acting his part with that complacency which so befitted the 'child of many prayers'. For Forrest Reid was a rebel from the start, whereas in Gosse's mind paganism and Christianity did, for a short time, manage to coexist. 'In my hot and silly brain', the critic wrote, 'Jesus and Pan held sway together, as in a wayside chapel discordantly and impishly consecrated to Pagan and to Christian rites.' (*Father and Son* [1907], p. 342.)

To Forrest Reid this sort of trimming would have been inconceivable, utterly foreign to his nature. But in spite of differing reaction to circumstances, for both of them the end of unreality signalized itself in very much the same way. Forrest Reid recounted in *Following Darkness*—and although *Following Darkness* is a novel, there is good reason for thinking the story a true one— how, one afternoon, having been told about a man who, using the oath 'God strike me blind', was immediately struck blind by a flash of lightning:

'. . . in my own room, standing by the window, I said aloud, and very deliberately, "God strike me blind! God strike me blind!" I waited with a mingled trepidation and incredulity, as if I had thrown some mysterious bomb into the unknown. A sea-gull flew past the window, white against the dark autumn sky: the leaves of the Virginian creeper trembled and grew still. I said again and in a louder voice, "God strike me blind!" But no flash of lightning followed. Down below, on the beach, the gray waves curled over with a slow musical splash. I looked into the sky, but it was calm and untroubled, and I decided that the story was a myth.'

(*Following Darkness*, pp. 25–6.)

Gosse's experience had not been dissimilar. His mother and

father, members of the tiny sect of Plymouth Brethren, lived in a continual, almost an hourly expectation of the total dissolution of the world. That which to normally constituted persons appeared as an inconceivably horrible cosmic disaster, seemed to them to be only the just and perfectly reasonable operation of Providence. It was in this atmosphere that Edmund Gosse's imagination became inflamed with premonitions and omens of the impending dread event:

'It was a summer afternoon. . . . I gazed down on a labyrinth of gardens sloping to the sea, which twinkled faintly beyond the towers of the town. . . . A wonderful warm light of approaching sunset modelled the shadows and set the broad summits of the trees in a rich glow. There was an absolute silence below and around me, a magic of suspense seemed to keep every topmost twig from waving.

'Over my soul there swept an immense wave of emotion. Now, surely, now the great final change must be approaching. I gazed up into the faintly-coloured sky. . . . I raised myself on the sofa, and leaned upon the window-sill, and waited for the glorious apparition.

'This was the highest moment of my religious life, the apex of my striving after holiness. I waited awhile, watching. . . . Still I gazed and still I hoped. Then a little breeze sprang up, and the branches danced. Sounds began to rise from the road beneath me. Presently the colour deepened, the evening came on. . . . "The Lord has not come, the Lord will never come," I muttered, and in my heart the artificial edifice of extravagant faith began to totter and crumble.'

(*Father and Son* [1907], pp. 342–4.)

Forrest Reid was not idle. He went, it is true, to Cambridge, to Christ's, abandoned the tea-trade. But Cambridge had nothing to offer him. Probably, at twenty-seven, he was too old. Writing many years later he looked back upon his time at the University as nothing more than a 'rather blank interlude'. He made few friends; though, surprisingly enough, his acquaintance with Ronald Firbank supplied a touch of colour to his life there. 'Firbank seemed to me unreal. I had never before met anybody in the least like him.' He was baffled by the 'polished surface'. 'The only time I ever saw the mask drop was on one winter evening, when, coming out of my sitting-room into the dimly-lit hall, he barked his shins on a coal-scuttle left there by my land-lady. Then he said "damn" quite savagely and naturally—as he might have at the age of fourteen—but a moment later the mask was resumed.' (*Private Road*, pp. 55–6.)

So, although he was very far from being the recluse some made him out to be, his most active life was now to lie in his books and his writings, and in the imaginative world that he created. Like Henry James, and like all genuine artists, his days were henceforth preoccupied with the struggle to solve 'the dear little deadly question of *how to do it*'.

This may not seem, at first sight, to have promised an adventurous career. But, as Algernon Blackwood once pointed out, 'the secret of a successful elevated life is to remain inconspicuous while yet attaining one's objective', and by this standard Forrest Reid's life must be adjudged 'successful' in the highest degree, with the success which could only have been achieved when, as Henry James again put it, 'of a beautiful subject his expression was complete'; for in the books he *did* attain his objective, he re-lived his own childhood and youth and created ideal lives of his own making. So, although youth disappeared, the spirit of youth, which is its essence, never died in him. In a sense—perhaps the deepest sense—he never travelled beyond the confines of his own adolescence. 'I could get on swimmingly until I reached my King Charles's head—the point where a boy becomes a man.' After that, he was forced to acknowledge,' something seemed to happen, my inspiration was cut off, my interest flagged. . . . I supposed it must be some mysterious form of arrested development.' Certainly all that was significant and lasting in his work was concerned with this period of life.

·   ·   ·   ·   ·

Of that work it is now time to speak. Childhood and youth are not themes which, until recent years, have attracted many writers in this country. There are plenty of novels which have children as characters, but quite remarkably few which show any deep insight into a child's mind and heart. It is comparatively easy to evoke the surroundings and emotions of children in general; it is harder to create an individualized child, a small living creature with the attributes, however undeveloped, of a recognizable human being. It demands an unusually intense and difficult and sustained projection of the imagination, which few writers are able to achieve. The Russians probably have the advantage of us in writings about childhood. In the work of Gorky, of Tolstoy, or of Aksakoff in his masterpiece *A Russian Childhood*, the theme has been more carefully explored than in any comparable books in this country. It may not be fanciful to trace in the Russian temperament something of the melancholy, brooding quality of mind, the backward- and inward-glancing regard, which seems to be favourable to such retrospective adventures of the imagination. For a book about childhood or a child *is* an adventure, with all the thrill of a voyage of discovery; and it is with something of the alertness, the elation, of explorers in an unknown terrain that the work of Forrest Reid should be approached by his readers.

At the outset we are confronted with problems of presentation and treatment. The French critic Edmond Pilon, writing about Alain-Fournier,[1] had encountered the same difficulty. There were, he felt, certain books 'd'une fragilité de pastel, et si diaphanes, si douces, si spécialement subtiles et tendres qu'on ne peut pas les toucher du doigt sans les froisser'. In speaking of books such as Forrest Reid's the conventional methods of criticism quickly prove themselves ineffective and even irrelevant.

Forrest Reid's books are the product of a vision. That vision, in a form ever purer and more intense, passed into the texture of his life and writings. In *Brian Westby*, which was one of the later and

---

[1] *Alain-Fournier*. No. 26 in the series 'Les Amis d'Edouard' (Abbeville, 1920), p. 28. (Quoted in March: 'The "Other Landscape" of Alain-Fournier', in *Publications of the Modern Language Association of America*, lvi (1941), 266–79.)

most personal of the stories, Martin Linton the elderly novelist
has been trying to explain to his young disciple what this means:

' "It's not very easy to explain," he confessed. "I expect . . . I
may have meant an *actual* vision—some kind of spiritual revelation
such as Wordsworth had in his boyhood among the Cumberland
lakes . . . one *can* have such a vision:—something which remains
ever after as an influence—which creates an ideal—and a longing
that it may come again . . . to those who *have* had it, the memory
of it is in everything they afterwards write:—everything, that is,
which has been inspired by a genuine emotion." '

Belief in this vision lies at the heart of Forrest Reid's work.
From his conviction of its reality sprang his whole theory of art:
'The primary impulse of the artist', he writes in *Apostate*, 'springs,
I fancy, from discontent, and his art is a kind of crying for Ely-
sium . . . in the most clumsy and bungled work (if it has been
born of the desire for beauty) we should doubtless find, could we
but pierce through the dead husk of it to the hidden conception,
that same divine homesickness, that same longing for an Eden
from which each one of us is exiled . . . all our life is little more
than a trying to get back there, our art than a mapping of its
mountains and streams.'

These are beautiful words, but they are also precise and considered ones. The strength of this impulse, and its influence on his
writing (as we shall see later when we come to consider some of
the novels in more detail) was very deep. The stories, he explains
in *Apostate*, 'are most real just where they may appear to be most
fantastic', and as frontispiece to *Private Road*, the book in which
he reflects on his work as an author, he places the words of
Hawthorne: 'I am half convinced that the reflection is indeed the
reality, the real thing which nature imperfectly images to our
grosser sense.'

In the stories themselves there are certain common elements;
three distinct themes continually recur. They are the themes of
youth, of nature, and of what, lacking a more precise word, must
be called the supernatural.

The theme of youth predominates. All that matters in Forrest Reid's work is concerned with the young. It would have been possible, in other hands, for these youthful heroes and occasional heroines of his novels to have produced a somewhat monotonous, even standardized, effect on the reader. We might have wearied of them as we so often weary of the children of fiction.

Here are two vignettes (neither taken from the novels) which may give an idea of the general quality of his approach. Both occur in his study of Walter de la Mare. The first is personal, and describes an unusual encounter in Belfast:

'One Sunday morning, a good many years ago, I came upon an odd little gathering in a public park. The park was situated in the Roman Catholic quarter of my native town, and the gathering was composed of about a dozen persons of both sexes, whose ages, at a guess, averaged between seven and ten. Both the hour and the place indicated that the members of this interesting group belonged to the elder faith, and the centre of it was a remarkably bright-eyed but far from lovely little girl, a year or two older than the rest. They all belonged to the poorest class; they all were ragged, untidy, and more or less unwashed; they all were spellbound, though the spell was broken every now and again by a general burst of laughter to which even the smallest contributed; and they all were listening to the bright-eyed child who, after one swift smile at the intruder, continued to read aloud from a torn and grimy copy of *Alice in Wonderland*. . . . It was an odd picture, singularly pleasing, yet, if one happened to be sentimentally inclined, singularly pathetic. The reader's accent was deplorable, her habit of suddenly pausing and reading on rapidly and silently ahead before returning to her impatient audience, was trying, but the genius which had created that fantastic dream tale for all time and for every child emerged triumphantly from the ordeal.'

And here is the second. He is discussing the poem 'Sooeep!' from Mr. de la Mare's *Peacock Pie*:

'Chimney-sweepers have always rewarded their champions by

inspiring them to write delightfully, whether it is in the prose of Charles Lamb or in the verse of Walter de la Mare: little chimney-sweepers, that is to say, for, as Charles points out, "old chimney-sweepers are by no means attractive". Mr. de la Mare's sweep is sufficiently grown-up to have a hoarse voice, therefore he has not quite the endearing quality of "those tender novices, blooming through their first nigritude, the maternal washings not quite effaced from the cheek—such as come forth with the dawn, or somewhat earlier, with their little professional notes sounding like the *peep peep* of a young sparrow". Always they are seen, out of the poet's tenderness of heart, in a clear morning world, though it must sometimes be raining and winter. But the poet sees them in the world he would like to give them: it is as if, in imagination at any rate, he would turn them loose in green summer meadows, to sport in the deepest grasses and under the bluest skies. Charles Kingsley gives Tom in *The Water Babies* nothing less than the whole fresh cool sparkling river for his home; and in that wild gleaming light of a rapturous innocence which floods the world of Blake's little blackamoors, they seem to stand with their naked feet bathed in the very dews of Paradise.'

Youth in Forrest Reid's novels is never a formula. He understood. He had a perfect sympathy for the complexities and the seeming inconsistencies of the young. In a passage which occurs in the early novel *Following Darkness* (which he omitted when that book came to be revised), he sketches with swift, firm strokes what the spirit of youth meant to him:

'In the foreground there must be the portrait of a boy, but painted in the manner of Rembrandt rather than Bronzino. By this I mean there will be less of firm, clear outline, than of light and shadow. The danger is that in the end there may be too much shadow; but at least I shall not, in the manner of a writer of fiction, have sacrificed my subject for the sake of gaining an additional brightness and vivacity. The spirit of youth is not merely bright and vivacious; above all, it is not merely thoughtless and noisy. It is melancholy, dreamy, passionate; it is admirable, and it is base; it is full of curiosity; it is healthy, and it is morbid; it is animal, and it is spiritual; sensual, yet filled with vague half-realised yearnings after an ideal—that is to say, it is the spirit of life itself, which can never be adequately indicated by the description of a fight or of a football match.'

(*Following Darkness*, p. 10.)

The theme of the novels demands that they continually balance on the razor-edge which separates sentiment from sentimentality. This razor-edge Forrest Reid trod with perfect assurance. The delicacy of the emotional and moral issues with which they deal are treated with a blend of sympathy and ironical insight which never once fails him.

There is nothing overtly sexual, little even of sensuality, in these books. Any trace of grossness would have spoiled the whole fragile construction and smudged its outlines. Realities are faced, as they must be sooner or later by any writer who cares for depicting the truth as he sees it; but there is no pandering to baseness for baseness' sake, no distortion or violence, no breath of sensationalism. Forrest Reid wrote from a standpoint which views innocence as the most deeply desirable of human qualities; and although much in the books is concerned with the forces which threaten that state, it is the values that accompany innocence for which the author most cares. In this sense, Forrest Reid's work is essentially moral in character, and his achievement a moral achievement.

The second element is the element of natural beauty. Or rather, to speak more precisely, it is the climate in which the stories take place. By no means all the books have settings of beauty, although in each novel there *are* natural descriptions of great beauty. The beauty is rather a beauty of *treatment*. The realistic scenes of Belfast life in the early books are, for all their squalor, invested at the same time with a strange twilight atmosphere, and the frequent pettiness and drabness of the lives they chronicle float in this eerie and subdued beauty. In later novels, such as *The Retreat*, beauty of landscape plays a much more direct part, is indeed what chiefly gives the story its special feeling and makes it seem, in retrospect, a long unbroken summer day. The feeling for nature always had a deep significance for Forrest Reid. The entire world of nature (he avowed in a cancelled passage of *Apostate*) was to him 'little else than emotion.' He enjoyed, by his own account, an almost mystical capacity for identifying himself with nature, for participating in the life of natural things. It was almost as if he were able to pass *into* nature. Once, indeed, he felt he very nearly had succeeded in doing this:

'It was June, and I was supposed to be working for an Intermediate examination, and had a book or two with me even on this blazing afternoon. It was hot and still. The breathless silence seemed unnatural; seemed, as I lay motionless in the tangled grass, like a bridge that reached straight back into the heart of some dim antiquity. I had a feeling of uneasiness, of unrest, though I lay so still—of longing and excitement and expectation: I had a feeling that some veil might be drawn away, that there might come to me something, some one, the Megistos Kouros perhaps, either with the winged feet of Hermes, or the thyrsus of Dionysus, or maybe only hairy-shanked Pan of the Goats. My state of mind just then was indistinguishable from that of the worshipper. . . . I was certainly prepared to join in whatever rites or revels might be required. My body seemed preternaturally sensitive, my blood moved quickly, I had an extraordinary feeling of struggle, as if some power were struggling to reach me as I was trying to reach it, as if there *was* something there, something waiting, if only I could get through. At that moment I longed for a sign, some definite and direct response, with a longing that was a kind of prayer. And a strange thing happened. For though there was no wind, a little green leafy branch was snapped off from the tree above me, and fell to the ground at my hand. I drew my breath quickly; there was a drumming in my ears; I knew that the green woodland before me was going to split asunder, to swing back on either side like two great painted doors. . . . And then—then I hesitated, blundered, drew back, failed.'

(*Apostate* [1926], pp. 212-3.)

The lyrical response to the loveliness of the earth and its seasons, half-mystical, half-sensuous, penetrated to and nourished the deepest roots of his imaginative life; and behind the cadences of his writing, as behind Mozart's music, often there seems to linger something, some unexpressed and inexpressible emotion, that trembles on the brink of tears.

'There was the beauty of an autumn afternoon in the Ormeau Park at dusk, when, with the dead leaves thick on the deserted paths, I had sat listening to a German band playing somewhere out of sight beyond the railings. Through the twilight, with its yellow twinkling of street lamps, the music had floated. The tune was the old *Lorelei*, but into the plaintive twang of those instruments all the melancholy of the earth had passed. It was as if the very soul of the empty park had found a voice, and were sobbing out its complaint to the November sky. . . .

'There was the beauty of the Lagan Valley, filled with the sound of hidden running water, where the sluggish river plunged down through foaming weirs. A beauty, in summer, when the dark soil had burst into a pagan riot of growth, rich and green and luxuriant; but in winter desolate enough, suggestive of broken, unhappy loves, of last walks together, while the grey light gradually faded from the marsh-lands beyond the tow-path, and the trees stooped down over their own dark images. . . .

'There was the beauty of the sea—an unearthly beauty, because it washed on the shores of my dream world. A strip of golden sand over which the dark blue water splashed in little creamy waves— thus it came back to me, forming always the same picture—a picture that more than any other was *my* picture. For, most of us, I suppose, have one picture that is somehow a part of our life, in which our life really takes place, and which is the last sight, perhaps, our dying eyes will see.'

(*Apostate* [1926], pp. 199-200.)

And behind everything, behind all beauty, lay the feeling of sadness; 'though I loved it, it made me sad . . . and . . . invariably awoke in me that old longing for a heaven that was not heaven, for an earth that was not earth, for a love that I knew I should never find either in heaven or earth.'

Finally, there is the supernatural, the dream-like quality. It was, as he admitted himself, 'inseparable from my conception of reality'. He didn't mean to suggest by this mere vulgar hauntings or ghost stories with their attendant array of mediums, poltergeists, and the rest; still less all the solemn paraphernalia of 'psychic investigation'. What he meant was something altogether more spiritual, more humane. 'After all, a sense of the supernatural need not be accompanied by fear', he once remarked. 'It may be aroused in broad sunlight; it may be no more than a suggestion of a deeper beauty, friendly and benevolent, existing behind the beauty of natural things. Such, at any rate, has been my own experience, and it was always a feeling unsought, a kind of expectancy, a state of mind far removed from dread.' This is the genre in which he and Walter de la Mare are indisputably the masters.

Forrest Reid discusses dreams in an interesting chapter of *Private Road*, but his interest in the phenomenal side of the matter is not really important in relation to the novels, although some of the plots do spring, unbidden, from dream-sources. In the books the supernatural has two functions. One is little more than decorative or dramatic, melodramatic even, an atmosphere rather than anything more tangible. Into this category fall the equivocal activities of the magician Flamel in *The Gentle Lover*, and Rex's unconvincing memoir in *Pender Among the Residents*. But usually the supernatural theme is more integral to the plot of the novel. Examples of this are the behaviour of Mr. Bradley, the mysterious organist, in *The Spring Song*; Ralph Seaford, the 'ghost-boy', in *Young Tom*; the angel Gamelyn, in *The Retreat*; the haunting of Denis in *The Bracknels*—and, of course, all of *Uncle Stephen*, which was his most sustained achievement in this kind.

The whole field of the supra-normal fascinated Forrest Reid. In its place we shall have to analyse the part which it plays in some of the novels, but it is mentioned here now as a persisting and fairly constant factor in their structure.

The values in the books are the values of the man, and do not change. Faithfulness, innocence, affection, integrity—integrity in the broadest sense; the scrupulousness which prevented him as a writer from ever venturing near the edge of that 'whirlpool of insincerity from which no man returns'—these were the qualities that he prized and admired. All these qualities he resumed in the single virtue of 'moral fragrance', that 'highest spiritual beauty of all', the beauty in which he acutely judged Yeats to be lacking, and of which his own books are so full.

Besides all this, Forrest Reid was a craftsman. All through his life he never ceased striving to perfect his style, to invest it with an unmistakable identity of its own. Writing didn't come to him easily or without pains and, as he was always the first to recognize, his development was unusually slow and hesitant. But with time and practice he overcame his problems one by one. Many of the short stories, for instance ('An Ending' or 'A Garden by the Sea' are examples), come off almost solely by reason of the craftsmanship which has gone into their construction. At first, however, errors of subject and treatment had led to delay in the discovery of his real themes. The wonderful final style, its delicacy and flexibility, was only achieved after long trial and error, and at the cost of occasional failure. This is what gives his work its peculiar technical interest.

' "Do you know what might be an interesting experiment?" muses Linton [and the accents are unmistakably the accents of Forrest Reid] ... "I think it might be interesting to read the books in the order in which he wrote them. In [the] first story, you see, he's only feeling his way—pretty blindly too—yet there *is* something, even in it, which he's trying to express. ... Nobody can do more than feel his way till he's acquired a method, learned his job, so to speak; and Linton was uncommonly slow in learning his. Besides, he often chose the wrong kind of subject; and in the beginning the writing itself was often bad. Still, after a fashion the books do fit together. I mean, he's got an ideal; and each of his books is an attempt to express it. . . . If he *could* bring it off, *could* produce it naked and complete—then I should think he might make a bonfire of the earlier things. They'd be only sketches and studies for the finished work." '

(*Brian Westby*, pp. 25-6.)

Forrest Reid *did* bring it off. The trilogy of novels about his young hero Tom Barber, which he wrote towards the end of his life, was his crowning achievement. No other writer, no one, has ever matched the skill and tenderness with which Forrest Reid explored, in these lovely and curiously intimate books, the mind and heart of an ordinary, but sensitive, small boy. In *Uncle Stephen* and *The Retreat* and *Young Tom* subject and style had coalesced, melted into each other, simultaneously reached their final point of development and produced, 'naked and complete', the work of art which all his previous books had been but a prelude to expressing. It is a far cry from the immature, the almost ninety-ish languors of *The Kingdom of Twilight* to the ease and charm of this later writing. Between the two there is a single point of contact—both, unmistakably, are the work of Forrest Reid.

And it is on a note such as this—giving some indication of the distance travelled in an authorship lasting half a century—that these introductory remarks may be best wound up. The ground has been cleared. The books lie before us and the adventure of their exploration, the adventure which 'all along [lies] in the interpretation, and therefore . . .[becomes] really most adventurous precisely in those quieter hours

When the soul seeks to hear; when all is hushed,
And the heart listens.'[1]

[1] *Private Road*, p. 243.

61

II

His Art: Five Novels

FALSE STARTS

Forrest Reid's first book, *The Kingdom of Twilight*, was brought out by Fisher Unwin in 1904; and rather more than forty years later he wrote *Young Tom*, which was his final novel. During these forty years he produced fifteen novels. He was in no sense a prolific writer, never a 'professional' one—the only novel, *Pender*, he did write as a more or less self-appointed task was an emphatic failure—but he continued to publish steadily to the end of his life.

His method of writing the early novels was simple: 'I write my first drafts always in pencil and on any odd scraps of paper that come to hand. From these I type a copy upon which I work, re-typing a page when corrections become too numerous. . . . I have invariably destroyed the original scribbles.' This was written in 1928, when he was being asked to present the MS. of *Apostate* to the Bodleian at Oxford; but in later years he made a practice of preserving the 'scribbles' and, so far as he found it possible, on uniform sheets. These he would send, when the book was in galleys, to his friend J. N. Hart, and by him they were bound up. He kept none of his manuscripts himself. In some cases Mr. Hart possesses both the original pencil draft and the later, corrected, typescript copy; and a comparison of the two versions is extremely revealing. Nothing shows more conclusively the enormous pains he took to perfect his art than these neatly scored pages, emended, cancelled, redrafted. He was frequently not satisfied until the page was a mass of corrections. Some of the omissions make fascinating reading: a great deal of the first draft of *Uncle Stephen* was taken out of the version finally printed. And some of the detailed alterations are as significant. Tom, at his father's funeral, 'Deliberately' (in the typed draft) 'fixed his attention on a creamy, black-spotted butterfly that [sic] had entered the avenue.' In the corrected copy 'that' has been carefully erased and replaced by the word '*who*'. It was apparently trifling details like this which, to Forrest Reid, bulked most important; his humanizing temperament would no more readily have deprived a butterfly of its identity than a human being. 'God's humblest, they', mused Hardy as he watched the insects playing round his lamp:

> '*God's humblest, they!' I muse. Yet why?*
> *They know Earth-secrets that know not I.*
> (*An August Midnight.*)

And to Hardy's humility and wonderment Forrest Reid gave faithful echo.

The novels fall, by virtue of developments in style, into two fairly clear groups, the dividing line being the publication, in 1926, of *Apostate*. What I propose here is to examine five of the tales—*The Bracknels, Following Darkness, The Gentle Lover, Uncle Stephen*, and *Brian Westby*—at some length, under a magnifying glass; not forgetting that they are stories, but mainly considering them from the point of view of their structure and form. Then I shall look at some of the characters in these and other novels, after that say something about the development of the style, and glance at the criticism, before finally attempting to arrive at some estimate of the ideas which underlie the books. In this way I hope that everything which is important in Forrest Reid's work will have been taken into account; but before looking at these representative novels some reference must be made to two early books. These are *The Kingdom of Twilight*; and *The Garden God*, which appeared a year later, in 1905. Partly because of the interest of what Forrest Reid himself has to say about these particular books, and partly too because both are now unprocurable and unlikely ever to be reprinted, some justification can be pleaded for pausing here to make an estimate of these two books; even although he looked on them as false starts, and subsequently expunged all traces of them from the canon.

The Kingdom indeed he regarded as more than a false start. He loathed this book. So profound was his dislike of it that for many years, by force or fraud, he used to seize and destroy any copies (including those in the Linen Hall Library at Belfast) on which he was able to lay his hands. Even though the wretched thing might find a place on their shelves, the later friends were sometimes surprised to find they were denied the imprimatur which would have made it possible to acquaint themselves with its contents; so complete was the anathema.

A copy of *The Kingdom of Twilight* lies before me as I write. In appearance it certainly *looks* harmless enough; but Forrest Reid's objections extended even to the format. This was 'cheap and flimsy, a feature of the binding being that it rapidly detached itself from the contents.' The binding of *my Kingdom* still remains loyally attached to its contents, but it is hard to disagree with what its author says about the value of these contents as literature.

To begin with, the book was a first novel. Forrest Reid was a fastidious artist, and to the more experienced novelist the book seemed, when he looked at it in retrospect, a disaster. Even when it was still in proof he realized it was bad: 'Eagerly I began to read, and I had read very few pages before the blow fell . . . the whole book . . . sickened me. . . . It seemed . . . a hotch-potch of purple patches, childish gush, and childish sentimentality.' (*Private Road*, p. 23.)

The plot is simple and, taken by itself, plausible: Willie Trevelyan, the hero, is a gentle, imaginative boy and his family are well-meaning but narrow in their sympathies. All that is responsive and affectionate in the youngster goes out instead to his friend Nick Grayson. But at the same time Willie has attracted, without being able to reciprocate, the love of his young cousin Eva Gower. This is the general scheme of the early chapters of the book. Later,

Willie goes—like Forrest Reid himself—into the tea-trade. He makes new, less suitable friends, falls under strange influences (and so, at this point, I am afraid, does his creator). One day, wandering by the sea-shore, he sees Hester Urquhart. They meet, fall in love, have a child, and marry—in that order. But Hester, as Willie's friends soon divine, is unscrupulous, a 'light woman'. At this point there is a gap. Book Five begins abruptly when their son, Prosper, is nine years old. Indirectly, we learn that Hester left Willie soon after their marriage. Willie and Prosper are busy with preparations for leaving London to go to Ireland, where they are to live in Willie's old home, by the sea. But the denouement swiftly follows. Returning from a visit to Eva, he finds Prosper fallen ill. A chill turns to pneumonia, the child dies. Willie, heartbroken, goes to his cottage by the sea—alone. Thither Eva, who loved——and still loves—him, comes to console him in his grief, while he embarks on the task of writing his autobiography. On this watery and somewhat indeterminate note the tale ends.

What vitiated the whole thing was the immaturity of the style, the unsuitable theme, and the irresolution with which both were handled. The young author had sent a copy of his work to Henry James, and Henry James, in his letter of acknowledgement, had gone straight to the heart of the matter. The book's inspiration flagged just so soon as he reached his 'King Charles's head—the point where a boy becomes a man'. This James pointed out, graciously but with firmness: ' I confess,' (he wrote) '. . . that *after* the middle, you strike me as *losing* your subject. . . . After the meeting with the woman by the sea—certainly after the parting from her—I felt the reality of the thing deviate, felt the subject lose its conditions, so to speak, its *observed* character and its logic.' Put more bluntly, what this amounted to was that Forrest Reid was trying to write about experiences of which he knew nothing, experiences, too, into which he could not imaginatively enter; and often about people he didn't understand as well. Hester Urquhart is a totally unreal figure and the richness of texture in the love-scenes is out of key with the rest of the book. Even Willie, the

E

central character, undergoes no significant mental development. And the portrayal of religious emotion is quite unconvincing. Nor did the style fit the theme; the 'over-waxen sweetness' whose absence in *The Garden God* was later to be commended by Edmund Gosse, was here triumphant all along the line; so also was the tiresome apostrophizing, the passages of Jamesian description, the lack of precision, the sermonic moralizing which choked the flow of narrative.

All these faults were the sign of an unformed style. In one sense perhaps the persistent over-writing was an advantage; it attracted attention away from the flimsiness, the aimlessness of the plot, and the lack of tightness in its construction. There is a danger besetting all first novels. It is that the writer's eagerness will turn such a book into a portmanteau, into which he can cast, without selection or discrimination, all his newly gained ideas and experience. Into this trap Forrest Reid stumbled.

In an early essay on Ernest Dowson, published only a year or so after this first attempt, Forrest Reid commented on the skill with which the poet had succeeded in reproducing so much of the atmosphere of Verlaine's work in his own verses. This success he ascribed, rightly I think, not to 'conscious imitation' but to a 'perfect sympathy' with the French master. It is, alas, the 'conscious imitation' rather than the 'perfect sympathy' which has gone to the making of *The Kingdom of Twilight*. The Henry James influence was, of course, the most pervasive:

'Above all he hated Monday mornings. Looked at from this extreme end of it, the dawning week seemed blankly interminable —a dull, dark prison, in whose walls Saturday afternoon, the single little bright window gleaming there, was so far away as to scarcely count at all, as to be a nearly invisible point of light in the prevailing gloom. What *was* visible, on the other hand, what was hugely and always visible, was just the day's endless routine, the wretched waste of precious hours . . . —the drudgery, the weary monotony of it all.'

(P. 110.)

And there were other, more dangerous influences—Pater,

66

d'Annunzio, even Huysmans. Only perhaps in the descriptions of Belfast and the surrounding countryside was he quite at ease, able to give a foretaste of his latent powers. Here is a slum-scene:

'Long, narrowly-paved, ill-lit streets of dirty little shops and dwelling-houses succeeded one another with a depressing continuity. An iron urinal, painted green, but looking black in the dull-yellow light of the gas-lamp above it, stood close to the foot-path, and formed a centre of attraction for a swarm of ragged children as lending an additional excitement to games of tig. Here and there the gloomy, grimy back of a warehouse, or factory, broke the monotony of the smaller houses. . . . At corners, and in doorways, groups of men and boys stood smoking, and spitting, and gazing at the passers-by. From one of the many black, narrow alleys there issued the oaths and obscenity of some drunken quarrel, and now and then the shrill, harsh laugh of a woman, mirthless, horrible, would rise above the gruffer undertone of her companion. Slouching, staggering figures zigzagged along, clawing at the walls, and coming every few yards to a standstill. At the door of a public-house the slow, silent invitation of a prostitute was stared into their eyes from a puffed, bloated face.'

(P. 69.)

Already he possessed this capacity for evoking scene and place, although the evocations still resembled each other more than the scenes they were designed to portray. But too often even these descriptions suffered from being written in the 'vicious medium that was neither poetry nor prose' which at that time did him duty for a style.

Artistically speaking *The Garden God*, Forrest Reid's next novel, shows an advance. The book was, of course, a *fin de siècle* one, with the mannered, cloying quality of decadent writing (Pater's *Child in the House*, which was one of Forrest Reid's enthusiasms at this time, has left a clear imprint on the style of *The Garden God*). Yet a sensitive critic might have traced, beneath the period influences and effects, the tentative stirrings of an original talent. 'La prose de l'auteur est soignée et se lit agréablement' its anonymous French critic had remarked;[1] and certainly there is more economy, a greater exactitude in the writing, passages, even, of real beauty. The author himself admitted later, in *Apostate*, to having had an idea 'that I liked it very much indeed'—although towards the end of his life he was to implore a friend, who possessed a copy, to relegate it 'to the darkest corner reserved for disowned juvenilia.'

The problem which Forrest Reid had set himself was a difficult and delicate one. 'The purpose of the book was purely lyrical', its effect, in Arthur Symons's phrase, intended to be that of 'a kind of poem'. The theme—'half dream, half reality'—is Greek, Platonic; the story of the slightest. It is cast in the form of a reverie, a 'tale within a tale'. The teller is Graham Iddesleigh, now, at the time of writing, in middle age. Musing over his childhood, he casts his mind back to his schooldays and particularly to his friendship with Harold Brocklehurst, and all it then meant to him. Harold, he remembers, had come, in the holidays, to stay with him. One day they went rowing and afterwards lay together, in sunny idleness, on the rocks. The scene, as it shapes itself in Iddesleigh's mature imagination, begins to take on the quality of an idyll:

'The sunlight made the water very clear and tempting. Floating faintly through the still afternoon came the notes of the church clock. From everywhere the salt, invigorating smell of seaweed just uncovered by the ebb tide was blown into their faces, and long trailing branches of it, golden-brown and grass-green in the sunlight, rose and sank with the swell. Here and there, a little lower down, sprays of a brighter colour were visible—pink and red and orange, like delicate, feathery coral. . . .

'After their bathe they sat on the rocks, baking in the hot sun. "How brown your hands and face and neck are!" said Graham lazily. "The rest of you seems so white. . . ."

'Then a sudden thought seemed to strike him and . . . raising him to his feet . . . he made him stand like the praying boy of the

[1] *Le Mercure de France*, 1 July 1906.

Berlin Museum, the "Adorante," his face and hands uplifted to the joy of the morning.

' "And now what else?" he murmured. "You are too young for an athlete. Your body is too slender. I will make you into a youthful Dionysus instead. Let me put this seaweed in your hair. It is a wreath of vine."

'He placed him so that he leaned against the black, smooth rock, and the soft melting lines of the boy's body shone out with an extraordinary beauty from the sombre background. Graham paused for a moment, and stepping back, shaded his eyes with his hand while he gazed fixedly at his work. A faint colour came into his cheeks and he advanced again. Very gently he pulled the brown waving hair over the boy's forehead, and a little lower still, giving to his face a more feminine oval. . . . He pulled his head, too, slightly forward, bending it from the shapely neck; and with delicate fingers he half lowered the lids of the dark, clear blue eyes, till the upper lashes, long and curling, cast a shadow on the cheek below; and he parted the lips, ever so softly, till a strange dreamy smile seemed to play upon them.'

(Pp. 82–4.)

It is only on the next page that, without any warning, we learn that Harold, on that very day, while they were making their way home, was killed—senselessly, instantaneously—by a runaway horse. Graham, prostrated by sorrow, finds himself haunted by the memory of the friend he loved, whose action had saved his own life. Weeks later, wandering into the little country church which stood near the place, he sees Harold in a sort of vision. He faints; but when consciousness returns it is only to bring his own sorrow and remorse with it. At this point the dreamer becomes aware, through his mood of melancholy retrospection, of his present surroundings, and the morbid little story, thus correctly rounded off, is brought to an end.

'The purpose of the book was purely lyrical.' Forrest Reid was right; yet, at the same time, one doubts whether, in the account which he gives in *Private Road* of its reception, and in particular of its reception by Henry James, he was being entirely candid with himself. 'Why'—he was later to ask—'should what had been academically acceptable for over two thousand years suddenly cease to be acceptable because I had translated it out of the world of dialectic into that of fiction? I had not altered it. It had been formulated by Socrates as an ideal, and as an ideal I had kept it.' (*Private Road*, p. 66.) Moreover, *Tim*, Howard Sturgis's novel, had appeared fourteen years earlier and had been (he pointed out) 'one of the most successful novels of its year'.

But it was not quite so easy as that. *Tim*, for all its sentiment, belonged to the main tradition of the Victorian novel. *The Garden God* was different, more pagan, and—while never approaching sensuality—altogether more sensuous in its treatment: the unmistakable note of subdued eroticism—as in the passage quoted—must have made that clear to the most superficial and impercipient reader. The point, admittedly, is a difficult one. But Henry James was—well, Henry James; and the date of *The Garden God*'s publication was 1905. A book in this vein, published today, would excite little comment on moral grounds. What we have to remember are the social shibboleths of the age, the proximity of the Wilde scandal, with the widespread and indiscriminate panic which it caused, and the repugnancy it aroused towards every unusual form of emotional relationship. But the particular causes of the distress which it gave to that great man lay deep in his subconscious mind, amounted to more than the disingenuousness which was all it appeared on a superficial showing to be. The subject treated in *The Garden God* was clearly one which Henry James viewed with both a shrinking distaste and, it now seems, a peculiar fascination. It was a topic which, more than once, he was himself drawn into treating obliquely. Much has been written, probably too much, about the emotional and moral issues concealed in *The Turn of the Screw*, but the 'protest of ignorance' which he makes in the preface to that little masterpiece of horror springs from the same compound of attraction and repulsion. The attitude appeared, as Forrest Reid justly pointed out, 'to be prompted by a strange moral timidity, which refuses to accept responsibility for what deliberately has been suggested'. (*Private Road*, p. 70.)

At any rate, the dedication of the book to Henry James was disastrous. All unwittingly, this simple act of homage had the effect of bringing their relationship to an end. Forrest Reid continued to send his books to James as they appeared, but from the Master no further acknowledgement was ever forthcoming. And the effect on himself was nearly as decisive. Never again was he able to regard Henry James in quite the same way: 'my admiration for the artist remained, but an admiration more human and intimate had been lost. The intelligence that had seemed so understanding seemed now less understanding.' (*Private Road*, pp. 69–70.)

'THE BRACKNELS' AND 'FOLLOWING DARKNESS'

Such were the early experiments, and their unlooked-for consequences. It was only after he had decided that he would leave the tea-trade and settle down to try his fortune by writing alone that he found his touch. *The Bracknels*, written after the Cambridge interlude, and with a full six years put between it and *The Garden God*, was the real start of his career as a writer; the first book into which he succeeded in putting something of his personal vision of life. Both it and *Following Darkness* are, in essence, stories of the development of one particular person—in each case an unusually sensitive boy. But in addition to this they are both stories about families. *The Bracknels*, indeed, in the original 1911 version, was explicitly sub-titled 'A family chronicle'. The books are each of them concerned with larger horizons than their predecessors; plots are more complicated, there is greater action, and an altogether broader canvas.

As originally conceived, *The Bracknels* bore small relation to the published volume. 'The process which had transformed *The Garden God* from a realistic school story into a lyrical romance was now exactly reversed. *This* lyrical romance I decided to turn into a realistic novel.' (*Private Road*, p. 84.) The 'lyrical romance' was the Moon Story, from which the final version grew. Forrest Reid expanded this tale into a full-length novel, 'treating the whole thing as a family chronicle'.

One's first impulse, I am afraid, is to doubt the wisdom of this conversion. Why, we find ourselves asking, was the Moon Story unsatisfactory? What were the motives that changed it into a 'realistic novel'? Whatever the answers, in the novel, as it was printed, there is a discontinuity—which is always apparent—between the 'family chronicle' and the mysterious dream-story which, at some stage, was woven into it. The book hovers between fantasy and realism without completely achieving either. At times, indeed, the dream-story comes perilously near to disappearing altogether. Much later Forrest Reid discovered how to handle the commonplace and the marvellous in a single narrative; here the experiment did not fully succeed.

It was an experiment, indeed, which required an adroitness in writing beyond the usual. *The Garden God*, an idyll 'removed from actuality and placed in an eternal summer' had been a vastly simpler affair. The difference between the two books was 'the difference between a drama and a lyric'. What Forrest Reid was attempting to do was to keep—intermittently—the mood of the earlier book, while at the same time placing it in a naturalistic setting, in a recognizable everyday world, incorporating a large cast and several subsidiary, and not always entirely happy, themes.

The hero of the book is Denis Bracknel. Denis, we soon realize, is 'different'; a difference which stands out all the more clearly when we begin to realize the kind of family to which he belongs. Mr. Bracknel is a self-made man, a Belfast merchant (and perhaps, we speedily begin to realize, none too scrupulous a merchant at that). He is dogmatic, unimaginative, and bullying; concealing beneath this domineering manner a soul possessed only by 'panic and emptiness'. His wife is a more pathetic figure, weak and melancholy and frightened. The children—grown-up now—are no more attractive. Alfred, the eldest son, is a coarse philistine and a waster, Amy and May, the two daughters, are foolish and flirtatious. And, many years younger than the rest of them, there is Denis. As he is the type of a character who occurs more than once in Forrest Reid's novels it may be as well to introduce him at once:

'The boy's share of personal beauty was meagre, but there was something pleasant about him. He was thin and sallow, with straight, black, coarse hair tumbling about a broad forehead. His grey eyes were dark and very peculiar, of a narrow, elongated oval, and set wide apart and slightly obliquely in his face, beneath thin black eyebrows, giving him . . . a most strange, an almost Oriental, look.'

(Pp. 22–3.)

The remainder of his family Mr. Bracknel finds he can understand, for they clearly belong to his own world: but Denis is an enigma to him. He has not the remotest conception of the secret inner life the boy leads, because his only idea, a predetermined one, is to force him into the family mould.

Into these surroundings there steps Hubert Rusk, Denis's new tutor. Rusk is twenty-three, only just down from Cambridge; young, earnest, inexperienced, but anxious to like and be liked by his pupil. Mrs. Bracknel soon seeks an opportunity of discussing the boy's future with him. Rusk is doubtful whether the usual kind of schooling will benefit the boy most:

'"Yes, don't you think so, Mr. Rusk? I have always thought so. But his father wants him to have a sound commercial education as well as—as the ordinary thing, you know."

'Rusk looked somewhat puzzled though he tried very hard not to. "Ah yes—a sound commercial education," he repeated vaguely. "What exactly does he mean by that, I wonder?"

'"By a sound commercial education? I'm afraid I don't know. I thought *you* would know. It is the expression he always uses." There was something almost plaintive in Mrs. Bracknel's tone.'

(Pp. 37–8.)

In this atmosphere Rusk does not find his new life an easy

73

one. Mr. Bracknel is overbearing, his wife nervous and helpless, Denis enigmatic, withdrawn, difficult to open out. The boy seems to live in a world of his own, and from what Rusk can pick up of the hints which are all he occasionally drops, that world cannot be a very pleasant one. Then, one day while they are out walking, Denis suddenly puts a question:

"'You're not superstitious, Mr. Rusk, are you?"
"'I don't think so. Not that I know of at any rate."
"'Not even a little bit?"
"'Oh, I won't say that!"
"'You're never afraid of something you don't understand?"
"'Something that may be going to happen?"
"'No, not exactly that. . . . It doesn't get as far as that. It's just a kind of feeling."
"'About what?"
"'That you're not altogether alone—when you ought to be alone—when you seem to be alone, I mean. . . . If you're walking across the lawn to the house, do you never feel as if there was something at a window high up, hiding behind the blind, and watching you?"
' "Oh, you're too full of fancies for me!" growled Rusk good humouredly. He laid a firm, friendly hand on his shoulder. . . . "What I'm afraid of at present is that we're going to get wet through."'

(P. 174.)

And then there are the daughters. With Rusk's handsome looks they both promptly fall in love. Mutual jealousy makes them enemies, and soon each is ready to stop at nothing to outbid the other.

At this point another favourite theme emerges. Denis is a moon-worshipper. One night when Rusk is lying awake he hears the boy creep out of the house. He follows silently, and is in time to see Denis making for the neighbouring plantation. Crouching in the brushwood at the edge of the clearing Rusk is astonished to see his pupil emerging into the moonlight 'moving through the dim, delicate beauty of the darkened wood, like a figure in a dream .

'For the boy was naked, and this simple fact, so unexpected and astonishing, had in some inexplicable way the property of banishing from Rusk's mind all hope that the whole thing might be merely an elaborate child's-play. . . . Denis advanced into the middle of the grove, and there was something in his movements, a kind of rhythmic precision and alacrity that was yet not haste, which gave Rusk a momentary impression that he might perhaps be walking in his sleep. The idea brought him a sudden hope, but of this hope he was doomed to swift disappointment when he watched the boy uncover the altar and place a large moon-shaped cake upon it. This cake, Rusk saw, was decked with white tapers —tapers which Denis was now lighting. When all were ablaze, he bowed low before them, as to some unseen and ghostly presence, and then proceeded to go through as amazing a ceremony as Rusk was ever likely to behold. He must surely have invented it, and yet it suggested to Rusk an actual survival from a half-forgotten pagan ritual. The boy poured out a libation. He burned incense as he moved about, waving it up to the mysterious, pale divinity that hung in the deep sky above him. The thin, aromatic smoke rose up in slender spirals, while the young priest, like a white, sylvan creature of a primeval world, performed his simple rites . . . somehow, as he watched it now, alone, at this hour and in this place, with the dimness of night and the stillness of motionless trees all around stretching away into what might have been the very womb of the past, he found it difficult to see it in the light of anything childish or trivial. . . . It was real—too real. What . . . was the relation of this naked pagan boy, with body bared to the whiteness of the moon, to the young Presbyterian, who sat Sunday by Sunday in his father's pew? . . . Suddenly, as Denis drew closer to him, he had a clear view of his face, and his heart sank. That strange, rapt, almost ecstatic expression was not the expression of a boy playing a game. . . .'

(Pp. 160–1.)

Rusk struggles on; but it is only his growing affection for

Denis, and the suggestion that he and the boy should go abroad for a year, travelling as tutor and pupil, that persuades him to continue after Amy has seriously compromised his position by a foolish trick. For by now he feels that he has captured the boy's trust.

The story shifts to Mr. Bracknel. A theft by a clerk at the office comes to light and Alfred, who has been driven to desperation by the smallness of the salary paid to him by his father, is implicated. Mr. Bracknel, who hates him for his idle habits, seizes this opportunity to get rid of him. He tries to force him to emigrate, but during the interview he loses control:

'Even in the present low state of his fortunes he [Alfred] was capable of deriving a genuine pleasure from his father's excitement. The situation struck him as extremely piquant. He produced his cigarette case.

'Mr. Bracknel made another movement towards him. His face was now purple, and the veins of his forehead and neck were swollen unpleasantly. A flake of froth actually appeared at the corner of his mouth. He raised his hand as if he were about to strike his son, and at the same instant stopped. For a moment he stood quite still, while his lips twitched, and his whole face was drawn as with some sharp sudden pain. Then he grasped at the table, missed it, and fell on the floor.

'Alfred gazed down at him callously, curiously, watching the colour ebb from his face and leave it a pale, sickly, waxy yellow. . . . His eyes were wide open, and he breathed slowly and noisily, a phenomenon which appeared to interest Alfred keenly. . . . Moved by a morbid curiosity, he bent lower over his father. Mr. Bracknel was not very pleasant to look at. His face had turned an ash-grey colour and his bulging eyes were fixed and glazed. His jaw, too, had dropped, leaving the tongue slightly visible between the false teeth.'

(Pp. 259–60.)

The shock of Mr. Bracknel's death is too much for Denis's already frayed nerves. It is decided that he and Rusk shall leave on their holiday as soon as possible after the funeral. But now the boy begins to suffer from hallucinations. On the evening of the day following the funeral he goes out, fails to return, and is at length discovered by Rusk and a search party in the shrubbery where he had celebrated his mysterious rites. But now they witness no rites, no moon-worshipping spectacle. Denis is found among the branches, hanged with his own braces, limp and lifeless.

And at that point the book really ends. In this original version, however, a small *envoi* was, at the publisher's demand, unwillingly and (I think) infelicitously added. In this postscript Rusk is made to return to Ireland, some months later, on a farewell visit before setting out for Australia.[1]

The Bracknels is better, much better, than either of Forrest Reid's two earlier books. About the moon-story theme, and its working out, there clings something of the quality of nightmare, but of a nightmare enacted in the wakeful light of day, which fills us with the same boding that we sense so powerfully in *The Turn of the Screw*. Denis, in fact, is killed through the agency of the same supernatural forces which overwhelm the boy Miles in James's story. Since *The Garden God* Forrest Reid had matured and shaken off those early influences which had arrested the natural development of his own genius. *The Bracknels* is the first-fruit of that greater maturity.

Where the book fails is in its lack of concentration, or integration. The moon-story theme, it must be repeated, is not a complete success. And there is wanting a certain sense of proportion. In the early chapters of the book we had not heard quite sufficiently about the moon-worshipper; and this has the effect, at the end, of making us unready for Denis's death, unprepared for the method he chooses, and confused and uncertain about his motives. Do we, in fact, really achieve that 'suspension of disbelief' which is essential if the boy's behaviour is to seem comprehensible to us? The denouement comes upon us too suddenly, for we had previously been given little inkling of the boy's fatal preoccupa-

[1] In the revised version, *Denis Bracknel* (published in 1947), this is omitted, the story ending with Denis's death.

tion, and cause and effect seem to have been connected by a chain that is not visible to us.

Basil de Selincourt, in his criticism of the book, went even further. 'I am inclined to wonder,' he commented, 'whether the moon episode is essential to the conception of Denis, and wonder whether you have not taken it really as a kind of luxury of the imagination.' (*Private Road*, p. 170.) This judgement is perhaps less an artistic one than a facet of the critic's own views on Forrest Reid's whole attitude towards the supernatural, views which are considered elsewhere;[1] but it is an attitude which is worth noting, however much it seems to run counter to the trend of Forrest Reid's genius.

A second weakness arises out of Forrest Reid's own interpretation of the book. Writing later, he saw the tragedy as essentially one which turned on a 'weakness of imagination'; a weakness, that is, in Rusk's own imaginative sympathy for the boy. It is doubtful whether this limitation in Rusk's understanding is made clear enough in the early pages. Perhaps the tutor's 'weakness of imagination' extended here to his creator; for Rusk's abundant stores of well-meaning sympathy, which have been so strongly emphasized, leave us rather unprepared for this explanation. The point really links up with the earlier criticism. The two motives for Denis's suicide are, firstly, the effect on his mind of Mr. Bracknel's death, taken in conjunction with his own unusual and highly-strung temperament, as evinced in the moon-worshipping theme; and secondly, Rusk's failure to enter into the boy's mind intuitively enough to have foreseen this danger and acted accordingly. In fact, both the moon-theme, and the analysis of Rusk's attitude towards his pupil, have been dislodged from their true place in the novel by the demands of the 'family chronicle'.

Hard on the heels of *The Bracknels*, a year later, appeared *Following Darkness*, the dedication to E. M. Forster, whom its author had recently met.

It seems to me, without any doubt, that this book takes its

[1] See pages 59–60, 170 et. seq., and 180–1 *infra*.

place beside *Apostate* and the Tom Barber trilogy as one of its author's two or three finest achievements. The novel has been compared in its emotional quality with Gide's *La Porte Etroite*, and one can easily forget, reading it today, that this too was a novel written before the first Great War. Its theme—the psychological development of a lonely and sensitive adolescent boy —is one which is very familiar today. Yet *Following Darkness* came out in the year before the appearance of Mr. Compton Mackenzie's *Sinister Street*, which is usually accounted the pioneer in this direction; and the psychology of the earlier book is, I think, much sounder than that in *Sinister Street*; and, for all the fine amplitude of his setting and surroundings, Michael Fane seems a far less plausible, less acutely individualized figure than the superficially less attractive Peter Waring. A more illuminating parallel —and one which Forrest Reid himself drew—is with Joyce's *Portrait of the Artist*, which appeared four years after *Following Darkness*. Forrest Reid's novel has none of the accumulated power and rush, the apocalyptic vision which flames and flickers over every page of Joyce's masterpiece, but Stephen Dedalus and Peter Waring were both subject to the same influences, the same temptations, the same spiritual torment and remorse. Joyce was Catholic-bred and Forrest Reid's youth was passed in surroundings dyed with the hues of an uncompromising Protestantism: yet the emotional life of these two Irishmen in their early years must have been strangely similar. The pervading atmosphere of Joyce's book—an Irish atmosphere—often recalls the more sombre parts of *Following Darkness*. And the idyllic scene where Stephen watches the unknown girl bathing by the seashore reminds us of Peter Waring's sight of Katherine Dale wandering on the beach at Newcastle:

'He looked northward towards Howth. The sea had fallen below the line of seawrack on the shallow side of the breakwater and already the tide was running out fast along the foreshore. Already one long oval bank of sand lay warm and dry amid the wavelets. Here and there warm isles of sand gleamed above the shallow tide and about the isles and around the long bank and amid the shallow currents of the beach were lightclad figures, wading and delving. . . .

'He was alone. He was unheeded, happy and near to the wild heart of life. He was alone and young and wilful and wild-hearted, alone amid a waste of wild air and brackish waters and the seaharvest of shells and tangle and veiled grey sunlight and gayclad lightclad figures of children and girls and voices childish and girlish in the air.

'A girl stood before him in midstream, alone and still, gazing out to sea. She seemed like one whom magic had changed into the likeness of a strange and beautiful seabird . . . her long fair hair was girlish: and girlish, and touched with the wonder of mortal beauty, her face.' (*A Portrait of the Artist as a Young Man* [1924 edn.], pp. 194–5.)

There is a less immediately lyrical effect in the passage from *Following Darkness*, and Forrest Reid is temperamentally unable to bring to the portrayal of Katherine the same emotion which fills Joyce's description, but read in its context the description, though briefer and less explicit, is equally delicate and evocative in mood:

'Owen and I were standing by the low sea-wall, looking out across the wet brown sands, when I saw her. It was a gray, cloudy day, and the air was full of mist and damp, which hung in heavy, livid-coloured veils over the black mountain-tops, and sometimes dropped half way down the slopes. The tide was out and the noise of the waves sounded remote and musical. The broad stretch of wet sand and shingle reached out to the cold, gray-green sea, with its white curling line of foam; and at the water's edge, a little bent forward, her light dress floating out behind her in the fresh wind, one hand raised, holding the brim of her big black hat, she moved along, a solitary figure against the broad line of sea and sky. It was Katherine, and as I watched her it struck me that the whole picture, from her presence in it, became curiously like a Whistler water-colour.'

(*Following Darkness*, p. 253.)

Or, in a different key, Peter's visit to the priest finds something of its echo in Stephen's confession to the weary old Father in an unknown Dublin church.

Following Darkness is a lovely book. First of all, the whole thing is drenched in natural beauty—the beauty of the Mourne Mountains and Slieve Donard, the beauty of Derryaghy, Mrs. Carroll's house, the beauty we associate with the early morning of a cloudless day at the start of summer. And there is beauty in the characterization, too. Each of the chief persons in the story is most exactly realized, their shifting relationships subtly charted. And yet although the book showed a greater feeling for form than its predecessor, and a new emotional dimension appeared in the account of Peter's unrequited devotion for Katherine Dale, with the public *Following Darkness* failed; though its author considered it the best book he had, up to that time, written.

The story is essentially the story of Peter Waring, and Peter's story is in some respects the writer's autobiography too. Forrest Reid usually disclaimed any attempt at self-portraiture in his work but he did admit, in some lines in the MS. of *Apostate* which were never printed, that in Peter's case 'a certain compromise had been effected' with reality.

The setting is the lovely Irish countryside, in County Down, between the Mourne Mountains and the sea. Here Peter lives with his father. That they are profoundly antipathetic characters we realize from the start. Peter's father is the village schoolmaster and his one ambition is that his son shall inherit and hold the same views, and particularly the same views on questions of religion, as he does. Of this there is, can be, no chance. The small household is an unhappy one:

'When I was with him [his father] I never felt quite at my ease, and this made me sulky and perpetually on the defensive. I was not more with him than I could help, and as we lived alone together, with only an old woman who came in every day to look after the house and do the cooking, it must have been easy for him to see that I avoided his society. I never pretended to myself to have any particular affection for him, and I don't even know that it would have mended matters if I had.

'One night, when I was about fourteen, I woke up in the dark, with the consciousness that it was very late and that I was not alone in my room. The next moment I knew my father was there, kneeling beside my bed. I lay absolutely quiet: I knew he was praying, and praying for me. Presently I heard him sigh, and then rise noiselessly to his feet, but I gave no sign. I heard him move away, I heard my door being softly closed, the faint click of the latch as it slipped into its place. I lay on with my eyes wide open, wondering why he had come in like this. I did not like it. It made me feel uncomfortable, as all emotions do when we are unable to respond to them. I believed my father cared for me far more than for anything else in the world, yet somehow that did not help matters. It was not the sort of love that begets love in return. Though he loved me, I felt he did not trust me, or rather that he believed I had an infinite capacity for yielding to temptation. By this time I understood that when my mother left home she had gone to somebody else. . . . But he explained nothing and I asked no questions. As I lay awake that night I thought of all this, and it occurred to me that it might have much to do with his extraordinary anxiety about my religious and moral life.'

(Pp. 22–3.)

But for Peter there is a single ray of consolation in the friendship he has formed with Mrs. Carroll. She gives him the sympathy, the encouragement, and the companionship for which he craves; she is symbolic too, of that wider world which is distrusted and hated by his father. When he is up at Derryaghy, loitering among its books and pictures, he is happy, he can escape from his father's dingy, restrictive world.

And then one day Mrs. Carroll's niece and nephew, Gerald and Katherine, arrive on a visit. The appearance of Katherine Dale releases all the boy's pent-up emotion: they go on an expedition into the country, and Peter realizes that he is in love, with all the passionate idealism of which first love is capable. It was a day of pure happiness:

' . . . we continued to trudge along, our feet white with dust. It really *was* very hot, and I was glad I had so little clothing on— merely a light cotton tennis-shirt under my jacket. When we reached a low grey bridge that spanned a shallow mountain stream we branched inland . . . the . . valley was wonderfully beautiful, widening out gradually, and gradually ascending; on each side of it steep dark mountains, covered with heather, and grass, and gorse, and hidden streams which flowed into the broader, deeper stream we followed. The colouring was rich and splendid—dull gold, bronze, dark green and even black, with the brighter purple of the heather woven through it, and the long, narrow, pale, silver streak of water, glittering and gleaming, far, far up, till in the end it was lost over the edge of a higher valley which crossed ours at right angles. . . . I looked at Katherine. She was very beautiful, and in a quite different way from her brother. . . . Her skin was very white, save where in her cheeks it flushed to a soft radiant glow. Her brown, crisp hair was pulled back straight from her forehead, though one or two little tufts had got loose and waved in the faint wind. Her nose and mouth had the same delicate beauty as Gerald's, but her expression was quite different, and it was there that her greatest beauty lay.'

Soon their picnic was over:

'We hid the basket under the heather. A quiet had fallen upon us, through which the noise of the splashing water seemed to weave itself in patterns and arabesques of sound.

'"Shall we go up higher?" I asked, and without answering me Katherine began to climb the hill-side, and I followed her over dry, springy, fragrant heather, and between huge mossy boulders that had lain undisturbed for centuries. . . . When we reached a place where the ground rose steeply for a yard or two I gave Katherine my hand to help her, and when we came to more level ground we still went on hand in hand. And with this light contact there came to me a strange, thrilling pleasure, intense yet dreamy, unlike anything I had ever known before. I did not look at my companion. When I spoke, telling her to avoid a patch of soft ground that had here spread across the path, the sound of my own voice astonished me, so unfamiliar was it, even trembling slightly; and I felt my limbs trembling. . . . I threw my hat from me and flung myself down among the heather. . . . Far, far below us, the sea, blue and deep, broad, beautiful and free, lay shimmering in the hot sun. . . . I felt my eyes grow moist, and I turned away my head that my companion might not see my face.

'Presently I looked round. Katherine was sitting beside me, gazing straight out at the distant sea. The broad brim of her black hat shadowed her face. The deep blue of her eyes seemed darker than before; they had the blue now of the eyes Renoir so often painted, and that I have seen nowhere else. . . . I wanted to be quiet. I thought if we sat in silence, if I held her hand; above all, if we sat in silence close together, her arms about me, my cheek against her cheek, the past might swim up into the present. . . . But instead of that we began to talk, to talk of things that did not matter, until, by and by, we got up to return home.'

(Pp. 66–76.)

At length the wonderful time comes to an end and Peter has to return to Belfast, to school. The scene changes. Instead of idyllic walks with Katherine on the hills and by the sea, he goes as a boarder to stay with his uncle and aunt.

For the latter he forms an instant dislike:

'Aunt Margaret welcomed me without effusion. She was an enormous woman, dark, middle-aged, and with a peculiar smile that always made me feel uneasy. Her lips parted and her teeth became visible, but otherwise her face underwent no change, the expression in her hard, shining, black eyes did not alter. It was, somehow, not a smile at all, but a grimace, and disappeared with a startling suddenness, leaving no trace behind it. When her face was at rest, her lips drew in, as if by some mysterious suction. She wore a wig, and . . . I had been told that she suffered from some obscure, internal disease, which at times caused her great

84

pain, but though she was white and fat and puffy, she presented no appearance of being an invalid. As she kissed me, a ceremony I would gladly have dispensed with, I became conscious of a vague, sickly ódour, reminding me of the smell of a chemist's shop.'

(P. 127.)

Their poverty, their ugliness, and their excessive piety could hardly be more distasteful to the boy:

'The furniture was cheap, flimsy, and uncomfortable. The curtains, the gaudy vases, the hideous wall-paper, were of the brightest and least accordant colours, and I even preferred our parlour at home, where, if the things were not less ugly, there were fewer of them. Several pictures hung on the walls, and one hung directly in front of me. It was an engraving, and represented a young man in armour visibly torn between a desire for virtue, embodied in a flaxen-haired lady in floating white drapery, and a deplorable weakness for all that another lady might be taken as symbolising. This latter person was a brunette, and rather more scantily, though quite decently, draped. She held a glass of champagne in her hand, waving it triumphantly aloft, like a torch.'

(Pp. 129–30.)

Life here and at school is dismal in the extreme. But he makes one friend, Owen Gill. Owen is an intellectual boy, and he opens Peter's eyes to whole vistas of which he had never dreamt.

'I saw a good deal of Owen. . . . On Saturdays and Sundays we usually went for long walks together, during which we threshed out the affairs of the universe, and built it over again. It was all quite new to me, just as was the peculiar type of Owen's mind, its extraordinary eagerness in the pursuit of ideas. My head already swarmed with an amazing mass of unsettled notions which buzzed in it like bees in a shaken hive. It seemed to me we never discussed anything less serious than the immortality of the soul. Owen was not sure of the existence of God, and I, so far as Christianity was concerned, was an Agnostic also. But to Owen it appeared to make an enormous difference, he was positively unhappy about it; while to me, though I did not let him suspect this, it was a matter of supreme indifference. . . . Sometimes, when we were talking, he would catch me by my arms and swing me slowly back and forward. Sometimes he would draw me close up to him till my face almost touched his, and his eyes seemed to look straight into my spirit, and then he would suddenly release me. He had a very quick and passionate temper, and was ridiculously sensitive, so that, though I employed infinitely more tact with him than I had ever done with anybody else, I occasionally offended him. Then he would leave me, his face as red as a turkey-cock, and his grey eyes dark and bright. . . . But the next morning he came up to me with a shy and shamefaced smile, saying he was sorry. At such times there would come into his voice so charming a gentleness that it was impossible to remain angry with him.'

(Pp. 162–4.)

The holidays came round again, the weary struggle with his father began once more. But the sweet image of Katherine still haunted his memory and imagination, and when Christmas arrived he sent her a small present.

'It had taken me a long time to choose something I thought she might care for. . . . I had got her a photograph of Francia's portrait of the boy Federigo Gonzaga . . . and over and over again I had pictured her opening the parcel, her surprise. It was two days after Christmas when the postman brought me a letter from her, but instead of reading it, I put it in my pocket. It was a fairly thick packet, so, though her writing was very large, I knew it must be a long letter. . . . All day long I thought of the pleasure I should have, and in the end I became so impatient that I went to bed about nine o'clock.

'I put the letter on my pillow, and placed a lighted candle on the painted, deal chest-of-drawers beside my bed. I undressed, got into bed, and only then, with eager fingers, tore open the envelope and drew out its contents.

'I looked at them as they lay upon the bright, patch-work counterpane, a single sheet of note-paper, and a New Year card in the form of a pocket calendar. . . . I glanced at what she had written. . . . She thanked me for my picture, which was very pretty. She would have liked to write me a really long letter, but there were some people staying in the house, and she had to look after them, and had only been able to snatch a moment to wish me a happy New Year. That was all.

'I blew out the candle and lay with my eyes wide open staring into the darkness.'

(Pp. 204–5.)

At Aunt Margaret's, next term, relations become more and more strained. George, their son, quarrels with Peter, and Peter leaves after he has taken his exams. At home, Owen comes to stay. Peter had anticipated, somewhat fearfully, a speedy clash between Owen's youthful dogmatism and his father's equally decided prejudices; to his astonishment nothing of the kind happens. Suddenly it flashes on him that Owen is really a totally different person to himself, does not share his world after all.

'It occurred to me, as I watched them and listened to them, that Owen and my father were perhaps more alike, mentally and spiritually, than Owen and I, though my father had but a fraction of Owen's fineness, and none of his generosity. They were related as a coarse weed and a delicate flower might be, but I was of a different genus.'

(P. 252.)

Meanwhile Katherine and Gerald come to stay again with their aunt. But a year has wrought its changes, and Katherine, woman-like, can no longer feel for Peter what Peter still feels for her. Like Agnes in *The Longest Journey* (whom she not a little resembles) her true character now works to the surface, Peter's very worship breeding in her a kind of sadism of which she is probably but dimly conscious. She is the 'cruel fair', and the more cruel because of this very obliviousness. She will not understand his love, refuses to take it seriously. Her impatience, wilfulness, and lack of imagination do the rest. After she leaves Derryaghy Peter, grown desperate, tramps out into the darkness one wild wet night and deliberately attempts to bring about his own death by exposure. Instead, he falls desperately ill with pneumonia, but manages to survive. He confesses the escapade to Mrs. Carroll, the one person in whom he can confide and who is able to soothe his harrowed emotions. She understands, helps him to see his grief over Katherine in some proportion, and gives him fresh confidence to face the future. And on this note, bringing 'calm of mind, all passion spent' the book gently closes.

A COMEDY OF MIDDLE AGE:
'THE GENTLE LOVER'

The Gentle Lover stands apart, in two respects, from Forrest Reid's other novels. To begin with, the story is much more concerned with adult characters. The theme of youth is there, of course, but in fact Brian and Sylvie Grimshaw are the only strictly youthful characters. And secondly, it is the only novel in which the setting is not Ireland, his own country. '*The Gentle Lover* was the direct result of loitering in Bruges and Italy'—and there *is* something leisurely and Edwardian about the book—'Its subject was a Henry James subject—one of those *amours de voyage* that Henry in his youth was so fond of treating.' Probably it was that 'Henry James subject' which prompted one reviewer to ask what would happen 'if the author would write a story with two or three duels, an elopement, and a shipwreck in it'. There are no shipwrecks in *The Gentle Lover*, not even an elopement, and the only duels are tea-table ones, but even so Forrest Reid treats the book with rather less than the appreciation which, I think, it deserves. Of course, it was derivative, and he couldn't hope to match the skill which James himself would have put into a *conte* of this kind. But to place the book on the same footing as *At the Door of the Gate* or *Pender*, is, it seems to me, perverse, altogether too low an estimate.

The early scenes are laid in Bruges, the 'sad Northern Venice'—the Bruges-la-Morte of Rodenbach's famous novel, that strange

stifling tragedy of a transferred love, whose atmosphere influenced
Forrest Reid—Bruges sad indeed, with her 'inconsolable towers',
her bells and her religious, her 'abandoned stone quays woven into
an idealization of melancholy by the cold arteries of the canals
which had long ago ceased to feel the pulsation of the sea.' The
spell of the city lies like an enchantment over the early pages of
The Gentle Lover.

Half-way through the book the setting shifts to Italy, to Florence: that 'most beautiful of cities, with the golden Arno shot
through the breast of her like an arrow', Florence the 'dense little
treasure-city' that Henry James painted in *Roderick Hudson*, with
its 'aesthetic aroma', its 'grave radiance', and its 'ancient, noble
landscape' all around it, sitting in the sunshine 'beside her yellow
river . . . without commerce, without other industry than the
manufacture of mosaic paper-weights and alabaster Cupids, without actuality or energy or earnestness . . . with nothing but the
little unaugmented stock of her mediæval memories, her tender-
coloured mountains, her churches and palaces, pictures and
statues.' And with Florence, Siena, dozing in her 'patient, sturdy,
sympathetic shabbiness', and Pisa, Pisa with the 'something fragile in its aspect, a quiet enveloping subtlety'.

Bennet Allingham, lingering in Bruges, accidentally comes
across a delightful youngster, Brian Grimshaw, and his equally
charming sister Sylvie. Discovering a common interest in painting, they all go off together in search of the Memlincks in the
Hospital of Saint John. There the children meet their mother and
aunt. The latter, Sophy Kilronan, proves to have been, long years
ago, one of Bennet's closest friends. Sophy Kilronan is as strong a
character as her sister Lucy is a weak one. Determined, emphatic,
perfectly assured, her imperiousness salted with a penetrating but
somehow kindly humour, she is really made of flesh and blood,
drawn from life itself.

But soon the Grimshaws decide to move on, to Florence.
Allingham, his loneliness brought home to him by his growing
affection for Sylvie, follows. But the gentle lover now has a

competitor in Mr. Halvard, a handsome young priest, whose acquaintance he made in Bruges and who also comes on to Florence. Halvard is really a weak character, for all his personal beauty, vain and an egoist, but he and Sylvie fall in love, and Allingham, as he must, acquiesces in this. The clergyman's religious scruples prevent him, however, from seeking to marry Sylvie, and he departs for Pisa. To Pisa, in a noble determination to persuade his rival to reconsider his convictions and ask Sylvie's hand in marriage, Allingham follows. He is unsuccessful. But returning later to the Grimshaws in Florence he learns, to his bitter disappointment, that Halvard has after all returned, and that the couple are going to be married. He returns to his hotel:

'As the hours passed, the lights in the rooms all round him were extinguished, till presently his alone burned. . . . All sounds within the hotel had ceased long ago, and Allingham himself, for all movement he made, might have been asleep. But he was not asleep. In the uneasy, noisy night, broken every now and again by the voices of strayed revellers, or the rattle of a carriage, or the hoot of a motor, he went back over all the pleasant days he had spent since that morning in Bruges when he had found Brian drawing the gateway and singing as he drew. And then Sylvie had come in, and they had gone, all three together, through the old grass-grown streets, and the bright joyous spring of youth had seemed to come with all its generous warmth into his life. The room was full of memories that drifted before him as he sat there in the crude white light. . . . And even as he grasped at them they were already fading, slipping from him, eluding him; and a feeling of intense loneliness shut them out, as a cloud shuts out the sun.

'. . . It was not so much that he had missed happiness, as that he had missed everything else as well. . . . He recalled the visions and ambitions of his boyhood—the bright, foolish dreaming that had ended in this. "No more—no more," he whispered, and an immense sadness descended upon him. He opened wide the shutters and looked into the darkness. "I shall never dream again," he thought, as he leaned over the window-sill, while the night air blew in his face. "Nothing will ever happen again that matters. . . . There will never be anything more—never anything more."'

(Pp. 311–13.)

There the book really ends, or should end. But perhaps the note of unrelieved gloom was too strong, for in the last chapter of all we are carried forward to one wet March afternoon in the following year. Bennet, quite unexpectedly, runs into Sophy in Pisa, where he has been living. He takes her home to his lodgings for tea, and learns that the Grimshaws are at the end of their tour and are leaving for England the next day:

'"Bennet," she asked abruptly, "why are you going away?"'
'"Going away?" he echoed. . . .
'"Have you anybody to go to?"'
'He shook his head.
'"Why don't you stay, then?"'
'"Stay here? In Pisa?"'
'"Not necessarily in Pisa; but stay with us. Come back with us to-morrow and stay with the Grimshaws. They'd be delighted to have you. . . ."
'He did not reply for a moment. Then he said softly: "But it would only be putting it off, wouldn't it? . . ."
'"Why not stay with us altogether, then?" Her voice had a gentleness that he had very rarely heard in it.
'He looked up. "But——" he hesitated. Then he said simply: "Stay with *you*, do you mean, Sophy?"
'"Yes, with me."
'Allingham's eyes turned to the window, where the light was fading. "I can bring—I can give so little," he faltered, at last.
'"You are lonely. When I first saw you, you looked dreadfully lonely and—and tired. . . . It has all been so stupid!" she continued impatiently. "I can't bear to think of your going on like this permanently. . . . Can't we be friends?"
'"We have always been friends."

91

'Her voice softened. "Yes—from the very beginning.... We have that at least."

'There was a silence.

'"But you know—you know everything, Sophy?"

'"Yes, I think I know everything."

'"And you would still be willing to take me?"

'She paused. Her eyes rested, with a beautiful and unwonted tenderness, on his dark, thin face. "I think we might build up something together," she said slowly, "that would be much nearer to happiness than anything either of us is likely to find alone."

'"I think so, too," he answered gravely.

'She held out her hand, and, as he took it, it was as if they had sealed their compact.'   (Pp. 317–19.)

The structure of *The Gentle Lover*, and certainly its dialogue, are an improvement on anything Forrest Reid had done in the previous books. The novel lacks the imaginative power of *The Bracknels*, but the characters are more varied, the irony more felicitous, the dialogue crisper and wittier. The plan of setting the book first in Bruges and then in Italy is a good one, gives variety to the narrative. The backgrounds are sketched in with delicate but telling strokes—never described at length. Particularly the atmosphere of Florence in the summer-time comes through. Allingham and Sylvie are making an expedition to San Miniato:

'Before them, full in the afternoon sun, rose the striped black and yellow marble façade of the church, with its huge bright mosaic of Christ Enthroned. Below, in the valley, the gray towers and red domes of Florence stood up above a mass of gray and brown houses, like tall flowers in a crowded garden. On all sides of the city were sparsely wooded hills, with white villas gleaming amid olive and cypress. The landscape, under the open blue sky, had a beauty of its own ... beginning and ending in itself, dependent for its charm almost wholly on the gray crumbling buildings that here and there dotted the hillsides.'

                                                          (Pp. 157–8.)

The evocation of Bruges is almost equally successful. Bruges always had a fascination for Forrest Reid, and he visited it many times. He wrote about it on two other occasions. In 'An Ending' the anonymous story-teller describes the effect the city came to have on him:

'About five o'clock he would return to his rooms, or to a little café in the Grande Place. Here sometimes he would sit, looking across the great paved square, with the belfry straight before him, towering up against the sky. He would listen to the carillon, never very long silent, and watch the birds fly out from the tower with the first sound of the bells, to wheel about it in the evening light. And insensibly the fascination of Bruges had wound its way into his life. . . .

'As the autumn advanced, and the evenings grew longer, he would take his walk sometimes on a grey misty afternoon that was soft as a caress. . . . The water grew paler under the rain; the outlines of things became blurred and dim; and solid buildings seemed to dissolve into a mist. The old houses, the old streets, the old bridges and canals, came to have a human appeal . . . and there were moments when his sense of loss became hardly distinguishable from the melancholy of Bruges itself, looking backward at the faint light of a vanished glory.'

(*Retrospective Adventures*, pp. 254–5.)

The conversation in *The Gentle Lover* is realistic and quick, much quicker than anything Forrest Reid had done before. The Grimshaws had been playing a little bridge, and Mr. Halvard has displayed his fine tenor voice to some advantage:

'" . . . I suppose you hear a great deal of music in London, Mr. Halvard?" she [Mrs. Grimshaw] asked, as the young clergyman approached the card-table.

'Mr. Halvard smiled gravely. ("He's just stinking with Oxford," whispered Brian, in admiration.)

'"Yes, a good deal. I find something like that to be almost necessary, with the work I am doing. . . ."

'"How nice that must be for you!". . . .

"'I suppose there's no use offering you either tea or coffee at this hour of the night, Bennet?" Miss Kilronan called out.

"'Have a ha'penny orr'nge, Mr. Allingham?" said Brian, approaching with a dish of that fruit. . . . "I'm going to eat my orange over here beside you . . ." the red boy said. . . . "It's too dark in this corner for Aunt Sophy to see me, and I'm going to eat it vulgarly. Do you mind?"

"'Not if you don't make a noise."

"'But I do. That's just where the vulgarity comes in. You must drown the noise by conversation. I think, on the whole, you'd better recite something. . . . There seems to be precious little juice," he murmured. "The noise will be something terrific, if I'm to get it out at all." . . . But Miss Kilronan's piercing eye had already detected these manœuvres.

"'*Brian*, what are you doing?"

"'Nothing, Aunt Sophy. . . . 'Where the bee sucks, there suck I,' " he added in an undertone.

'But Miss Kilronan came straight across to them. "How can you be so disgusting? . . . Get a plate and a knife at once, and behave like a gentleman."

'Brian frowned, but obeyed, and Miss Kilronan sat down beside her old friend.

"'Why have you chosen this dark corner, Bennet? One would think you had been put here in disgrace!". . . .

"' 'A cœur blessé—l'ombre et le silence,' " he murmured. . . .

"'Poor Bennet! Who has wounded your heart?"

"'All of you have helped. I feel that I am supplanted. Nobody wants to show me photographs of the Bargello."

"'But you know the original?"

"'What difference does that make? And then, to crown all, I am exhibited as a horrible person who imbibes whisky and soda —incidentally setting a bad example to Brian—when everybody else is rejoicing in coffee. It was you who betrayed me, Sophy."

"'It would have served you right if I hadn't betrayed you. Wait till next time."

"'Next time it won't matter. My reputation is lost."'

(Pp. 186–9.)

The central figure in *The Gentle Lover* is, of course, Allingham himself:

'There was in his manner, in his way of saying things, a some-what tentative quality, which only very enthusiastic persons found irritating. To such persons he appeared over-tolerant, and very likely they ascribed his lack of dogmatism to indifference. For if he made a statement he seldom pressed it home, and there was that in his voice, in his slightly hesitating manner, which seemed to imply a consciousness of an infinite number of points of view there for his interlocutor to choose from, any of which was quite as likely to be right as the one he had himself selected. This, com-bined with an absence of small talk, and a failure to appear amused when he wasn't amused, tended at times to produce an impression of aloofness and unsociability. . . .'

(P. 9.)

Sylvie, on the other hand, fails to come across. Her tenderness produces an effect of indeterminate dimness which softens the edges of her personality. Katherine Dale was, of course, an idealized character too, but Katherine lives in the mind long after Sylvie's pink and gold have been forgotten. But Brian, her brother, the 'red-haired happy boy', is one of Forrest Reid's most charming youngsters, lively, mischievous, witty, without reserve.

The passage where Brian goes to Sylvie's room in the evening to tell her that Allingham has left Florence, is one of the most touching in all the books. Sylvie, with feminine intuition, in-stantly guesses that Allingham has gone to Pisa to plead with Mr. Halvard, and to try—against his own best interests—to bring that over-scrupulous clergyman to see reason:

'She was standing in the middle of the room when he entered, as if she had come upstairs for something and had forgotten what she had come for, or been fascinated by the darkness that seemed from outside to press and surge against the window with a sinister suggestion of life. . . .
'"Sylvie!" he said.

'At that she turned, and a faint flush came into her cheeks.

'"Are you going to bed?" he asked.

'"No; it is quite early, isn't it? . . ."

'Brian had walked over to the window, and he now pulled down the blind. With his back to her he said softly, "Mr. Allingham will not be coming to-night. . . ."

'There was something in the gentleness of his voice that touched Sylvie extraordinarily, and for a moment, as she realised the delicacy and loyalty of his affection for her, even the figure of Mr. Halvard, and all his beautiful words and thoughts, faded. Her eyes rested on her brother. "Did they tell you where he was?" she asked.

'"No."

'Then, in the silence that followed, suddenly she blushed crimson, for it seemed to her that Brian knew and that he had told her, that he had cried aloud, "He has gone to Pisa, to Pisa." Yet nothing had been spoken, he had not even looked at her, his eyes were fixed on the carpet at his feet as he sat there on the side of the bed.

'Her blush passed slowly, but the boy had seen it, and he had coloured too. If only he had not been a boy, if only he had been her sister, then she could have flung her arms round his neck and cried; and the relief, the relief that that would have been! But instead, they could only sit there side by side, while the room seemed brimmed up with all that was unspoken. A touch, and the whole thing would have come crashing down upon them; but that touch was not given; and hours and hours seemed to pass, and yet Brian, when she looked up, was still there, the light shining on his red hair, as he sat gazing down at the carpet, his hands, on either side of him, on the pale counterpane.

'"Are you going downstairs again?" he asked, "or shall we read something? . . . I have a book of Mr. Allingham's here. I don't know whether you will like it—it is poetry. . . . Shall I read some of it?"

'Sylvie nodded, and he began:

96

'"*Sailorman, I'll give to you*
  My bright silver penny,
If out to sea you'll sail me
  And my dear sister Jenny."

'"*Get in, young sir, I'll sail ye*
  And your dear sister Jenny,
But pay she shall her golden locks
  Instead of your penny."

'*They sail away, they sail away,*
  O fierce the winds blew!
The foam flew in clouds,
  And dark the night grew!

'*And all the wild sea-water*
  Climbed steep into the boat;
Back to the shore again
  Sail they will not.

'*Drowned is the sailorman,*
  Drowned is sweet Jenny,
And drowned in the deep sea
  A bright silver penny.'

'He read on and on, one poem after another, and Sylvie, sitting with folded hands, appeared to listen . . . but . . . She had never cared for poetry; in the form of literature, at all events, it had no existence for her.   But her brother was too young to understand that. To him beauty was a thing we can always share —above all, with those we love; since who should comprehend it if not they?'

(Pp. 294–7.)

It is a long passage, but it has seemed worth reproducing here because it shows all Forrest Reid's delicacy of perception and his skill in hinting at those undercurrents of emotion which, because hidden, are so much the deepest. And the quotation from Walter de la Mare is characteristic too. Forrest Reid sometimes fitted poetry into the texture of his own prose at just that point where it would have its desired effect of heightening the atmosphere which he had himself created. It was not a device he used very often, but when he did it was always effective, always unexpectedly successful.

Then, finally, there is Allingham's feeling for Sylvie—all gentleness and tenderness and unspoken devotion. And there is pathos too; because Allingham, the gentle lover, is old enough in years to be her father, with all that must imply in difference of outlook and experience: and because too he can yield this young girl he loves to the man by whom she has been captivated.

> *My love is thine to teach: teach it but how,*
> *And thou shalt see how apt it is to learn*
> *Any hard lesson that may do thee good.*

'Peu de gens savent être vieux' runs the maxim, and it is because he is one of those few who, in La Rochefoucauld's words, 'know how to be old' that Allingham can accept this, accept it even against the promptings of his own heart.

'UNCLE STEPHEN'

Eighteen years separate *The Gentle Lover* from the appearance of *Uncle Stephen*. The two books are as different from each other as two books by Forrest Reid could well be. *The Gentle Lover* was two things: it was a conventional love story, and it was an Edwardian comedy of manners played in a European setting. In *Uncle Stephen* there is *no* love story—no love story, that is, which poor Sylvie would understand—and there is no European setting, because Uncle Stephen lives at Kilbarron. But there *is* Tom; and he more than compensates for the absence of the rest.

Tom Barber is the last of the small boys Forrest Reid created, and for that reason, and because he is an important person in his own right, he had better be brought in immediately. Tom is an ordinary boy; but Forrest Reid was no ordinary artist, and when we have put down the last of the three books he wrote about him we feel that he is known to us very intimately indeed.

'I loved writing this book [its author confessed later]. . . . During the two years spent on it Tom grew to be extraordinarily real to me—real, I think, in a way none of my other characters has ever been, so that sometimes for a few minutes I would stop writing because he seemed to be actually there in the room. I knew the tones of his voice, I caught glimpses of him in the street, and one evening, after finishing a chapter, I put down my work to go out for a walk with him.'   (*Private Road*, pp. 235–6.)

It is true we only know one or two of the events of Tom's outward life—know that he stayed at Greencastle one summer holiday, and know the marvels that occurred there, know that he and his great friend Pascoe flew kites, dug aquariums in the garden, raced caterpillars on their desks during school, know that he made friends with Alfred (a hedgehog), Roger, Barker, and Pincher, the friendly dogs, Edward the squirrel, James-Arthur, the boy on the farm, all the innocent inhabitants of his world; know, even, that he struck up acquaintance—of a sort—with the local messenger boys at Kilbarron; though some of these latter, one must suspect, were not quite so innocent—as the following interesting and democratic piece of dialogue may show:

' . . . just round the corner was the Royal Cinema, whose coloured posters he stopped to study in the company of a red-haired message boy. . . . The butcher's boy had seen it [the film] on the previous night, had in fact seen it twice, and soon they were in the thick of its entanglements. Tom gazed at a distraught female clinging passionately to a cold and aloof young man.

'"Is she his love?" he asked, for he had these quaintnesses of vocabulary.

'The butcher's boy stared stolidly at the lady. "What d'you mean, his love?" he presently said. "She's a tart."

'"Oh," said Tom.

'"Can't you see he's spurning her?" the butcher's boy continued. "He's got a girl already. His girl's the other girl's sister."

'"What other girl?" asked Tom.

'"The tart. His girl's the tart's sister, but he doesn't know that, because she calls herself another name."

'"Who does—his girl?"

'"No, the tart. What would his girl change her name for? Have a bit of wit."

'"But why should the tart change hers?" asked Tom, bewildered.

'"Ah, you're silly. Tarts always chooses fancy names—foreign names. I don't believe you know what a tart is."

'"Yes, I do."

'"Well then, what you talkin' about." The butcher's boy gave him a scornful look, mounted his bicycle, and rode away. . . .'

(Pp. 83–4; 1931 edition.)

But as well as these and other, less exacting, everyday happenings, his thoughts are almost as familiar to us as our own, and this is because we know them through the understanding, gentle sympathy of a perfect artist. As familiar, but far more beautiful. Some of the passages which describe Tom's reflections are as good as anything Forrest Reid ever wrote. Here is one which will serve to introduce him:

'Tom's expression altered. The freckled face—redeemed from marked plainness by a pair of singularly honest and intelligent grey eyes—became stilled as the water of a pool is stilled. He might have been listening intently, or merely dreaming on his feet. Probably the latter, for when he awakened it was as if the hands of the clock had suddenly jumped on, leaving a little island of submerged time unaccounted for. It was strange: a few minutes had been lost for ever: he had been here and yet he had not been here! . . . *Could* you be in two times at once? Certainly your mind could be in one time and your body in another, for that was what had happened—he had been back in last night. But suppose his body had gone back too! Then he would have vanished! Uncle Horace would have said, "Where is Tom?" and somebody would have answered, "He was here a minute ago: he was standing over there: he can't be far away." Only, he *had* been far away. As far away as last night—and in his bedroom. This odd experience seemed to make all kind of things possible. Somebody might come to you out of *his* time into yours. You might, for instance, come face to face with your own father as he was when he was a boy. Of course you wouldn't *know* each other: still, you might meet and become friends, the way you do with people in dreams. The idea seemed difficult and involved, but doubtless it could be straightened out. Dreams themselves were so queer. When he had dreamed last night, for example, he was almost sure he had been awake. What he wasn't so sure of was that it had been a dream at all, or at any rate *his* dream. . . .'

(P. 11.)

What is skilful about writing like this, isn't only its effortless charm and aptness of expression. Or even the delicate picture it calls up of a dreaming, sensitive child. The thing that strikes one is that Forrest Reid knows exactly *what* a child thinks, and even more, exactly *how* a child thinks. One might almost add 'and *when* a child thinks' for this dreaming fit of Tom's took place during his own father's funeral service. Tom, we feel sure, was devoted to his father; but Forrest Reid knows Tom, and knows also that that is what Tom—and every other sensitive small boy in similar circumstances—in fact *does* think.

Tom had, in his late father's words, 'a distinct taste for the marvellous', and *Uncle Stephen* is a book about marvels. When it opens Tom's father has just died, and left with his stepmother and her family—all of them older than himself and with one exception unsympathetic—Tom's thoughts find themselves constantly reverting to his mysterious Uncle Stephen. Uncle Stephen is an enigma. At the Gloucester Terrace house he soon discovers that there exists a conspiracy of silence on the subject. Something—though what that something is no one seems to know, or if they do know seems ready to tell—*something* has happened to cut him off from the rest of his family and relations. No one, for instance, seems to have written to tell Uncle Stephen of his father's death,

let alone invite him to the funeral. It is all very mysterious and
Tom cannot understand it. But he has got hold of a book written
by Uncle Stephen and, although some of it is in Greek and some
of it he cannot understand, it has made him determined to visit
its author. This plan he confides to only one person, his young
stepsister Jane Gavney. She assists him to make his escape.

The journey to Kilbarron, accomplished by train and on foot,
is a long and arduous one; but when Tom arrives, clutching his
brown-paper parcel, a very curious thing happens: for in answer
to Tom's somewhat timid 'Does Mr. Collet live here?' the
housekeeper immediately replies: 'Why, it must be Master Tom!
I'd given up expecting you, Master Tom, and was getting ready
to go home.' Tom stops suddenly in the bewildering realization
that he had been expected. But even stranger, a few minutes
later, when Mrs. Deverell takes him along to the study, is his
meeting with Uncle Stephen himself:

'He had, in his nervousness, a blurred impression of high book-
lined walls, of a soft floating light that dimmed and shaded off
into a surrounding darkness, but above all, though at what seemed
to be an immense distance from him, of a figure seated by a table,
a figure whose grave, kind face and silver hair were surmounted
by a black skull-cap. There was a perceptible pause and an intense
silence. The room rapidly became brimmed with this silence,
which passed over Tom in wave after wave, so that he might have
been deep down under the sea. His heart was thumping, his cheeks
burned, and all at once an unutterable misery swept over him.
His mouth quivered; he was at that moment on the very verge of
tears; but he forced them back, biting on his lower lip. At the
same time the seated figure had risen, looking tall, though
slightly stooped, in a black costume that vaguely suggested an
earlier period than the present, and which showed only a touch of
soft white linen at throat and wrist. But this movement seemed
to have the effect of decreasing the distance between them, and
Tom advanced. It was all strange enough, for no word had yet
been spoken, and Tom came forward slowly, step by step, his

arms hanging by his sides, his head drooping a little. He came on and on till at last he felt a hand resting on each of his shoulders, and at this he looked up into eyes of the darkest deepest blue he had ever beheld. His own eyes were misty and again he was biting on his lip, but he felt a hand brushing lightly over his head, and then more firmly, so that, obedient to its pressure, he tilted it back a little, and at the same time closed his eyelids. The hand came to rest, still pressing lightly on the tumbled hair, and Tom all at once had the oddest and loveliest impression. He didn't know whence it came—perhaps out of the Bible—but he knew—and it was as if he had never known anything so deeply, so beautifully—that Uncle Stephen had blessed him.'

(Pp. 63–4.)

But the next day facts have to be faced. His stepmother has to be written to, Uncle Stephen's lawyer consulted, Mr. Knox, the local clergyman, approached about a tutorship. In the evening, on his way back to the house, Tom explores the grounds. Soon he discovers a mysterious house, catches sight of a boy looking out of one of its upper windows—looking at *him*. A glimpse of his face Tom has, and then he vanishes. In front of the house there is a narrow lawn, a terrace, a pool, and in the middle of the pool, the statue of a young boy.

When he gets back it is to find Uncle Stephen and Mr. Knox discussing plans for his future. It is agreed that Mr. Knox and his uncle shall teach him between them. Tom, standing in the road after seeing off Mr. Knox from the end of the drive, senses that he stands at a cross-roads:

' . . . he turned round and through the gate looked into the green avenue from which he had just emerged. Within *there*, was something not so simple. While he lingered there deepened in him a strange impression that he was on the boundary-line between two worlds. To one world belonged Mr. Knox and his meetings, and Tom was standing in it now, as it might be on the shore of a pond. It stretched all round these stone walls, but within them was the other, and as soon as he passed through that gate he would become a part of the other. Here he was free to choose, but if he took a step further all would be different. What he should enter seemed to him now a kind of dream-world, but once inside, he knew it would become real. In there was the unknown —mystery—romance: the ruined garden, the stone boy holding his empty urn above the pool, the boy he had seen at the window, Uncle Stephen. As he stood at the gate Tom at that moment was not very far from seeing an angel with a flaming sword guarding it. His body thrilled when the call of a bird rose through the silence. He took a little run forward, tugged at the bar, pushed: and the latch dropped back into place as the gate clanged behind him.'

(P. 111.)

The following afternoon Tom again makes his way to the secret house, and sits by the fountain. Here he meets the boy he saw at the window the day before. His name is Philip. They agree to bathe together in the morning. Meanwhile, Uncle Horace, his stepmother's brother, has arrived by car. He quarrels with Uncle Stephen, and Uncle Stephen refuses to give Tom up. That evening, after he has gone, Tom, as if intuitively guessing that henceforward his future is decided, tells Uncle Stephen about Philip. For answer, Uncle Stephen lights a candle, and leads Tom down the passage.

'Tom stood on the threshold of a room he had never seen before —Uncle Stephen's bedroom. . . .

'The room was not large—not so large as Tom's own bedroom —and it was far more simply and sparsely furnished. A low narrow bed in the centre of the floor, a wardrobe, a chest of drawers, a dressing-table and a single cane-bottomed chair—there was no other furniture than this. There was not even a carpet, only a rug beside the bed; and the grey walls were bare—the whole room had a monastic bareness and austerity, except that, in the open space beyond the bed, there was something wonderful.

'It was wonderful because—time-stained, ancient, battered—

without arms, and with the legs broken off below the knees—
it yet had all the beauty and radiance of a God. Motionless he
stood there dreaming, with a lovely mildness in his open countenance. He was a spirit, and Tom felt himself to be in the presence of
a spirit—of a beneficent guardian, who had made sweet and sacred
this place in which he stood.'

(Pp. 160-1.)

This statue is the statue of Hermes, Uncle Stephen tells him—
Hermes who was the boys' God. The effect of the statue on Tom
is curious, half-fear, half-bewilderment. All that Uncle Stephen
can get from him is that, 'you, and him, and Philip, and—even
the boy at the fountain:—it was as if you all were one person. . . .'

After this the story moves swiftly. Some days later, lying by the
river with Philip and thinking him asleep, Tom, urged by an
obscure prompting, softly whispers in the other boy's ear. 'Two
words he whispered involuntarily, though it was only after he
had spoken them that they reached his consciousness, producing
a slight shock.' The two words were: 'Uncle Stephen'.

The climax of the story is reached a week or two later: Uncle
Stephen decides that Tom must know everything. He tells Tom
to go to the cupboard in the wall of his bedroom and bring him
the box that lies there:

'Tom sprang to his feet. The cupboard, as he pulled back the
door, revealed itself as but a couple of shelves, and on the upper
one of these was a flat wooden box, its corners brass-plated, its
lid overlaid with a criss-cross pattern in brass filigree. It could not
contain much. It was about twelve inches long and a third of
that in depth. . . .

'The box was lined with olive-green silk, and appeared to contain merely a few old letters, among which Uncle Stephen fumbled before he drew out from beneath them a flat leather case
which he opened by pressing a spring. Tom bent nearer. Only
his breathing was audible. Within the case was a thin slab of ivory
on which was painted the portrait of a boy.

'"Do you know him?"

105

'Tom did not answer. He was gazing not at the picture but at Uncle Stephen himself. The pupils of his eyes were slightly dilated and his face had grown very white.

'"There is a name," Uncle Stephen said, "and a date—there inside the lid. The date is that when the likeness was painted; the name is the name of the sitter, of the boy. Read it aloud."

'Tom read in an oddly muffled voice. "Stephen Collet. 1880."

'. . . "It is your name," whispered Tom, " . . . that *is* you, Uncle Stephen—that boy?"

'"It was—once."

'"And it is Philip."

'"There never was a Philip, though I took that name when I ran away. . . ."

'"I *think*, you know," said Tom slowly, "that deep deep down I must have had a sort of suspicion. I don't even now feel frightfully surprised."

'Uncle Stephen turned to him doubtfully, but Tom pursued his idea. "You see, I couldn't have liked Philip so much if he hadn't been you."

'But Uncle Stephen did not look convinced. "You have a considerable capacity for liking people," he said.

'"Yes," Tom admitted. " . . . you know, Uncle Stephen, I once almost asked you if you were Philip. It was that night, you remember, after Uncle Horace had been here: the first time I was ever in this room. I couldn't understand then, and I was very silly about it—but it was because I felt there was something I *didn't* understand. And one day I called Philip by your name. It was because his eyes were exactly the same as yours. . . ."'

(Pp. 223–8.)

Tom next asked Uncle Stephen for an answer to the question that had really been worrying him all along: had Uncle Stephen known of his existence before they met, had he been expecting his arrival at Kilbarron that evening a few weeks ago—and if he had, how could he have guessed that he, Tom, was coming?

Uncle Stephen's explanation, though it would have seemed

incredible fifty years ago, is perhaps not so incredible in the light
of much recent speculation:

"'I had heard of you—yes", came the reply, "—from a friend
of your mother's. But it was very little—a phrase or two in a
letter. I don't know what there was in it that impressed me, gave
me a definite impression which persisted and deepened. For many
years I had lived alone, and possibly that may have had much to do
with it. I cannot say. I can give no rational account of what happened, but you became very real and very dear to me in imagination. . . . Before I dreamed that afternoon, I had been thinking
of you, thinking too of my own boyhood. Then the scene arose
in my mind in which these two boys met. It arose spontaneously:
I did not seem to be making it up. At a certain point it must have
passed into a dream, for I definitely woke up, and I knew by
looking at my watch that the afternoon was nearly over. But I
really thought very little about the matter until you came with
your story. That seemed incredible, and yet I had to accept it.
I knew there was no boy at the other house—besides, what you
told me *was* my dream. I ought to have left it at that. Unfortunately I knew exactly the conditions under which this accident—if
it was an accident—had taken place. I determined to repeat everything. And you came to me again with your story and this time
it had advanced a step. I knew it must be dangerous. Even if some
strange connection *had* been established between present and past,
I knew it could not be safe. Therefore I should not have gone on,
because it involved not only myself, but you.'"

(Pp. 226–7.)

Tom, with great difficulty, persuades Uncle Stephen to let him
visit the old house in the grounds—but, alas, 'Philip' (or Stephen)
is not there. Tom drops asleep. When he awakes it is to see Philip,
the same Philip he had known, before ever he had spoken about
him to Uncle Stephen—lying before him on the bed. Haltingly,
Tom tries to make a clean breast of it all, explain everything. But
either Philip cannot grasp Tom's attempts, or else Tom himself
cannot make sense of what he is trying to describe. In desperation,

Tom leads him back to the big house. Mrs. Deverell declares that there is no sign of Uncle Stephen. Tom, now thoroughly frightened, is forced to explain this by concocting an elaborate falsehood about Uncle Stephen being called away unexpectedly. Then, with an effort, he tells Philip everything, persuades the unwilling boy to sleep in Uncle Stephen's room in an effort to transform him into Uncle Stephen again. The attempt is a failure. Philip next expresses the wish to visit Coombe Bridge, a village some distance off, where, he declares, he 'lived when he was a boy'. Thither the two boys make their way, and from there, after some vicissitudes, and an exhausting night tramp, they return to Kilbarron. Tom is too tired even to walk, and when they reach the grounds Philip has to carry him on his back. In this weary condition the two travellers reach the house where Tom had caught his first glimpse of Philip.

'They took off their shoes and prepared for the night. The window was wide open, but so still was the air that outside not a leaf stirred, and the candle flames stood up straight and motionless. The moon had dimmed and there was a faint reflection of daylight in the sky. Stephen blew out the candles.

'"We're here at last," he said, "and now do you know why I wanted to come?"

'"It's too late to talk," Tom answered drowsily. "Wait till the morning."

'He was already on the threshold of sleep, with the door ajar and infinitely alluring. "Good night," he whispered.

'Stephen did not answer. Tom leaned closer. Then he shut his eyes, and almost instantly sank into the dark unconscious world which lay below his dream-world, and in which, from night to night, his life was mysteriously renewed.'

(P. 324.)

When Tom wakes it is to find the sun shining and Uncle Stephen bending over his bed. Uncle Stephen tells him that he 'awoke', in his own room, an hour before, and came straight over to the other house. But more curious still is the behaviour of Uncle

Stephen's memory: for from the time the two boys left Coombe Bridge on their return journey, until their arrival at Kilbarron, everything is clear. It is what happened *before* this which is doubtful: "'There must have been a complete break somewhere. A break in consciousness, I mean—*my* consciousness. It is like this:—I can *think* back over last night, remember what I thought and felt; but of what came earlier I have only vague impressions, as if I had *watched* the earlier scenes.''' (Pp. 326-7.)

But meanwhile Tom has been explaining the many practical difficulties in which the whole business has landed them. Among other things, the total disappearance of a perfectly normal boy has to be accounted for. Uncle Stephen's plan is simple. Their only course is to leave the country, possibly for a year, or longer, until any repercussions which there may be will have had time to die down. He will explain everything to Mr. Knox and together he and Tom will set out on their travels. While Uncle Stephen is busy with the tutor Tom slips off to the other house, the scene of all their adventures. Sitting on the soft turf by the pool he sinks into reverie:

'His thoughts sank into a kind of dreaming. They floated over the past and the present, drifting to and fro, rising and sinking, like loosened seaweed on a swelling sea. . . .

'"Down—down—down." He dabbled his hand in the water of the fountain, and gazing into the shallow pool, began to sing in an undertone that one word. It was because he was looking down through the dark greenish water: yet there were poems by Sappho—fragments of poems—which contained no more than a word or two, but which were somehow beautiful and sufficient, like that broken statue of Hermes. . . .

'"And golden pulse grew on the shores. . . ."

'He looked farewell at the stone boy watching over his garden. . . . The stone was warm. The sun had warmed the curved pouting mouth and the smooth limbs and body; but when Tom's lips pressed on those other lips the eyes were looking away from him, and dimly he felt that this was a symbol of life—of life and of all love. No, no—not all—not Uncle Stephen's. Uncle Stephen's eyes were fixed upon him, looked straight into his spirit, that was why he was different from everybody else. "Good-bye," Tom whispered into the delicate unlistening ear. . . .

'All the most beautiful things he knew had come to him through Uncle Stephen. They had been there, perhaps, like anemones in a wood, waiting to be discovered:—still, it was a kind of gift if somebody brought them to you, or brought you to them. And not an ordinary gift, for they were things which could not be worn out or broken. Uncle Stephen was his master and he was Uncle Stephen's pupil.'

(Pp. 337–9.)

Of what the extracts which I have quoted from *Uncle Stephen* do not give an idea, is the atmosphere which bathes the surroundings in which this dream-tale takes place. Readers of Mr. de la Mare's novel, *The Return*—a book which Forrest Reid greatly admired, and by which he was, I think, indirectly but quite clearly influenced in some of his own work—will understand when I compare the spell created in the two books. Tom reached Kilbarron by moonlight: and this first crepuscular arrival set the note for the whole atmosphere of what was to come. We seem indeed to see Tom, as he makes his journey, passing out of the sunshine into the shadows, and this is an extraordinarily effective foreshadowment of all that lies ahead of him.

Most of the plot of *Uncle Stephen* takes place in the secret garden of that strange 'other house' which so fascinated Tom: it was indeed the 'strangest house he had ever seen, built of wood and thickly covered with a dark, small-leaved ivy' and 'thatched with pale yellow straw over which climbed trailing boughs of Old Man's Beard'. The roof 'jutting out to form a narrow cloister below, was supported by trunks of trees—the natural, unhewed trunks, bulging and crooked—and they too, like the walls, were densely coated with layer upon layer of ivy. The unusual depth of this vegetable growth was what indeed gave the house its strangeness, its at first sight startling suggestion of life.

It *was* alive. Watching it intently, Tom imagined he could see the walls—though ever so slightly—swelling and contracting in a slow breathing.' Set high up above the eaves, in the thatch, was a latticed dormer-window, dark and uncurtained. 'Tom saw nobody, yet he had a feeling that someone was watching him, and he never lost consciousness of this. . . .'

The setting is equally strange, full of boding, producing an indescribable feeling that this haunted sylvan world is utterly cut off, isolated in its loneliness from all human contacts:

'A narrow lawn of moss-thickened grass sloped down from the stained door-steps to a grass terrace, where a further flight of balustraded steps descended to a pool rimmed with stone. On an island in the middle of the pool stood a naked boy holding an urn tilted forward, though through its weedy mouth no water splashed. The fountain was choked. A tuft of grass had found a roothold in the hollow of the boy's thigh; and on one side of him crouched an otter, on the other was an owl. All round the pool were rough grey boulders coated with mosses, dark green creepers, and trailing weeds. Between the stones sprang scarlet and yellow grasses, hart's-tongue fern, and bushes of cotoneaster, berberry and lavender. His garden must have been blown to the fountain boy by wandering winds, or dropped by passing birds. On the dark surface of his pool floated the flat glossy leaves of water-lilies, and the lonely little sentinel gazed down at them, or at his own black shadow, or perhaps he was asleep, awaiting the spell-breaker.'

(Pp. 103–4)

Uncle Stephen is the only book of Forrest Reid's which depends for its effect entirely on our belief in the supernatural theme. This theme is the inspiration of the book, and it is obvious that the whole thing stands or falls by its success. That it *does* succeed I think there can be little doubt. Where the book falters is rather in the *use* of the dream-transference theme. Until Uncle Stephen's revelation, little more than half-way through the book, everything goes smoothly; only after this point does the story seem to lose impetus. It is as if Forrest Reid, having worked up his tale to its imaginative climax, finds that he has a number of characters on his hands and no particular idea of what they should do next. Perhaps this is putting it too strongly: but certainly the second half of the book, from where Tom wakes in the other house to find Stephen beside him—seems to be invented, not imagined. Beautifully invented, of course—but invented none the less. The effect of the boys' journey to Coombe Bridge is to introduce a fresh dimension of space into the tale; as if, by walking out of the setting of the story, they were to walk out of the story itself and break its texture. It is hard, indeed, to see what purpose the expedition to Philip's birthplace can have served, unless we are to imagine that contact with the spot helped Philip in some way to recover his identity as Uncle Stephen.

The book's original title had been 'My Uncle's a Magician', and in the first draft it was 'simply . . . a story of magic and mystery'. Unfortunately the effect, as it stood, was a melodramatic one. The difficulty then was: how to fit this early story—as indicated by its title—into the later, more conventionally constructed framework? There was no alternative but to 'rewrite the whole thing as realistically as the nature of its content would permit.'

'As realistically as the nature of its content would permit'—there was the rub. At first difficulties of technique made the task appear insuperable; it was only when these were seen to be irrelevant (this by Walter de la Mare, who acted as consultant), that the problem solved itself: 'the real story remained precisely what it had been all along—a story of sacred and profane love— the machinery being merely a way of *telling* it.' (*Private Road*, pp. 234-5.) The suspicion, however, remains that this process was not altogether a successful one, and perhaps the weakness of the book's ending confirms these suspicions. We feel that Tom's and Uncle Stephen's difficulties are resolved too neatly; that the story is *brought* to an end—by the contrivance of its author—rather than allowed to work itself out through the previous happenings in the plot. As a curtain at the finish of light comedy, the ending would serve; but it does not do justice to the real inspiration in the beginning of the book.

But all this is to drag ghosts into the sunlight. *Uncle Stephen* is an intimately personal thing; it *is* what its author called it, 'a story of sacred and profane love'; and it was, in certain passages which the author cut out of the final printed version, more intimate still. 'What was real was the emotion of which the story was the symbol. The imagination of Tom was the focus, and Tom was absolutely real, even if a rather special little boy, who "felt through all this earthly dress bright shoots of everlastingness."' (*Private Road*, p. 235.)

Uncle Stephen is not a book that can be rationalized. The beauty of the book lies in the beauty of the idea behind it, not in the correspondence of that idea with some tangible reality. We must take it on its own terms; its author's terms. And possibly on Tom's terms too; for Tom's reverie at his father's funeral may have had a significance for subsequent events which escaped us at the time, perhaps one *could* (in *Uncle Stephen* at all events) be in 'two times at once'; perhaps somebody *could* 'come to you out of his time into yours'; perhaps, above all, it could really be that you were dreaming when you thought you were awake.

> *All that we see or seem*
> *Is but a dream within a dream.*

And here, possibly, lies the clue to the understanding of *Uncle Stephen*—that the book only yields up its shadowed, tenebrous beauty when we see the whole thing as purest moonshine, lifted on to that mysterious plane where the laws of the world we know cease to be valid, and where everything is indeed 'a dream within a dream'.

'BRIAN WESTBY'

Brian Westby is a realistic novel. In this respect it lies at the opposite extreme of the scale from *Uncle Stephen*; there is no dream element, no intervention of the miraculous, no 'wandering between

H   113

two worlds'. All is constructed, put together. And yet the book is a masterpiece. Read in the *right* way—and that is essential to a real understanding of its meaning—this story has a greater emotional impact than anything else he ever wrote. Forrest Reid was never to write a masterpiece, probably never *wanted* to write a masterpiece—in the sense to which that much-abused word is usually put—but this book, 'in the line of his own idiosyncracy', *is* perfection.

It is rather a special line. What Jules Lemaître says about criticism—that a work of art confers its reward only in the degree to which we can imaginatively experience the emotion of its characters—is true here. The success of the book depends on our response to the friendship theme at its centre. Unless we can *become* Martin Linton the whole thing loses its force, falls apart. If we *can* project ourselves into Linton's imagination then, I think, we may feel ourselves in the presence of something different only in scope and degree, and not in kind, from *Dominique* or Turgenev's *First Love*.

The story is told with marvellous skill and economy. The artist, said Schiller, may be known rather by what he *omits*; and everything that is inessential here has been pruned away, all those loose-ends that twine themselves round a plot and destroy its outline. The resulting narrative is stripped, but never bare; economical, but never bleak.

This narrative is simple, the chief characters number no more than three, yet the whole thing hangs together, each part being dependent on every other. One of the most testing questions we may ask ourselves when we are confronted by what we believe to be a work of art is: 'What part of this picture, or piece of music, or book, could have been eliminated without diminishing its essential force?'—and when we are baffled in this search, and yet still retain our original conviction of the work's greatness, we can, in nine cases out of ten, be assured that what we have been considering is indeed a masterpiece. This exacting test *Brian Westby*, by virtue of its perfection of form, survives. It is not heroic, but as we read we think to ourselves: 'this was inevitable, this was how it really happened, it could only have happened thus and thus, and in no other way'; and we realize that it is consummate art. It follows from what has just been said that the book has an underlying simplicity of theme. This theme is the growth of Martin Linton's affection for Brian, the climax to which it leads, and, in the last pages of the book, the denouement that follows.

There are, then, only three characters who matter; and the first of these we meet is Linton. Our initial view of him is through the eyes of Brian. Brian is contemplating him as a possible character for his novel—which is a first novel:

'He was middle-aged to begin with—rather late middle-aged—round about fifty, say—for his hair was streaked with silver where you could see it. And he had lived a more or less unactive life—unactive physically. . . . Sedentary—that was the word he wanted—a sedentary life. He was a bit slouchy, too, and his complexion was sallow, not sunburned. He didn't look awfully well, and—not awfully happy either. . . . What next? Well, the next was more commonplace: anybody could see that he was careless about his clothes, which needed brushing at this moment. . . . Brian got no further, for just then the man turned and he found himself looking straight into his eyes, which were dark and intelligent, and at the same time both old and young, tired and very much alive.'

(Pp. 59–60.)

To this we may add one or two facts which Brian could *not* have observed. Martin Linton was a novelist. Recovering from a serious illness he decides, on an obscure prompting, to return to Ballycastle. It is a strange prompting, for he has not visited the little Ulster seaside town for almost twenty years—since his honeymoon, in fact. His marriage with Stella failed miserably, failed in a surprisingly short time. Since then there had been the books, and what he supposed one might call success, but something had been missing, his life had been incomplete, a failure.

'And he knew, when he looked deliberately back over the years, just where it had failed. Happiness is only made by affection. Nothing else in the long run matters. The responsibilities and anxieties that accompany affection are in themselves blessings. He had no responsibilities, no anxieties, and he felt that he had lived long enough. . . .'

(P. 19.)

Since his illness the old inspiration had not returned. Life appeared flat, stale, without colour. Nothing seemed to matter. His capacity for enjoyment and the springs of his invention alike seemed to have dried up. And at that gloomy point in his musings he noticed Brian.

The boy was sitting on the shore, against a sand-dune:

'Linton looked at him as he sat there, nearly in profile. He was very untidy and very attractive, with his flaxen ruffled hair breaking into loose curls over his forehead, and his fair skin. He was wearing a rough brown jacket, a tennis-shirt, and an old pair of baggy grey flannel trousers held up by a knotted scarlet necktie instead of a belt. He gave Linton the impression of being a part of his surroundings—of the sun-bleached sand-dunes, the deserted shore, the blue tumbling waves, the open sky. He gave him the impression of being more *in* nature than anyone he had ever before met. He looked as if the cleanness of the sea-wind was in his blood; he looked as if something of the impersonal beauty of sea and sky and shore had passed into him and become human. And suddenly Linton found himself thinking of the young horsemen on the Parthenon frieze, riding by in proud humility. He was like *them* too, although his features were quite unlike. Or rather it was that both were like the same thing. And now he knew that this was what had first struck him. The boy had reminded him of the world he loved best, the spirit he loved best, the beauty he loved best, the only beauty that had the unspoiled freshness and simplicity of nature.'

(P. 27.)

But there is another, almost greater surprise in store for Linton: for the book lying by his side is a copy of his own first novel. He represses his immediate impulse, which is to reveal himself.

116

The boy, Linton learns, is on holiday at Ballycastle. He, his mother, and his sister are living in rooms in the town. Brian is looking for a job, and meanwhile is writing his own first novel. But by now Linton's deception has led him further than he intended, has put him into a false position, and he finds himself forced to assume the uneasy role of an anonymous friend of the novelist. But the difficulty of the situation does not deter him from arranging another meeting the next morning.

The day dawns blue and cloudless; it is true summer weather. They walk along the shore and Brian decides he will bathe. Linton prepares to watch:

'He sat down and dangled his feet over the edge, while behind him the boy undressed and put on his bathing-suit. Soon he was ready. There was no timidity about his bathing—no preliminary trial of the water's temperature such as Linton himself would have made—he plunged in at once. Splash!—a shower of glittering spray—and Linton watched his strong young body gliding through the clear green water—first downward, and then in a wide upward curve that brought him to the surface. He shook the water from his yellow hair; his blue eyes were dark and bright with pleasure; he turned and shouted back something—then swam out towards the entrance of the creek. He swam powerfully and easily, with rhythmic unhurried strokes, and Linton watched him with the oddest emotion of pride and affection. Odd, because of course it was absurd—just as if the boy belonged to him. . . . Then he thought:—If only he *did* belong to me; if only he *was* my son—how different everything would be! And instantly he knew that even to imagine this, even to pretend it, was a happiness.'

(Pp. 106–7.)

During their outing Brian lets drop his identity, tells Linton that he is really Brian Linton and not Brian Westby, that his mother married a second time, shortly after he was born, and called him, the child of her first marriage, by her second husband's name. And again Linton, by an effort, keeps silence.

But soon Brian resolves to arrange a meeting between his new friend 'Mr. Martin' and his mother. His mother, too, wishes to meet Brian's mysterious acquaintance. But Linton, for reasons which he cannot, of course, reveal to Brian, is obdurate. Brian, naturally, is offended. But the older man is helpless to take any other course. He knows Stella's implacable hostility towards all his ideas, knows she has forbidden Brian to read his books, knows, above all, that if he was to reveal his identity to her now, all would be lost.

Linton resolves to tell Brian everything. He can see no other way out. The boy must know. A few days later they go on an expedition to Fair Head. The best way which Linton can hit on of breaking the truth about his own identity is to show the boy a story he has written. Brian, he hopes, will in this way tumble to the truth:

'"Clayton awoke with a slight shiver," Brian began. . . . "I say: you've written quite a lot!"

'Linton submissively had handed him a bundle of small square sheets. "Not really very much," he said. "And I don't know whether you'll be able to make out my writing."

'"I can make out to begin with that you've pinched the hotel note-paper," Brian told him gaily. "And I *can* make it out: it's as plain as print."

'He began to read, and for several minutes there was no sound except the turning of a page, and from far below, the faint whisper of the waves. Linton . . . sat watching Brian, and waiting. . . . Would he recognize it? It all depended. Depended on how far he had a sense for such things—an ear—a *flair* . . . his face was very grave. Sometimes he would turn back and read half a page over again: now and then Linton could see his lips moving; now and then he appeared to stop reading altogether:—only he never once looked up. . . .

'He had reached the last page, and still without a word or a glance at Linton, he turned back to the beginning. But at this Linton leaned forward and took the manuscript from his unresisting grasp. Brian said nothing. . . . The boy's face was troubled, but it was—even more—deeply, painfully shy. . . .

'The minutes of suspense which followed were the most poignant Linton had ever known. He had an intense desire to speak, but was as tongue-tied as Brian himself. . . .

'Yet they could not go on like this: he must break the silence or it would never be broken. "Have you guessed?" he asked; and the answer came at once, but in an oddly husky voice, "Yes, I think so."'

(Pp. 224–6.)

The only immediate effect this disclosure has upon Brian is to make him renew his pleas that Linton should interview Stella face to face and clear up the whole matter. But Linton remains inflexible. Stella he has never seen for twenty years, yet he *knows*, in a way the boy, who is her daily companion, could never do, that it is all hopeless.

Brian in fact, although he does not properly realize it, is on the horns of a dilemma. His inexperience, and the natural optimism of youth, makes him blind to the truth that between his father and mother there can never be accord, never, even, agreement to differ. For that their conflict is too deep-seated. His own feeling for Linton, Linton's very presence, must sooner or later make a decision inevitable. The growing inevitability of that decision he does not foresee, he will not recognize its existence even, until events force him to do so.

The decision, when it has to be made, will be no easier for the delay. Brian's feelings for his mother are mixed. She seems to him narrow, intolerant, restrictive, remote from and unsympathetic to his real feelings and interests. And yet she loves him; that he knows. And her love elicits from him a response. After all, she *is* his mother, in her own strange way she cares for him and Claire more than for anyone else, she is manifestly devoted to her own mistaken view of what is necessary for his happiness. And, above all, Brian knows *her*. He has known her all his life, knows her as he knows no other human being. And she, he feels, in spite of all the limitations of understanding, knows *him*. And Linton—his father—what of him? They are friends, it is true; perhaps even more than friends. But here all is novel, untested.

'"Suppose you are forbidden to see me," Linton asked, "what will you do?"

'"I don't know. I'll kick up a row for one thing."

'"And then?"

'There was no reply, and after waiting a little while, Linton spoke. "I don't think you understand your mother. She is very determined, very thorough, very sure she is right. Can't you guess what her views are when she wouldn't even allow you to keep my name—*your* name? That was going pretty far. I hadn't disgraced it. Did you think I had?"'

(Pp. 231–2.)

That evening, in the rain and the darkness, Linton climbs the hill to their house. Late as it is, he sees a lighted upstairs window and, while he stands there in the shadow, glimpses Brian for a moment silhouetted against it:

'The light remained . . . and Linton continued to watch it. This was not the walk he had promised himself; moreover the rain was growing heavier; but an emotion he was powerless to beat down held him rooted to the spot, and he leaned back against the loose stone wall that topped the bank, his gaze immovably fixed on the window.

' . . . Linton wondered what he had said to his mother—how much he had told her—what attitude he had taken up—and what had been the end of it? What*ever* he had told her, Stella would not have made it easy for him; and for that matter he had not made it easy for him himself. . . . "I should have gone away," he mused sombrely. "To stay on when my staying was bound to lead to this, was pure selfishness." . . . Brian might wonder; might be hurt, disappointed, perhaps; might miss him for a little; but very soon he would get over it. . . .

'And yet Linton could not believe that to go like this really would be best. It would entail an unqualified, an absolute self-

120

sacrifice. . . . And in a sudden final flash of self-knowledge he spoke aloud the truth: "I cannot live without him."

'His eyes were still fixed on the lighted window. . . . It was as if a magic circle had been drawn on the night, and he stood within it—alone with a lighted window. He did not feel the rain. . . . For the light flashed its continuous message—it held him, it filled his mind—and in it he saw things, heard things, remembered things. . . .

' . . . The only thing that could make him give it up would be Brian's own desire that it should end, and so far he had expressed no such desire. . . .

'And there was Brian's affection for him—a boy's unspoken affection—all freshness and brightness and delicacy—half-hidden and half-revealed, like the first spring buds softly unfolding on trees and hedges. . . . No—he could not give him up. . . .

'Suddenly, without even a warning flicker, the light upon which Linton's eyes were fixed went out, and he found himself alone in the darkness. So abruptly it happened that he had the sense of a physical shock, violent and brutal. Instantly the empty dreary night was there, and he became conscious of the rain and the cold —and of his own body chilled and cramped and wet, while far down below, on the desolate shore at the cliff's edge, he heard the remote, unresting crying of the sea. . . . He knew it was useless to wait, yet still he could not go. He watched and waited—waited absurdly, unreasonably—for the light to come again. It might: he knew it would not, but it might: and in the grip of a blinding emotion he felt he could not go while there was even that remote chance.'

(Pp. 236–41.)

It is a magnificent scene, and one that is deeply symbolic. The contrast between Linton's faithful vigil in the streaming rain and the blind inhumanity of that suddenly disappearing light, is one of tragic force. And when, a few pages later, we learn the boy's thoughts during that period of waiting, the full irony of the situation reveals itself. Linton is less wise, perhaps, than Allingham in *The Gentle Lover*, whom he a little resembles in character and situation; and certainly he is more selfish. He will not give up the prospect of happiness which offers itself to him without a struggle, will not accept the implications of the situation which is developing—and this only makes his personal tragedy a harder one in the end.

Next morning, Linton, from the hotel, sees Brian on his way into the village. Seizing this opportunity, he calls on Stella. But it is the same Stella he knew all those years before, the same uncompromising, unbending Stella, high-principled and quietly, maddeningly stubborn. Either Linton must leave Ballycastle, or she and Brian will go themselves. For her there can be no middle way, no compromising.

Brian returns. Stella, sensing that she is near defeat, plays her last decisive card. The card which she plays is traditionally a woman's last—the card of weakness. The boy finds his mother alone, on her knees, in prayer. The scene that follows is a clever one, for in it Stella (who is throughout the book a significant character, despite her comparatively rare appearances) uses every means, novel and well-tried alike, to break down the boy's loyalty.[1] To the reader this last desperate gamble is to all appearances a failure, for she and the boy quarrel, violently. Beside himself, Brian rushes from the house. Hurrying to the hotel, hysterical with excitement and anger, he goes straight to Linton:

"'I've come to you. . . . What do you want me to do?'"

By a supreme effort of self-control Linton resists the temptation to profit by the boy's immediate reaction. Is his present feeling a

[1] It is worth pointing out that Forrest Reid's grasp of the aspects of feminine psychology involved in this situation is accurate and deep. Perhaps indeed it may be accounted *too* deep to be wholly true and convincing. Certainly nothing in the book, no single touch, is ever allowed to diminish the unattractiveness of the picture of Stella with which we are presented. She is one of the few, the very few, wholly unsympathetic characters that Forrest Reid drew. A close study of the implications of her role in the book offers (I think) a suggestive commentary on certain deep-seated elements in Forrest Reid's outlook.

lasting one, is he really going into this open-eyed, ready to accept all the consequences, with his mind made up? That is what Linton must be sure of.

They go down to the shore. When the boy is calmer Linton talks to him, tells him what it is that they are planning, and its gravity, tells him there can be no going back once their decision is taken; and of the tragedy it would be if that decision was wrongly made. At last he is convinced that the boy is really resolved. No time must be lost; they must leave that same day:

'Linton looked at him for a moment, gravely and steadily. "You're sure you'll be able to manage it, Brian," he said slowly, "and that nothing or nobody will stop you?"

'"There won't be anybody," Brian answered. "And even if there was, how could they stop me; what could they do?"

'Linton did not know: he did not see himself how anyone could stop him. "Well," he murmured; "I shan't see you between this and five o'clock:—I think it would be better not to." He looked at him again, and this time he smiled. "It will be all right," he said softly. "At least, I'll do everything in my power to make it all right. You believe that, don't you? You can trust me?"

'"Yes, of course," Brian replied. "It's much more the other way. I mean, it's you who'll have to trust me."'

(P. 291.)

And there I break off this narrative. The last half-dozen pages of *Brian Westby* are more poignant, more filled with suspense than any others which Forrest Reid ever wrote.

But some words which stand on the title-page of *Brian Westby* form a fitting epilogue. For 'sometimes', run these words, 'the problem is more difficult of solution, when the voice of duty seems to call in opposite directions, and sympathy and inclination themselves are divided. In such cases it is well to consider the claims of the past, for that at least is known, like an old friend; whereas the present is still untried, and the future may be an illusion.'

What contributes more perhaps than anything else to the

effect created upon us by *Brian Westby* is the skill with which the story is told. Looked at simply as a piece of ingenious story-telling the book is a triumph. And this is perhaps the best place to glance at his method of handling the novel. In *Brian Westby* Forrest Reid made use of an unusual expedient to which he resorted in no other novel. The greater part of the action takes place, by turns, from the point of view of each of the two chief characters. With the exception of the necessary passages of narrative and dialogue, the whole book is cast in the form of a series of *internal monologues*. That is to say, what we are reading about in chapter two are Linton's own thoughts, impressions, feelings when he first sees Brian on the shore. In chapter three the roles are exactly reversed; we are now watching the same scene, the same actors, but through different eyes—Brian's eyes.

An example will give a clearer idea of this technique, and its effectiveness. Linton is trying to persuade the boy to see him again:

' . . . an intense desire grew up within him that this their first meeting should not be their last. Only the strength of that desire, indeed, enabled him to overcome his shyness and the fear of a repulse, and to ask the boy . . . if he would come out with him —somewhere—anywhere—in the afternoon. . . .

'He was acutely disappointed when the boy said, "I'm afraid I can't. I promised to play tennis with my sister this afternoon." . . .

'"Thank you very much," he presently added. . . . "I suppose you're staying here?" was a still later thought.

'Linton seized on it as an encouragement. "Yes," he answered at once. "At the hotel."

'Then he waited, but the boy, contrary to his hope, did not suggest a further meeting on another day. . . .

'"I may see you tomorrow?" he then suggested.

'But the boy did not answer and Linton felt himself colouring. Didn't he *want* to see him? . . .

'"Yes," said the boy, without looking at him, "if you're sure it won't bore you."

'"It won't bore me," Linton said simply.

'"Are you sure? I don't want to take up your time, you know."

'It was Linton's turn not to answer. Somehow this reluctance, or diffidence, or mere politeness, depressed him. . . . All the same . . . he made a further effort. "We might talk things over," he said. "A good many of my friends are writers, and I might be able to help you in some way."

'"Thanks," said the boy slowly after a pause—as if the idea of being helped had its less attractive side.

'. . . "I really would, you know," he went on persuasively, "very much like to see something you've done."

'The boy became lost in thought: apparently it took time to reach a decision.

'"*Will* you bring something?" Linton asked, with the sense that this was final.

'Then the boy made up his mind. "Yes, I'd like to," he said.'

(Pp. 37–40.)

And now the same little drama is played again, but from the other angle:

'. . . he couldn't help feeling that the stranger's curiosity wasn't mere curiosity. . . . This . . . even in his own mind, was a whispered thought, and he wouldn't have uttered it aloud for worlds. Nevertheless he became practically certain of it when his new friend invited him to come out again in the afternoon.

'He wanted to accept, and he would have accepted if he hadn't promised to play tennis. Having explained this, he still stood considering it. But he must go now if he was to bathe before dinner, and the sea, with the sun glittering on it, looked extraordinarily attractive. . . . Suddenly he became conscious of his silence and said, "Thank you very much," in a voice which sounded dreadfully stiff and formal. . . . He wanted to make a suggestion . . . about their meeting again. Ought he to make it? Oughtn't he to wait till it was made to him? Well, he *would* make it, whether he ought to or not. He struggled for another moment and then heard himself muttering "I suppose you're staying here?"

'"Yes, at the hotel."

125

'And nothing more followed. What Brian had really meant had not been understood; or if it had been, was not taken up. . . .

'He noticed that his companion . . . appeared to be feeling some difficulty or embarrassment. Perhaps he *had* understood, and didn't *want* to make a definite arrangement. In the end, all he said was, "I may see you tomorrow?"

'And he said even that half-heartedly, it wasn't much more than a mumble. Brian didn't know what to make of it. . . . The very fact that this man seemed to show a particular inclination to be kind to him increased his diffidence. He hesitated, fumbled, said something about not wanting to take up his time; and the moment he had done so knew he had blundered. . . . Then unexpectedly the man said, "We might talk things over. A good many of my friends are writers and I might be able to help you in some way."

'It was very decent of him, and Brian thanked him again. Only he . . . would rather, he thought—at first at any rate—see what he could do by his own unaided efforts. . . .

'"*Will* you bring something?"

'It was rather pressing—the way he said it. Brian was ashamed of hesitating so much; it seemed so ungracious. He suddenly made up his mind, and his face cleared. "Yes, I'd like to," he answered.

'And for some queer reason, as soon as he had said it, it became true; he felt he *would* like to. . . .'

(Pp. 66–9.)

The adroitness with which these two pieces complement each other—their wonderful psychological insight—the immense effect produced upon us by this acquired sense of double intimacy—the command of every shade and inflection of thought, feeling, and expression—the use of indirect speech to reveal the whole of what is passing in a single mind—all this makes the experiment, in sheer skill of writing, a *tour de force*.

When the question arises of the place this book must be given in any comparative estimate of Forrest Reid's output it is difficult to give any exact reply. *Brian Westby* is a book of narrow emotional and physical scope. The action occupies a week or two only, and it all takes place in a small, confined setting. There are really only two characters, they scarcely ever leave the stage, the book is entirely concerned with them. Yet in spite of, or rather because of these limitations the book's power and concentration is enormously increased. Greater emotional issues are treated here than in any of the other books, issues which put *Brian Westby*, for purposes of comparison, on an altogether different plane from the other books he wrote; what we *can* admire, without qualification, is its skill; and that, in the final analysis, may be such as to make it for most people perhaps more a writer's than a reader's novel; although to every reader who can understand and feel and suffer with Martin Linton, helplessly in thrall to the 'throbbings of noon tide', the meaning of the book must be plain and overwhelming. For Linton's is the tragic predicament of that man in Rossetti's little poem 'The Mirror':

> As who, of forms that crowd unknown
>   Within a distant mirror's shade,
>   Deems such an one himself, and makes
>   Some sign; but when the image shakes
>   No whit, he finds his thought betray'd,
> And must seek elsewhere for his own.

III

Character and Setting

Tout paysage est un état d'âme.

All that mattered in the world of Forrest Reid's creative imagination was, as we have seen, concerned with the young. It is they who fill the pages of the novels and give his work its particular character. Many of the books have been imaginatively conceived from the viewpoint of a boy, with all the consequent enrichment of character that this process has afforded. Enrichment, and also range. What is *not* apparent to the casual reader of the novels is the breadth of characterization they contain. The worlds of Owen Gill in *Following Darkness* and of Grif and Palmer in *The Spring Song* are as different from each other as both are from Tom Barber's or Brian Westby's; and the identification which Forrest Reid manages to achieve with each of them in turn is what gives the work as a whole its variety. For the books *are* about one world, do have a single theme, but that theme is one capable of infinite variations and modulations and transpositions of key. The world of youth is a many-faceted one, contains within it possibilities of good and evil, beauty and ugliness, drama and tedium, often as great as and usually more intense than any that grown-up life can parallel. The range is not so wide; but the vividness and concentration are enormously increased.

There was one character Forrest Reid realized more fully than any other, and we will begin by looking at him. Tom Barber was almost the last of the characters he created, and in the three books in which he appears we live with him at his own level continuously. Tom has been singled out by one critic as representing the 'ideal image of childhood', and though Tom himself would perhaps have been alarmed, and his creator somewhat amused, by this periphrasis, it does, in a sense, touch the truth. Tom is a *real* boy, not ideal and certainly not an image, but he is at the same time something more, something nearer to his author's heart than a mere character in a book. What that something *is*, cannot be put into words without falsifying the very idea it is meant to represent, but that it does exist behind Tom himself the sympathetic reader will at once perceive. Tom *is* representative, but representative of something very special, representative only in his particularity. This is given an added emphasis by the stolidity of Tom's friend, Pascoe. Pascoe is a severely practical small boy, full of common sense and innocent of any imagination whatsoever, but in his own way and within his own limits he is perhaps almost as much a success as Tom himself. He is at all events the perfect foil. Pascoe it is who turns a walk to Glenagivney from 'an idle excursion into a scientific expedition'. Tom, lying in the heather, lazily watches him in his industrious botanizing:

' . . . Pascoe, with his mouth pursed up and an intensely serious expression on his whole countenance, looked somehow both amusing and attractive. "Would you be surprised if we saw an angel?" Tom asked him, but it was the kind of question Pascoe evidently regarded as merely symptomatic, for he neither stopped working nor answered.

'"The worst of botany books," Pascoe presently remarked, "is that unless there's a coloured picture, or you happen to know the name of the plant already, they don't help you much. . . ." '

(*The Retreat*, p. 175.)

Tom is no botanist, but he *has* seen an angel, he saw him on that very path to Glenagivney a few days before. One does not readily think of angels as human beings, or at least as other than very idealized ones. But *his* angel (although, when he sat down, seeming to possess 'a most peculiar lightness, like a butterfly poised on a leaf') was very much a human being, a boy—'a very ragged boy, with bare feet, no jacket, and rents in his shirt and trousers through which his skin showed. He had hair the colour of the bleached ears of wheat, and the brightest eyes Tom had ever beheld.' (*The Retreat*, p. 154.)

That walk was also memorable for something quite different, for during it Tom had his first encounter with a goat. A shrewd goat evidently, a goat with an unusual sense of humour, for having tipped Tom gently into the ditch, thus obliging him to crawl along it to safety before he could reach the highroad again, she then mounted guard over the basket containing his picnic. How to regain this vital object was Tom's problem. Should he attack, or appease? The latter course didn't seem to be much good:

' . . . the rich greenness of the lane seemed to make any additional offerings rather superfluous. . . . The lane was a kind of caprine Paradise. All she had to do was to stretch her neck and she seemed jolly good at that. The grass was long and juicy . . . and . . . There was also deadly nightshade, Tom perceived, but nothing was deadly to goats. She was now sampling some furze prickles. Still, an offering was his best chance . . . and holding the bunch at arm's length before him, he returned.

'The goat seemed surprised to see him. It was as if they were meeting for the first time. She gave conventional little bleats of astonishment as he approached. What a dear little boy! And so kind! Where *had* he got all those lovely things? Surely they couldn't be for her, and really they were far too pretty to eat! She took jolly good care all the same to gobble them up as quickly as possible, and in the process made them sound so crisp and succulent that Tom felt half inclined to try a mouthful himself. He cast the remains of his bouquet at her feet, lifted the basket, and this time walked away with dignity.'

(*The Retreat*, pp. 159–60.)

There is not the space, alas, to quote this charming incident in full, but it shows us quite as much of Tom's character as the goat's: Tom is no hero in the obvious sense of physical bravery. But he is resolute, he is determined, and although something of a dreamer, he is shrewd too. Above all, he is affectionate:

' . . . Deeper and deeper he sank into his thoughts. He supposed it was true that it took a long time really to get to know people, and that he was always in too great a hurry. Certainly he was in too great a hurry to tell them he liked them, and it hadn't answered well in the past. They didn't want to be told. They didn't want—those he *had* told—even to be liked; . . . Nor were words ever satisfactory. What you said always sounded either too much or too little. You could hear it yourself—either horribly gushing, or else so feeble and dry that it expressed nothing. The only true communication seemed to be not words at all:—when Uncle Stephen stroked his hair, for instance.'

(*Uncle Stephen*, p. 156.)

Besides his own affection for Uncle Stephen there are two other people in the novels who in turn feel affection for him. The first of these is Deverell. Deverell is a young poacher, son of Uncle Stephen's housekeeper. He is an uneducated creature, usually taciturn and surly, but in a mysterious way Tom's appearance on the scene has the effect of unlocking his heart: and in unexpected fashion the means is presented to the younger boy of repaying his gratitude. Deverell is in his own queer way sensitive, but he is also a ne'er-do-well; one night he housebreaks, and something leads him to suspect that he may have been observed. Tom, seeing his nervousness and pitying him, wins round Uncle Stephen to letting him give the young fellow money with which to clear the country. He takes this to the cottage where Mrs. Deverell and her son live, and the two friends have tea together:

'Deverell's chair suddenly grated on the floor as he pushed it back. . . .

'"Mr. Tom, I wished I'd known you five years ago."

'Tom smiled faintly. "You wouldn't have wanted to know me five years ago. I was only a kid."

'"Yes," said Deverell slowly, "I suppose so. It's queer, isn't it, how things is always like that?"

'As he looked at the dark unhappy eyes that were turned on

131

him, Tom too had a feeling that human affairs were hopelessly ill-arranged.

'Deverell rose and began to clear away the tea-things. Tom helped him. When at last everything was tidied up the young poacher turned to the boy. He laid his hands heavily on Tom's shoulders. From this position they moved round till they clasped the back of his head. And Tom remained absolutely still, his face curiously grave.

'"Wish me luck, Mr. Tom," Deverell said at last.

'"Yes, I wish you good luck."

'Deverell's hand passed awkwardly over his hair.

'"You can kiss me if you like," said Tom simply.

'Deverell bent down.'

(Uncle Stephen, pp. 213–14.)

This is from that 'story of sacred and profane love', *Uncle Stephen*, and it is interesting to compare the passage—economical, direct, and objective as it is—with that scene on the rocks drawn many years earlier in *The Garden God*.[1] Here Forrest Reid is content to allow Tom and Deverell to speak for themselves, and the result is more tenderly moving and far more authentic than that earlier effort, when we felt the presence of the writer growing unpleasantly intrusive. In the earlier passage the emotion generated was artificial; that is, an emotion which was produced in us only by virtue of the emotion it produced in Forrest Reid himself. It was his own feelings which Forrest Reid was describing, not the sensations of Harold Brocklehurst and Graham Iddesleigh. In the passage from *Uncle Stephen* the emotion stirs in our minds from our contemplation of the circumstances of the scene itself; the author does not interpose himself; the account is at first-hand, objectively and simply reported.

The same delicacy and discretion is employed in recounting Tom's friendship with James-Arthur. The boy is a farm-hand. His feeling for Tom is less emotional, but more responsible, more fatherly. And Tom's admiration—for he is a smaller boy in *Young*

---

[1] Quoted on pp. 68–9.

Tom than in Deverell's book—is stronger in proportion. One day he and James-Arthur go bathing in the river, and Tom watches the older boy as he prepares to dive in:

' . . . while he stood up on the bank in the sunlight, he slapped his sturdy thighs in pleased anticipation. Even at this early date of summer his body was sunburnt, and in Tom's eyes he somehow did not look naked. He had simply emerged from his soiled and much-patched clothing like a butterfly from a chrysalis, and the contrast between his fair hair and the golden brown of his body and limbs appeared to the smaller boy as attractive as anything could be. In fact James-Arthur, merely by divesting himself of his clothes, had instantly become part of the natural scene, like the grass and the trees and the river and the sky, and the dragonfly asleep upon his water-lily. Tom told him how nice he looked, and, while James-Arthur only smiled and said he was a queer wee lad, it was easy to see that secretly he was not displeased.'

(*Young Tom*, pp. 33–4.)

In this passage pastoral and Greek influences mingle together in a sunny unity. The description *looks* easy enough to write, but in reality work like this, the blending of extreme simplicity of manner with extreme simplicity of matter, only comes with long pains. If it is true that the object of art is precisely to conceal the art by which its effect is achieved, Forrest Reid succeeded in doing this. The books—the later books, that is—seem, to the reader, to write themselves. And no higher tribute than that can be paid by reader to artist.

Tom is a gentle creature; and in this he has much in common with Griffith Weston, the hero of *The Spring Song*:

'He was not in the least a handsome boy, but his expression was pleasing. He looked quiet rather than shy; he looked intelligent, sensitive, and sweet-tempered. His eyes, beneath their drooping lids, had something of that sleepy gentleness which characterizes the angels and youths of Perugino, but the wide space between

them gave the whole countenance, with its beautiful forehead, a
kind of grave nobility and innocence.'

(*The Spring Song*, pp. 1–2.)

Grif is a dreamer; and in his book, which is itself full of the freshness and lightheartedness of springtime, the boy's adventures are
not dissimilar to Tom's. He has the same mystical experiences in
nature, the same strong imagination readily stimulated, the same
love of animals, the same essential *aloneness* of spirit. And although
some of the experiences Grif went through—notably those at the
hands of Mr. Bradley—were more daunting than any Tom had to
undergo, both boys share a certain resoluteness of character
coupled with an entirely natural sensibility which is peculiarly
attractive.

And just as Tom's sensibility and imagination conjured up
Ralph Seaford—or Ralph's spirit—in Granny's house, Tramore,
so much the same thing happens to Grif down by the river one
perfect summer's day:

'He grew drowsy. . . . He was getting sleepier and sleepier,
but it was so delicious lying here in this half-dreaming, half-
waking state, that he could not resist the temptation to remain a
little longer. His eyes were nearly closed, like a cat's eyes when it
sits in the sun. He seemed to see, through the green dimness of the
trees, a whiteness as of some one moving, some bather like himself perhaps, but more probably a faun or a wood-boy. And he
knew that it was not really either one or the other, but, like many
little boys, he could continue knowing and not knowing at the
same time, while the idle dreams that flitted through his mind
seemed to be pictures he could watch. . . .

'Somewhere among the tall rushes by the water a flute was
being played. It played a strange tune,—sad, yet with a certain
gaiety singing through it, and with an odd little twirl at the end. . . .

'Grif was very happy. Now that the music was ended he had
the clearest sense of its reality . . . it was as if a warm physical
touch on his cheek had awakened him. Where had the music gone
to? He only knew that it had crossed the river and floated over the

fields. Yet, if he had had wings . . . he was sure he could have followed it. And he was sure it would have led him to some definite place, which he would have recognized at once as *the* place, the end of his journey, the home of his hidden friend.'

(*The Spring Song*, pp. 172–4.)

The world of the Seawrights in *At the Door of the Gate* is as different from all this as it could well be. We are plunged into all the narrow, humdrum, purposeless activity of lower middle-class Belfast life. The prevailing atmosphere is one not of squalor, but of a sort of all-enveloping seediness and decay mingled with gloom and spiritual frustration. This atmosphere fills the book, even the passages of descriptive beauty are pitched in a sombre and melancholy key:

'They crossed the dreary expanse of the bog meadows, passed the Cats' and Dogs' Home and the huge football-ground, with its hideous walls of corrugated iron, emerging on the upper road at a spot directly opposite the cemetery gates. Here the ground rose steeply, its green surface broken by innumerable white and grey monuments, and threaded with dark trim paths. The hard silhouettes of a few cypresses, and the softer outlines of the trees in the park alongside, stood out against a pale blue sky; while beyond, yet quite close, was a dark low range of hills, the air from which blew down, fresh and cold. . . . In this portion of the cemetery, allotted to the poorer classes, no cypresses grew, but the trees, a little thinned by autumn gales, were planes and beeches. Between their branches the grounds of the park were visible, while with every puff of wind dead leaves were whirled in showers about the graves and along the cinder paths. Here they danced, rustled, pirouetted, fluttered like brown desiccated butterflies, before they took up a temporary resting-place in some sheltered nook, or under the lee of the wall. A faint damp smell arose, filled with suggestions of melancholy and languor. . . .

' . . . above the city proper, hung a blue cloud of smoke, through which tall mill chimneys and the grey spires of churches pierced, slender and dark. Farther still, over Belfast Lough, the atmosphere cleared again, and the clouds, streaked with silver, drifted like fantastic birds, the swan-maidens of fairyland.'

(*At the Door of the Gate*, pp. 29–32.)

Although they are brothers, Richard and Martin Seawright share little or nothing in common. Martin is Mrs. Seawright's favourite because to her he seems open, frank, where Richard is silent and uncommunicative. But it is really Martin who is the weak character, and the front he shows to his mother is a deception. In reality he is a hypocrite and a drunkard and a prig. Richard, for all his rough edges, is as honest as the day. But he cannot help feeling jealous of the place Martin takes in his mother's affections, and this poisons his own relations with Mrs. Seawright, paradoxically makes him resolve to himself that he will not seek the very affection he wants so much. And Mrs. Seawright is an ordinary mother, nothing more, and to an ordinary mother such an attitude can be interpreted in only one way. *At the Door of the Gate* is primarily a book about grown-up people and their fortunes, but we see enough in the first hundred pages of the novel to realize the plight of a shy, proud, and intelligent boy in a home that is hopelessly unsympathetic to him.

This predicament—which was also, we remember, the predicament of Peter Waring and Brian Westby—was a favourite one and Forrest Reid obviously sympathized with it.

When he wrote about children Forrest Reid did not only write about boys. Lewis Carroll, as we saw, was fond of saying he liked all children, except boys. Forrest Reid wasn't so exclusive in his attitude as the author of *Alice*. Some of his best minor characters belong to the fair sex. There is the wholly delightful Anne, in *The Spring Song*, with her unshakeable and adenoidal loyalty to 'Balmer' Dorset; there is Jane Gavney in *Uncle Stephen*, Tom's stepsister and the one member of that disagreeable family whom he likes and who likes him. Jane Gavney plays a very minor part in the book, but the quality of her feeling for Tom—half admiration, half bantering affection—is exactly right. The scene where she goes to Tom's bedroom and talks to him in the dark—a dark-

ness illuminated somewhat fitfully by the rays of a torch—is curiously touching, reminding one in some respects of that scene
between Ellen and Boyne in Howells' novel *The Kentons*, by
which Forrest Reid was very moved, and of which his own scene
is perhaps an echo. There is Mrs. Seawright's adopted daughter,
Grace Mallow, in *At the Door of the Gate*, a grave and carefully
drawn figure, wholly feminine; and thinking of Grace one must
think also of Rose Jackson, the worthless foolish creature whom
Richard marries. We see Rose almost entirely from Richard's
point of view, but we are not untouched by pity for her, and
Richard's own gradual awakening to an understanding of her
essential frivolousness is one of the best-done things in that otherwise not very successful book; in this respect being in an exactly
opposite position to Sylvie Grimshaw, who is the one character
that fails in an otherwise very different and more successful story.

But perhaps the best of all these characters is Katherine Dale.
She is a very real portrait, a complete essay in feminine psychology
and nowhere more so than at the point where her relations with
Peter go wrong. Katherine's character was discussed in the previous chapter, and I am not going to quote from her book again,
but here is an extract, rather a long extract, from *At the Door of
the Gate*. Richard takes Grace out skating. He has realized his
tragic mistake in marrying Rose, and Grace, although she bears
her own husband no ill will, has realized on her side too that it is
Richard she loves, has loved all along, and not Campbell. The
piece I am going to quote will, I think, show how mistaken is the
view which seeks unduly to narrow Forrest Reid's range as a
novelist, and will also give another indication of the extraordinary sombreness he can bring to the evocation of landscape or
mood:

'The scene that met their eyes was bright, gay, animated. Overhead, the cold grey sky was already streaked with the scarlet of an
early sunset, against which the leafless trees stood out black and
naked. The lake stretched from its wooded banks, white, with a
thin crisp coating of snow, which crackled like powdered crystals

137

under the steel blades of the skates. A low continuous hum rose from the ice, growing rapidly louder as they approached the bank. . . . Beginners flapped about like large ungainly birds with clipped wings; the more proficient glided along in rhythmic, effortless curves. . . .

'His beauty had never appeared to her to be more wonderful than at that moment. The wintry background threw into relief his warm brown colouring, and the grace of his movements was delightful to watch. . . .

'She let herself go, losing all fear in the consciousness of his strength and skill. . . . On every side came the murmur of voices and laughter. Bright spots of colour—the hats, the dresses of girls —took on a strange brilliance against the background of dark trees and frost-bound woodland. A sea of life seemed to catch her up on its strong, exhilarating tide. She had a sense of freedom, of space, of motion rapid and easy like the flight of birds. And she was side by side with Richard, her hands clasped in his hands, her body swaying with his. She was rapt in the exquisite happiness of being alone with him, so close to him. It was as if they were alone together, yet were breathing the pleasure of all those other skaters, an atmosphere of joyousness warm as sunlight, wherein her own joy lived deliciously. When he spoke to her, and she turned slightly, she looked straight into his dark eyes; and their bodies seemed to blend together in one being as they sped on towards the flaming sunset.'

(*At the Door of the Gate*, pp. 253-5.)

And later, in the evening, tired but content, when they sat together in front of the fire, Grace

'. . . let herself sink deeper and deeper into the net of strangely mingled happiness and sadness which had wrapped itself about her. . . .

'A silence fell upon the room—a silence so prolonged that it might have followed upon some momentous confession. . . . She was thinking of their childhood—of him, Ricky, the playmate of her childhood, whom even then she had loved—that

beautiful, strange, sullen boy. . . . He was the first to speak, but
she did not hear what he was saying, so filled was she with the
dream that for hours she had been living in. Her head drooped a
little, and at last rested against his shoulder. She saw his beautiful
dark face, and his beautiful eyes, in which a smouldering light
burned. She pressed her cheek against him and all her spirit
trembled. . . . Then she drew his head down and her lips pressed
softly against his cheek.

'She felt him draw back . . . and . . . knew that when she
had kissed him she had really kissed only her dream. . . . Her passion had blown upon him, but it had been like a breath upon a
mirror, passing like a breath. . . .

'Suddenly Grace got up. "I must play to you," she murmured. . . .

'She played very softly, in a kind of undertone, but she played
as he had never heard her play before. An intense longing, a desire,
unhidden yet conscious of its hopelessness, seemed to have passed
into the music. It was not music that he listened to, but the torture
and the resignation of a spirit. . . .

'She finished, and then began again—the same music—always
the same.

'"Stop!" he cried abruptly, and she stopped at once, turning
her head a little and looking at him timidly.

'But his face wore a strange, almost resentful expression, which
she did not understand. She looked into his eyes—far—far. It was
like looking into an eternal night in which her vision wandered
and was lost—a blackness that stretched back and back. Her soul,
naked and shivering, seemed to stand on the fringe of that darkness, as a suicide by the edge of a pool. . . . Her soul . . . cried out
to him: "I love you—I love you. . . ." The cry was stifled and
lost: it came back to her smothered and thin as from an infinite
distance.

'While she stood there submissively before him, the thought
of her unhappiness and of her possible happiness came to him as
the sublest of temptations. In a world of shadows what could it
be but one shadow more, and why should he withhold it? He

took a step forward with the air of a somnambulist whose mind and purpose are caught in the obscure grip of a dream. At the same instant, reading his wavering thoughts, she held out her arms to him and their lips met. With that, indeed, came a moment of fear. But as he kissed her—as he clasped her to him and felt her arms tighten about his body—the despairing passion of her answering kiss seemed to cut off sharply the last possibility of retreat.'

(*At the Door of the Gate*, pp. 257–61.)

This long passage gives some impression of Forrest Reid's strange, gloomy power, and the cumulative force this power can achieve in the production of its dark and mysterious effects.

The minor characters are always among the most effective and successful. Forrest Reid had an acute eye, a novelist's eye, for the little idiosyncrasies and traits of character that are often, on a casual view, all that distinguish one human being from another. The restricted scope of the books never gave him much opportunity to exercise this gift, and he often preferred to indicate character by the oblique method, but when he was able to use his powers of observation in a straightforward piece of character drawing the results were nearly always felicitous.

Richard Seawright, like Forrest Reid himself, was put into the tea-trade. When he arrives at Wynch Brothers to apply for the vacant position he reports to the chief clerk. Mr. Lambert Jackson is a dreary, and at the same time a pathetic creature:

'Richard advanced to the counter on his right, and stood there waiting. He saw a tall, thin, elderly person working at a desk, but was too timid to try to attract his attention, so the tall, thin, elderly person continued to work for several minutes in obliviousness to the fact that he was being examined most minutely. Richard indeed thought his appearance remarkable. He had sandy hair and a sandy beard. His teeth were very white and very prominent, jutting out, like tombstones, with an effect of a perpetual and somewhat ghastly smile. Hollow-cheeked, pale, he looked, if not exactly emaciated, extremely anæmic. He wore a grey tail-

coat, and as he worked at his ledger displayed astonishing lengths
of bony wrist and knuckly fingers. Presently he raised his head,
coughed, and two very pale blue eyes, so pale as to be almost
colourless, encountered two extraordinarily dark ones. . . . The
tall thin person advanced with a white, skull-like smile, and in a
high-pitched voice wished him "Good morning."'

(At the Door of the Gate, pp. 49–50.)

Jackson is indeed an almost Dickensian figure, and almost comi-
cally Dickensian too are the hopelessly discredited experiments
in the spiritualism in which he believes with such vague yet perfervid enthusiasm. The account of the Swedenborgian meeting,
to which he drags Richard, and which is addressed by the American woman evangelist, apparently gave offence to many Sweden-
borgians at the time; but however that may be, the atmosphere
of a revivalist meeting is captured exactly:

'The President, a person who on week days obviously exercised the profession of shop-walker, approached them, shook
hands damply, and mentioned that Mr. Jackson would find a
couple of seats on the platform. He led the way as if the hosiery
department were situated in that vicinity, and Richard found himself in an extremely prominent position, facing the audience.
. . . They were far from beautiful, but they had a quality of ugliness that was eminently expressive. The hard white light pouring
down from the ceiling illuminated, mercilessly, faces pale, tired,
unhappy. It seemed to Richard that he had never seen such queer-
shaped heads, such odd features, such weedy or bulging forms, so
many of the stigmata of degeneration, of unhealthy living, unhealthy parentage.'

Presently, after a hymn and a few prayers, the professional
evangelist came forward:

' . . . she rose, standing in profile against the pink background,
like a figure in an audacious poster. Her large Jewish face was of
the colour of old ivory, and terminated in a series of chins. The
black eyes were hard and bright, the mouth square, the expression

somewhat forbidding. . . . She faced her congregation, colossal, commanding, and spoke with a strong American twang. Her grammar was appalling and her voice cracked, but it was apparent that she was accustomed to hold an audience. . . . She began . . . speaking without notes, a stream of disconnected sentences, usually foolish, invariably vulgar, yet with something behind them that fascinated her listeners. . . . With a startling irrelevance she announced that she believed in "free love". "Love one another," she quoted, "but remember that you must love proper. When I talk of free love I mean good love. That's what so many men mistakes, *and* women. You can't be a Christian unless you're a spiritualist, and you can't be a spiritualist unless you're a Christian."'

(At the Door of the Gate, pp. 132–4.)

At the Door of the Gate is a book full of character observation. There are the cheerfully vulgar McGlades, and the equally vulgar and equally cheerful McVintys. The description of the Seawrights' expedition to Slieve Donard on 'the Twelfth'—Orange Day—is a memorable piece of humourous writing. But there are some delightful lesser characters in nearly all the novels. Here, for instance, is Pascoe's Aunt Rhoda:

'Aunt Rhoda was a slight, small, and wiry-looking old woman, visibly of extreme energy both of mind and body. Tom had hitherto seen her only from a distance and through bushes, digging in her garden; on which occasions she had been wearing a kind of purple tam-o'-shanter, top-boots, and a very short skirt. She was now wearing a wig, though not with any attempt at deception, since obviously it had been chosen as a compromise between the age she felt and the age she actually was. . . . She was dressed in black, with a lot of soft black lace at her throat. Her hands, yellow and dry as parchment, were even more wrinkled than her face, but they flashed with emeralds and diamonds, for she wore at least half a dozen rings. . . . The wig was piebald, and the small wizened mobile face beneath it reminded Tom irresistibly of a monkey's. The dark, observant eyes, younger than the wig and ever so much younger than the wrinkles, increased this resemblance. And perhaps the strangest thing about it all was that Tom did not think Miss Pascoe ugly. The standard might be simian, but the effect was sympathetic and attractive.'

(*The Retreat*, pp. 238–9.)

And there are many more, of all ages, but mostly they are the young. Of these there is a whole gallery: Grif's young brother Jim in *The Spring Song*, and his sisters Anne and Barbara; or Palmer Dorset, that sagacious and persistent young Sherlock Holmes whose astuteness in detection so fascinated Dr. O'Neill, Trefusis, the boy poet in *Pender* ('an imaginary portrait' of that youthful Irish prodigy, Master Romney Robinson); Gerald Dale, Katherine's brother, Max Sabine or Mr. Holbrook or Miss Jimpson in *Young Tom*; and many others.

It was typical of Forrest Reid's humanity that he never introduced a character for technical purposes alone, simply to solve a problem. Even those whose appearances in the novels are briefest leave a clear mark of individuality behind them. They *are* persons. Even the half-pathetic little guide who attaches himself to the Grimshaws in the picture gallery at Bruges[1] is an all too familiar figure:

'They passed through the courtyard of the Hospital to the old chapter-room where the Memlincks hang. A gray, fussy, little curator, armed with several magnifying glasses, instantly descended upon them, like a demon of the Arabian Nights, and swept them impetuously before the "Adoration of the Magi".

'"Memlinck's masterpiece. Look close; you see the hairs," he hissed ardently, drawing the reluctant attention of his visitors to the sprouting, three-day beard on the chin of one of the kings. "The man looking through window is portrait of Memlinck himself . . . Memlinck—portrait of Memlinck . . ." He turned in swift pursuit of Brian, who had made his escape, and silently gliding a magnifying glass between him and the head of a weeping Madonna, whispered: "Tears!"

[1] Mr. J. N. Hart remembers the original of this character well.

143

'Much was put into that hoarse monosyllable. The coldness and indifference, the unhallowed levity, the stealthy or hurried departure without "tipping," of thousands of mean and ungrateful sightseers, swam up through it. . . . He looked round. "Tears!" he announced again, this time to Sylvie. Yet almost at the same moment he was at Allingham's elbow. "Burgomeister's Daughter." And the magnifying glass passed swiftly and triumphantly over the transparent head-dress. "Burgomeister's Daughter —Lace!" The words sounded this time almost a note of challenge.'

(*The Gentle Lover*, pp. 9–10.)

Phemie and Mary, the cook and housemaid in *The Retreat*, even William the gardener, are real human beings, though we catch no more than glimpses of them.

But there is one class of characters who never play a major part in the stories and yet occupy too large a place to be dismissed in a few lines along with these charming but less important folk. In nearly every novel Forrest Reid wrote, there is one recurring type. Occasionally he is a clergyman or priest, but more often he will be a doctor, a doctor of the old-fashioned, family kind. This person has two functions to perform. He will act as a point of reference to whom the chief youthful character can turn for advice (and incidentally at the same time, by his intervention, form a useful device for advancing the plot), and he will also provide an ironic commentary on the action itself. It is difficult in fact not to see a good deal of Forrest Reid himself in this persistently reappearing figure. In *The Kingdom of Twilight*, his very first book, we meet him in the person of Dr. Grayson, and thereafter in Mr. Escott, that most unclerical cleric in *At the Door of the Gate*, Father O'Brien, the genial, but slightly unreal, Jesuit in *Pirates of the Spring*, Dr. O'Neill in *The Spring Song*, Dr. Birch in *The Bracknels*, and even (because she in fact fills very much the same role) Mrs. Carroll, in *Following Darkness*. Uncle Stephen is the apotheosis of the type, but because Uncle Stephen is really very much more than a mere onlooker, being a central character in the book, he falls outside this group. Where we see the 'uncle-doctor' type in its fullest development is perhaps in Doctor Macrory. Doctor Macrory comes into *Uncle Stephen*, at the beginning, but *Young Tom* is really his book. He is ironical, detached, and understanding, and with him Tom can feel an ease which his father, however fond of him he may be, cannot inspire. The doctor is, in fact, that not uncommon type, the bachelor who understands children better than their parents. He soon sees where Tom's interests lie, sees that he has the temperament and imagination to which beauty makes instant appeal. He also detects in him the makings of a classical scholar. And because Tom is a sensitive little boy he feels at once that he has gained the doctor's confidence, and in return gives him his own. Doctor Macrory, driving him over in the car to Granny's house Tramore for a few days' stay, takes the opportunity to discuss with him the suggestion that he should take up Greek:

'Tom had done a little, a very little Latin with Miss Sabine, but his classics ended there, and he didn't know what to think. In his uncertainty he suggested that there mightn't be anybody to *teach* Greek. At Miss Wallace's, for instance, where Pascoe had been, there hadn't been anybody to teach science; yet that was what Pascoe was most interested in, because he was going to *be* a scientist.

'Doctor Macrory's glance again rested upon him, with an oddly reflective expression. It quite often did, Tom had noticed, proving that he was really interested and not just pretending to be; which was one reason why it was so much easier to talk freely to him than to Daddy.

'"Possibly he is," Doctor Macrory answered; "but unless I'm singularly mistaken you're not: Greek for you every time. . . . I really mean what I say, Tom, about learning Greek. I haven't met Master Pascoe, but the fact that you and he propose to make an aquarium together doesn't mean that science is at all likely to be in your line. You haven't that type of mind. If you're interested in natural history, it's only because, like the Greeks, you're fond of animals—which is a spiritual quality, and has nothing whatever to do with science."'

(*Young Tom*, pp. 55-7.)

All these characters were products of the imagination. And so, to close this chapter, I am going to mention a living character. Or rather, someone who was once alive, because the boy in question—'gay, responsive, affectionate, and with the merriest laugh I have ever heard'—went as a young man to Australia, rode out into the Bush, and, from that day to this, was never heard of again. In his childhood, before he became a sailor and went to sea, this boy, Kenneth Hamilton, had been Forrest Reid's constant companion.

The essay called 'Kenneth', in *Retrospective Adventures*, gives an account of his youthful literary experiments. 'Kenneth'—we are told—'has been writing now for more than a year, yet his works are still very little known. They appear for the most part in *Kenneth's Magazine* (illustrated)'. At this point it becomes necessary to explain. *Kenneth's Magazine* was a rather unique literary effort. It ran for nine issues, and although only one copy of each appeared—for the impersonality of print never came between this journal and its readers—the single copy always enjoyed the liveliest circulation among the editor's collaborators and friends. The editor himself proved a vigorous occupant of his chair, and in the editorials—which combine cajolery, threats, and promises in the nicest proportions—contributors and readers alike were kept constantly reminded of their responsibilities. Indeed, as the identity of these two classes tended fast to become indistinguishable, these reminders were usually of a somewhat double-edged nature.

I have seen the set of *Kenneth's Magazine*, and a disarming and attractive undertaking it is. The illustrated cover sets a note of gay inconsequence from the start—it can usually be found to refer to one of the more *mouvementé* incidents in the serial within—and the contents, verse and prose, are accompanied by cheerfully libellous sketches and caricatures. The whole succeeds in conveying a most vivid impression of the trials, triumphs, and disasters of authorship.

Kenneth's works consist mainly of short stories, though there was also planned *John Milton: A Critical Study*, quickly abandoned, 'owing to the surprising and unsuspected dullness of *Paradise Lost*'. The tales are vigorous, full of action, and have little truck with niceties of dialogue or reflection. The action is, indeed, as vivid as anyone could well wish, being mainly concerned with pirates, criminals, and such fry, and their illicit but undeniably exciting deeds. 'Not one of them—not even *The Young Viking*, not even *The Hero of Sheldon College*—would be published by the S.P.C.K., while what that society would make of such a thing as *Split, the Burglar* may be left to imagination.' It was in this exciting company that Forrest Reid's short story 'The Accomplice' (which was later printed in *Retrospective Adventures*) made its début.

There are, of course, attempts at other genres—there are even love stories. But, it must be admitted, they lack the fire of the adventure tales. There is, lastly, the poetry; and here there *is* a complete change. The poems, surprisingly, are 'extremely personal, and usually rather sad.' Some of them, such as the 'Ode on an Infant Leper who Died as Soon as Born', are really *too* sad, and 'our response is proportionately feeble'. 'Fireside Memories' was included by Forrest Reid in his essay, but there is another poem I want to quote which so far as I know has only appeared in the small MS. volume (prettily bound up in wall-paper) which contains Kenneth's verses.[1] The theme (which had greatly struck the small boy's imagination) was the recovery of the sonnets which Rossetti had buried in Lizzie Siddal's grave at Highgate. Students of Pre-Raphaelitism will condone the small piece of poetic licence which has here made the poet himself undertake the gruesome work. The poem is entitled simply 'Rossetti'. Here it is:

[1] Future bibliographers and others may care to have the collation of this unique item, which is: Verse and Prose/by/Kenneth Hamilton/ [Copied out by] Forrest Reid/1918

The night was dark,
  The weather cold;
The fierce watch-dog's bark
  Made him feel less bold.

The spade deep
  In the earth he dug;

The shrill sound of some farm cock's voice he
heard, and he shuddered: and the trees moved as
if some ghostly form was near,

But bravery fought his fear.

At last the sound
Of wood was heard;
He stooped well low
For he knew the coffin was so near.

The board he lifted;
Then the coffin in the deadly dark he saw.
He wedged the lid open,
And saw in sleep divine—his wife.
The work of his life
Lay beside her,
Bound in her flowing hair.

This is a dramatic poem; but to end the chapter, and as a complete contrast, here is a poem—never published in the books—by Forrest Reid himself, which he called 'By the Nursery Fire'; and setting it down here, alongside the other, is, I think, the most sympathetic way of celebrating the delicate relationship between teacher and pupil:

Quiet he sits, and quiet now
The dreams that shadow his sweet eyes
Brimmed up with gentle innocencies.
This firelight full of wondrous things,
This dusk through which a fairy sings,

From darkest corner of the room,
For him are fraught with memories.
Twilight for him holds naught of gloom;
The creaking stair, the shaken blind,
The leaves brushing the window-pane,
The ghostly patter of the rain,
Make but a music in his mind,
Whose spirit hath its own soft light
Brighter than candles in the night.

IV

Style and Ideas

Style is not an embellishment, as some people believe; it is not even a matter of technique; it is, like colour to a painter, a quality of vision, a revelation of that particular world which each of us sees and others do not. The pleasure which an artist gives us is that of making us acquainted with one more world. . . .

PROUST, '*Lettres de Marcel Proust à Bibesco*'
(*La Guilde du Livre, Lausanne, 1949*), *p. 177*

. . . all beauty is in the long run only fineness of truth, or what we call expression, the finer accommodation of speech to that vision within.

PATER, *Essay on Style*

What we mean by style is, I suppose, only the more or less perfect expression of a writer's individuality. . . .

FORREST REID, '*W. B. Yeats: A Critical Study*', *pp. 56-7*

I have called this chapter *Style and Ideas* because they are, I think, inseparable. This is as it should be; for in the work of a genuine artist one can only spring from the other. This is, quite literally, true: and it is a truth that has lately been much neglected. Elegance of expression is not a quality which can be analysed in a vacuum. Style without matter, in short, is little more than a mockery; and just how wearisome such writing may be, readers of those little books by Arthur Benson much esteemed in the early years of the century, *Through a College Window* and its companions, still remember. Nor, by itself, is mere excellence of matter any more certain of achieving a permanent place in literature, for otherwise we should find ourselves paying very much more for the eleventh edition of the *Encyclopaedia Britannica* than the bookseller at present asks, or than we are ready to give. Style alone, as Sir Thomas Browne so memorably intoned more than three hundred years ago, preserveth from the iniquity of oblivion. But it can only preserve what will be worth the preservation. It is, of course, a question of adjustment; one must know exactly what one wants to say and one must also know exactly the *way* in which it should be said. If the 'fundamental brainwork', which Rossetti postulated as essential to great poetry, has been honestly done, it is almost axiomatic that style—a style—will follow. The style of the lawyer, picking his way through an intricate legal argument, or the style of the historian, will be different from the style of the novelist or the poet. That is obvious. But if each of these writers really *knows* what it is that he wants to express, the style to fit the expression will spring to the mind, in those mysterious rapt moments between the germination of an idea and its committal to paper, unbidden. Style is, after all, only the proof of mastery, of excellence, and whether it is put to use in the unravelling of a complicated intellectual problem, or in the transcription of quite personal visions and ideals such as Forrest Reid's it is very much more than mere adornment, *is* that 'quality of vision', that 'fineness of truth' of which Proust and Pater both speak. This is the heart of the matter.

'"You don't want to write the kind of stuff which can't be read a second time until the first reading is forgotten—which depends on mere surprise for its interest."' So Linton counsels Brian as they sit planning the story they are going to write together. '"There must be something behind—or rather all *through* your work— a spiritual atmosphere. It seems to me that this alone can give it richness. Art isn't just life in the raw: it is a selection from life: it *is* a vision:—life seen through a temperament, as Zola said. And its quality depends on the quality of that temperament far more than on the material out of which the actual pattern is woven."' (*Brian Westby*, pp. 165–6.)

But there is something more to it even than this. That something is simplicity, the quality in writing which Pater spoke of as *diaphaneitè*, or translucency. For words, as that great critic observed, 'should be indeed things—the word, the phrase, valuable in exact proportion to the transparency with which it conveyed to others the apprehension, the emotion, the mood, so vividly real within oneself.'

This effect Forrest Reid never ceased striving to capture. 'I must confess', he wrote in a passage of retrospect, 'that the older I grow the higher value I set on simplicity.' This simplicity, or transparency, is not the highest quality of style, but it is the most effective. 'Les plaisirs que l'art procure ne doivent jamais coûter la moindre fatigue.' Forrest Reid did not reach that ideal without much disappointment and some failure. 'To a realist', he remarked in *Private Road*, 'it is a severe handicap to be by temperament romantic, unless, like Flaubert, he is sufficiently resolute to keep the two elements in his nature separate, and write alternate books in which, without confusing, he expresses both of them. I think I found the way eventually, but for a long time . . . I fumbled.' (*Private Road*, p. 145.)

This is an important clue to understanding one aspect of his development as a writer. He matured much more rapidly as a prose-writer than as a novelist. In *Private Road* he recalled how it became his habit to carry about a notebook in which he would dash down immediate impressions, to be worked up at leisure later on, and perhaps even to be fitted into one of the novels. In this way his powers of description were constantly exercised. The real difficulty lay elsewhere.

In books like *At the Door of the Gate* or *The Gentle Lover*, in parts of *Following Darkness*, and in *Pirates*, the fusion of romantic feeling and realist technique does not take place, and that is why these particular books, despite passages of beauty and many individual excellences, do not hold together as works of art.

The work falls into three stylistic phases: the first, during which he produced the two early books, that were failures, written during the years when Forrest Reid was feeling his way, written under influences that did not suit him; a middle period which starts with *The Bracknels* and includes *Following Darkness*, *The Spring Song*, *The Gentle Lover*, and the study of Yeats; and the last period, which began with *Apostate* in 1926 and continued until his death, during which his style was constantly developing.

The earliest influences were Pater and James, and they were transitory ones, as they were bound to be, for 'they did not really suit me'. The effects upon his style of his admiration for these two artists, when he was first subjected to their influence, were not salutary. Pater, in particular, is not an author imitated with impunity.[1] Yet in the long run contact with them did more good than harm; for he soon ceased to echo them directly and, once freed from a slavish admiration, he was able, by close study of their practice, to draw those lessons that were truly relevant to the formation of his own style. What he finally retained from Pater was not the sickly preciosity that was all most of his followers achieved, but a feeling for the value of words, as exact and delicate units of meaning, for the balance and euphony of a sentence, and the rhythm of a paragraph. From Henry James he learnt to appreciate the importance of structure and form, as providing the setting, the framework for well-proportioned prose; and also the need to master those technical problems that beset the inexperienced novelist. But neither James nor Pater explicitly taught the need for clarity. This was left to a French writer; for it was only with the discovery of Anatole France, much later, that he saw his way. 'I could not imitate that style,' he wrote, 'but somehow it set me free to discover my own'; because, with its 'charm, its natural grace, its simplicity and lucidity' it seemed to link itself with the Greek ideal towards which he was striving. Anatole France was the impetus that led him to the radical reorganization of his style —a process which, once begun in *Apostate*, was to continue for the rest of his life.

And as the style changes, so do some of the ideas. Certain elements in the writings persist, but others appear and then vanish, and others again reach their fullest development only towards the

[1] Corroborative evidence of this is supplied by the statement of Field-Marshal Earl Haig, who declared that his style was formed by Pater. For this rather macabre discovery I am indebted to Mr. Stephen Gilbert. 'The influence' Mr. Gilbert adds, 'is difficult to trace.'

end of his life. I want to look at four of these elements and try and trace their influence in the books. The four elements are realism, suspense, dialogue and narrative; and, lastly, irony.

Forrest Reid was a writer in the tradition of Turgenev, the author who had, in his own words, 'blended reality and beauty more perfectly than any other artist'; and in these books it is often easy for us to forget the realism for the beauty. The atmosphere which fills many of the stories is so powerful, the effects are so delicately captured, that reading them for the first time one is inclined to overlook the care and thought, the craftsmanship, that have gone into their construction. Where they fail—as in *Pender*, or *The Kingdom of Twilight*, or *At the Door of the Gate*—it is precisely because an imaginative pattern has *not* been imposed on the book, because it has not been felt but invented. Consequently the craftsmanship has received no impetus from the imagination, and the whole affair limps along through as many chapters as its author can manage to sustain; until, sighing with relief, he is able by an arbitrary twist of the plot to rid himself of a task for which his enthusiasm has long vanished.

Forrest Reid's greatest success in matching realism with romanticism was, of course, in *Brian Westby*: but at present the book I want to examine from this point of view is *Apostate*. *Apostate* was Forrest Reid's autobiography. Or rather, it was an autobiography of the first seventeen years or so of his life; these were the only ones which were significant to him. The book is a lovely and curiously intimate document. It was written in a style different from any style he had employed before; it was, indeed, as if by writing about his own childhood and boyhood and living through those 'early days' in imagination he had freshened the springs of his artistic life. Probably Forrest Reid had been passing through that bleak period, familiar to many artists of middle age, which often forms a kind of cæsura in their work; a period when the first creative impulse has spent itself, and the author lies becalmed, his sails unstirred by the accustomed breaths of inspiration. *Pender* and *Pirates of the Spring* had shown some evidences of such a failure of power, of an exhausted imagination; *Pender*, indeed, Forrest Reid later acknowledged to be a 'manufactured book', no more and no less, with none of that 'compelling urge' which a real work of art must have behind it. It is as if the spiritual reawakening which the writing of *Apostate* produced in him was mirrored in the clear, limpid purity of the prose itself. This book, then, marks the rediscovery at the same time of an altogether new style in which he could tell his own personal story. It is not a conventional autobiography—one would hardly have expected that—but it is a novelist's autobiography. That is to say, it is told in a series of dramatized scenes, very unimportant most of them by conventional standards of importance, but holding for the author an intense, if often irrational, significance. Forrest Reid told the story of his life as if it were a novel, and the book triumphs as much on account of its skill in selection and construction as in the transparent beauty of its prose or the tale which it has to tell.

I said that in *Apostate* the realism and the romanticism mingled in a single work of art. It was the first book in which Forrest Reid was successful in blending them. Perhaps the clue to his ability to do it here, rather than elsewhere, lay in the character of the book itself. It was autobiographical. Renan, in his *Souvenirs d'Enfance et de Jeunesse*, commenting on the fact that Goethe selected as the title for his memoirs 'Truth and Poetry', remarked that the author thereby signified that 'a man cannot write his own biography in the same way that he would that of anyone else. What one says of oneself is always poetical.' This is completely true of *Apostate*. Here is a passage which will illustrate this:

'When I was about six or seven I used to be taken out each morning by my nurse, Emma, to the Botanic Gardens, at that time not yet transformed into a public park. There was a large conservatory there, and the wing of the building where the palms and cactus grew had a glass door bordered with red and yellow panes. On chilly October days I was very fond of flattening my nose against one of these coloured windows, and peering out into an exotic world. . . . The damp warmth of the greenhouse atmosphere, the moist earthy smell of the ferns and creepers and mosses growing there, helped to deepen the illusion that I was far away in the virgin forest. Tigers and panthers burned in those shrubberies, and scarlet, green, and blue parrots screamed soundlessly in the trees . . . but . . . I had not been brought out to spend my morning in an overheated conservatory which gave Emma a headache; and though I did not yield without demur, in the twinkling of an eye I would find myself back again in grey October and the unromantic Gardens, where perambulators rolled leisurely, and everything was dull and domestic.

'Looking back through Time [continues Forrest Reid—and this is the point, surely] is very much the same as looking through that greenhouse door. The shapes of things remain unaltered, but there is a soft colour floating about them that did not exist in the clear white light of morning. Only, again, I am not sure—am not sure, I mean, that this clear white light ever did exist for me. I cannot help thinking that I was in those days very much what I am now.'

(Apostate [1926], pp. 5–7.)

Forrest Reid's realism followed the course of his own writings, as we watch them emerge from the shadows which crowd so thickly in some of the early books into the clear sunshine of the later novels. Realism of the sordid and Zola-esque kind could find no place in, for instance, the Tom Barber books; the realism which could minutely describe the phenomena attending Mr. Bracknel's death-throes,[1] or the sordid horror of death in a railway train:

'She [it is poor Rose in *At the Door of the Gate*] was aroused from her reverie by a slight noise; her fellow-traveller had dropped his newspaper. . . . His head leaned back against the cushion. . . . The purplish glow had faded from his cheeks, leaving them a pale, yellowish white, like discoloured wax. He was . . . clean shaved except for short side whiskers of a reddish grey; and he sat with his mouth slightly open, while his pale and rather prominent eyes stared so fixedly at her that she got up and moved to the other end

[1] See page 76.

of the carriage. . . . Yet from time to time she could not help glancing at him. . . . He no longer looked at her, but at the photographs of coast scenery on the wall immediately before him. A curious nervousness began to creep into her mind. She shut her eyes and tried to sleep, but found herself constantly opening them to cast a furtive glance at the man in the corner, at the hands and at the fat pale yellow face, which swayed and jerked grotesquely with the rocking of the train. She had never seen anybody who gave her such an impression of absolute limpness as this man, who appeared to be at the mercy of each jolt of the carriage.

'She shivered. The hands were curiously unhealthy, pale like tallow, with a reddish down growing half way up the broad flat fingers . . . each time the train swayed she saw the man make a sudden spasmodic jerk in his seat. . . . And the glazed eyes never moved. Then all at once it struck her that the eyelids had not blinked.'

(At the Door of the Gate, pp. 284–6.)

In the novels which followed *Apostate* the darker side of Forrest Reid's genius is entirely absent. This is unlikely to have been intentional; but it did mean that Forrest Reid was at last finding his real subjects, and it so happened that treatment of these subjects called no longer for this kind of writing.

Instead, the realism of the later books is less oppressive, less cheerless, altogether lighter in tone. It is hard to convey this without extensive quotation, as the feeling is diffused throughout these books; in part, of course, it was dictated by the shift of emphasis in the subjects he chose, but it was also in no small measure due to the revivified style in which *Apostate* was written, the style which, once discovered, he never relinquished, and indeed continuously developed and loosened for the rest of his writing career.

That development was a development towards *simplicity*; and perhaps as much as anything else it was what influenced the texture of the style. This was what had attracted him towards Anatole France. He was not directly influenced by Anatole's cool, ironical, limpid style, but it did, in his own words, 'set me free to discover my own', set him free from the really quite unsuitable, though superficially attractive Jamesian style, and from that 'vicious medium', half-poetry, half-prose, which was the legacy of Pater and the writers of the nineties.

It was the consciousness of how far he had advanced as a craftsman since his first attempts that prompted him, towards the end of his life, into revising two of his earliest novels, *The Bracknels* and *Following Darkness*; and at the time of his death he was preparing to perform a similar operation on *The Spring Song*.[1] To study carefully the parallel texts of *Following Darkness* and its rewritten successor, *Peter Waring*, is to receive a rich lesson in the uses and possibilities of English prose. Some there are (E. M. Forster is one) who regret in the later book what they consider the loss of a delicacy and freshness which marked the earlier version; but of the technical gain achieved by the revision there can be no disputing.

The things that Forrest Reid had to say could not really be said until he had detached himself from these influences and produced a style of his own, corresponding to the uniqueness of his private spiritual vision; and this the discovery of Anatole France enabled him to do. If he had clung to the earlier styles not merely would he have been unable to express the things he really wished to say, but in all likelihood he would never have succeeded in producing a real work of art at all. It is probable, too, that the healthy scepticism which was latent in Anatole France's view of life helped to keep his own work free from the sentimentality which would have fatally marred its fineness of grain.

The feeling of suspense is closely connected with Forrest Reid's power as a story-teller, which in turn depends upon his technique of realism. The element of mystery in so many of the tales helped to create this effect, in many of them was chiefly what that effect *was*. The short story 'Courage', printed in *A Garden by the Sea*, is

[1] Most of the pieces which appeared in *Retrospective Adventures* were also subjected to careful revision before being reprinted. There seems to be something peculiarly Irish in the urge to revision. Yeats, George Moore, A.E., and even Bernard Shaw all made a practice of literary second thoughts.

an example. Michael, who is a small boy, has gone to stay with his grandfather in the country, and coming up from the station he notices a high stone wall lining the roadside. When he arrives at the rectory he learns from one of his grandfather's servants that the house he has seen is empty, empty because it is haunted. He determines to explore it. When some days later he climbs into the deserted building, the first thing he sees is a portrait of a lady with a boy beside her. He is reminded of his own mother, from whom he has received a letter only that day. She was better, she told him, but she must only write a short letter, she is so tired. . . . The boy goes upstairs. The house is fascinating, and before he has realized how long he has been exploring, darkness falls:

'He sat motionless, trying to realize what had happened—and listening, listening . . . with this consciousness of awakening life a fear came also. He listened in the darkness, and though he could hear nothing, he had a vivid sense that he was no longer alone. Whatever had dwelt here before had come back, as a beast returns to his lair, and was even now, perhaps, creeping up the stairs.'

Summoning up all his courage, he dashes down the stairs and is on the point of rushing out of the house when a strange thing happens; for he feels—feels with the force of a conviction—that someone is telling him he must climb up the dark dreadful stair-case again, that 'there was something he must do . . . and if he left this undone, then he would have failed'. The mysterious message, he knows—though he cannot tell how or why—comes to him from his mother. There is no compulsion, he is free to run away, to escape, as all his instincts urge him; yet that would be to let *her* down, and although he knows he would be forgiven, he would feel wretched, humiliated:

'He steadied himself against the side of the porch. The cold moonlight washed through the hall, and died out in a faint grey-ness half-way up the first flight of stairs. With sobbing breath and wide eyes he retraced his steps, but at the foot of the stairs he stopped once more, dreading the impenetrable blackness of those awful upper storeys. He put his foot on the lowest stair, and slowly, step by step, he mounted, clutching the banisters. He did not pause on the first landing, but continued straight on into the darkness, which seemed to close about his slender figure like the gates of a monstrous tomb.

'Groping his way, he opened the door of the room . . . and was at first conscious only of a sudden, an immense relief, for [the] . . . room . . . seemed blessedly empty. Then, close by the window, in the pallid twilight, he saw something. At first hardly more than a shadow, a thickening of the darkness . . . .'

(*Retrospective Adventures*: 'Courage', pp. 243–5.)

We remember also the brief, intense poignancy of Linton's vigil by the sea-wall at the end of *Brian Westby*, the hunt for Denis at the close of *The Bracknels*, Andrew Rutherford reading the secret notebook in *Apostate*, the melodramatic fight between Richard and Martin Seawright in the last pages of *At the Door of the Gate*. This ability to hold his readers' attention at the critical moments, to build up an atmosphere compact of expectancy and brooding anticipation, is one of the gifts of the story-teller. Forrest Reid's plots—until in the later books plots almost disappear—were always constructed with care. Those of his books that can be accounted failures shipwrecked on quite other rocks than these.

One of the lesser rocks was dialogue. Dialogue is the breath that gives a novel life, and still more, that inexpressible quality, *tone*. To create natural conversation is never easy for the inexperienced writer, and Forrest Reid was not alone in finding it one of the most intractable of all the novelist's problems. It would perhaps be hardly fair to disinter some of the earlier tragedies in this line, and much of the dialogue has an atmosphere of quaintness which its author never intended it should acquire, but a passage like this (from *The Garden God*) shows that Forrest Reid was not proof against falling into one of the classic traps which are laid for the beginner. Graham Iddesleigh is describing his dream-life to his friend Harold:

'"As soon as I fell asleep I saw him—my dream-boy. I awoke, it seemed, on the sea-shore, at the very gate of his garden. And I heard his voice calling me—calling, calling. . . . Who he is, what he is; if he indeed be your spirit, or if you only remind me of him, I suppose I shall never know. At times I think he must have been born with me, and have grown with the growth of my soul."'

(*The Garden God*, p. 78.)

Not only was there the failure to respect the contrasting roles that dialogue and description must play in narrative, and the impossibility of making one of them perform the tasks of the other: the dialogue itself sometimes went wrong. In one of the last scenes in *The Bracknels*, Denis, unnerved by his father's death and hysterical with fear, seeks some comfort from his tutor Rusk:

"'Why are we like this, Mr. Rusk? Why should we be different from other people? But we are—we are. We are all tainted. There is something wrong with Alfred—with me—with all of us. . . . You must go away; you can do nothing. Why should you stay among us? This house is haunted. It is not meant for you. For us it is different—that is the air we have breathed for long—long. We are tainted—we are tainted.'"

(*The Bracknels*, p. 272.)

This is not the language we should expect from a boy of fourteen, even a hysterical boy, and even sensitive and intelligent boys of fourteen do not refer to themselves as 'tainted', nor do they talk about the 'air we have breathed' when they refer to an unhappy home life. This is not to be unsympathetic; but passages like this do show that Forrest Reid had not yet gained full control of his medium. It is not a serious flaw and in many books would pass unnoticed; here it strikes a note that is false, and because the surrounding harmony is so delicate we can hear this slight dissonance the more clearly.

Forrest Reid persevered, and in time became as skilful in managing conversation as in anything else; and in addition his own style acquired an easy, almost a colloquial quality that earlier it had lacked. The colloquialism is never smart or hackneyed, but in the later books it is there, or nearly there, most of the time, and his graceful use of this device gives a recognizable flavour to his prose, as well as being a token of the human feeling that lay behind it. It was just that 'perfect expression of a writer's individuality' which he himself admired in authors such as Katherine Mansfield, Henry James, and Norman Douglas.

The colloquialism, or near-colloquialism, was one expression of a strong individuality; another was the calculated use of emphasis. When we listen to Forrest Reid what we *hear*, what we can hardly help hearing, is a tone of voice, someone speaking; the inflexions and stresses, hesitations and insistencies, all the tricks of expression of the human voice come through to us, rising straight from the printed page. It was, I think, the late Logan Pearsall Smith who, speaking of Henry James, once undertook to recognize the master's art from reading no more than a single sentence. The claim was excessively confident; and it is not one which his admirers would perhaps care to make on behalf of Forrest Reid. But I think that most people with any claim at all to know the books could with reasonable certainty claim that a paragraph of Forrest Reid's is unmistakable, and in many of his writings one could, I think, spot his hand in the first few lines. In an essay on Hugh Lofting, he prefaces his remarks about the author of the Doolittle books with some reminiscences of his own on the subject of literature for children:

'*Misunderstood*—read aloud by a grown-up sister—did not exactly bore me, but its two small heroes, Humphrey and Miles, produced a sense of irritation not unmixed with scepticism. . . . This antipathy never reached the point of positive loathing inspired by *Little Lord Fauntleroy*; it consisted rather in an uneasiness, a feeling that I was being made to listen to what ought not to be talked about—to what no real boy ever *would* talk about. In short, I disliked the *kind* of sentiment, which was not my kind. . . . I could tell of one tragic Christmas when I received no fewer than three books by that dreariest of imposters, G. A. Henty, and of the

disgraceful scene that followed. At thirteen one *does* look a gift
horse in the mouth, or at least I did.'

(Retrospective Adventures: 'Hugh Lofting
and the Nursery Shelf', p. 103.)

The trenchancy and the characteristic emphasis—making the
whole thing seem alive, felt—can hardly be missed. Nor can the
gentle humour which flickers over the surface of the writing, and
which was always latent in his books. There is acute literary
criticism here, but so attractively and persuasively is it set out
that only on a second reading does the full *sense* of what Forrest
Reid is saying reach us. This ability to strike exactly the right note
of intimacy, of engaging ease, so that we become, as it were,
silent participants in his own dialogue with himself, is a very difficult achievement of literary art. If it is successful the whole thing
is lifted to a personal and friendly plane, and more can be said—
or hinted at—on that plane than on any other. This is of course to
wander beyond the small paragraph quoted, but the implications
of it do serve to introduce the last characteristic of Forrest Reid's
style which I want to discuss.

Forrest Reid was a master of irony. Not a bitter or mordant
irony, not even a very detached irony, but irony of the kind that
accompanies a dry humour and a shrewd and tolerant understanding. It is the irony, grim in manner but kindly in intention,
of many of the 'uncle-types' in the novels: of Dr. Macrory, for
instance, or Dr. Birch, though it was not confined to a single
character, or a single type of character. Irony might be defined as
the sense of humour of a reserved but good-natured person whose
experience at the hands of life has not been uniformly fortunate.
There is a disillusioned, but quite unembittered realism—perhaps
the realism of Ulster—in Forrest Reid's sense of humour. And
there is never anything pawky or ungenerous or fixated about
his attitude—never anything which makes us think of it as giving
more than a pleasant salt to his prose. It acts as a protection against
sentimentality, but it is never a vehicle for cynicism. Cynicism,
with its implications of worldliness, resentment, staleness, was

utterly abhorrent to Forrest Reid and alien to his view of life.

The view of life that *did* underlie his writing was as much his own, as characteristic and personal, as his style. Everything that happens to a man after he has left the magic confines of childhood and youth becomes, on this view, inessential. With the onset of maturity all that really matters lies behind, all the vividness and colour has ebbed out of life. '*Your image gone, and the whole crystal blind.*' Significantly, disappointment in love, or failure to win reciprocated affection, is a frequent theme in the novels; and this conscious disillusion runs like a melancholy undertow beneath the equable surface of the writing. Allingham fails with Sylvie, Linton with Brian; Ricky makes the wrong choice in marriage and suffers, Peter Waring loses Katherine Dale. And it is perhaps significant as well that two at least of these, Allingham and Linton (in both of whom it is possible to see projections of the author), fail because they are too old. They can no longer recapture the buoyancy and flexibility of youth and, lacking that magic, are left

> *. . . more desolate, more dreary cold*
> *Than a forsaken bird's-nest. . . .*

The directness, the freshness, the wild visions and the quickly fired enthusiasms have vanished, all vanished, never to return.

> *TheMoon doth with delight*
> *Look round her when the heavens are bare;*
> *Waters on a starry night*
> *Are beautiful and fair;*
> *The sunshine is a glorious birth;*
> *But yet I know, where'er I go,*
> *That there hath past away a glory from the earth.*

Wordsworth's experience, and Forrest Reid's too, are not uncommon ones; the sense of exile, of deprivation, is one that has been very vividly shared by sensitive beings of all ages. Always it was towards

... those first affections,
Those shadowy recollections,

that, despite their ever-receding distance down the corridors of
time, Forrest Reid turned back his gaze, and from them he wove
the stuff of his books. The memory of the experiences themselves
might grow dim in the mind, the images crumble, but the
emotions associated with them did not, remained for him as they
did for Wordsworth, still 'a master-light of all our seeing'. 'If I
had never written a line, and were never again to write one, that
would not alter my conviction', he wrote, 'that the years of childhood, boyhood, and adolescence are the most significant. What
follows is chiefly a logical development—the child being father of
the man.' He found few to follow him in this view; in fact he
claimed Walter de la Mare as his sole fellow-believer. But the
'minority of two' were not on that account discouraged. The
explanation, Forrest Reid thought, for the neglect of such an
important truth had to be sought in the average person's refusal to
live anywhere but the present: 'most people have forgotten, lost
interest, and their time-consciousness, I think, is less liable to ebb
and flow . . . with no overlapping, no swaying backward and
forward, no return either in imagination or dream.'

All this is not to say that Forrest Reid's vision of youth was an
idealized one. He was, before anything else, an unflinching realist
who faced the fact that youth is a strange mixture of the good,
the bad, and the merely odd. Of this no one was better aware than
himself. Youth in the books is never a formula and the characters
are never used to point a moral or act as mouthpieces for their
own or other people's views. In this his books are unlike those
written by his old friend E. M. Forster. In each of Mr. Forster's
novels moral issues are treated, and the characters represent ideas
which are greater than themselves, much in the manner of a
medieval morality. The morality in Forrest Reid's books—for
there *is* a clear, though unconventional, scheme of moral values
to be found in the writings—is rather different and far less explicit.
We may perhaps put the difference in this way: morals in Mr.

Forster's world are less *integrated into* his art than *inculcated by* that art: the Schlegels and Wilcoxes in *Howards End* are both plot and moral at one and the same time, and the art, and the plot in which that art shows itself, can only exist at all by virtue of the moral ideas which conditioned both of them. Take away the moral element and the book means nothing, would not, in fact, exist at all. There is a moral to be drawn from *The Bracknels*, or *The Gentle Lover*, or *Brian Westby*, but each of these novels exists in its own right and if we do not care to draw the moral conclusions that wait there for us we shall, looking at each book as a novel only, be little the losers. The judgements in Mr. Forster's books are much more bound up in the art with which the story is told, and the story itself is imagined, and takes its shape from, certain definite moral ideas in Mr. Forster's mind rather than from an initial act of disinterested creation.

Since 'E. M.' seems to have come in here, it may be as well at this point to try and discover what it is that he and Forrest Reid share. He has none of Forrest Reid's sensuous delight in beauty, indeed his conception of the beautiful is, one feels, rather a rational one, a sweetness and light diffused from Cambridge, whose pure intellectual rays never lighted on Belfast. Nor by the same account could the mystical immersion in nature we find in so many of Forrest Reid's books have made strong appeal to one who was always laconic and precise—though none the less effective—in his descriptions of the world around him. Where E. M. Forster and Forrest Reid really find common ground is in their feeling for youth, for naturalness, for innocence, as against the intolerance, the narrowness and the unimaginativeness which masquerades as 'experience'.[1] For pretentiousness, whether in art or life, neither of them has a moment's patience. Mr. Graham, the hypocritical literary snob in *Brian Westby*, with his comparisons of Dickens and Thackeray, his everlasting 'Where do you place Matthew

[1] 'Mr. Forster's heroes are the sort of men Forrest Reid's boys might have grown into, if Forrest Reid had allowed his boys to grow up.' In this connexion the above remark by an anonymous reviewer (in *The Times Literary Supplement*, 27th July 1951) is perhaps suggestive.

Arnold?'—'Where do you place Shelley?' is a figure who stands in the same dock as the unhappy Mr. Bons, bewilderedly making his journey through the heavens in the Celestial Omnibus.

Some of these themes, as they appeared in E. M. Forster's early stories,[1] are ones which later became familiar in Forrest Reid's books. In (for instance) 'The Story of a Panic'[2] there is, beneath the surface, symbolism, and Forrest Reid was not a symbolist. But in the story itself a parallel does exist with the predicament of Denis in *The Bracknels*, surrounded by his insensitive, dull-minded relations. For the priggish, conventional, middle-class English clergyman and maiden aunts in Mr. Forster's tale cannot understand the startling change that has overtaken poor Eustace, any more than Mr. Bracknel or Rusk can bring themselves to sympathize with Denis's crisis of the nerves and imagination. In both cases the obtuseness of the respectable and the elderly leads to death. Gennaro jumps out of the window and is killed on the asphalt path below; Denis hangs himself in the shrubbery. They are the victims which Society periodically exacts from among the nonconformists who, however unwittingly, have failed to obey its unwritten code. And in both cases the writer's sympathy lies with the victims as against their oppressors.

Both men, in fact, pin their faith in any tolerable human future on that 'aristocracy of the sensitive, the considerate and the plucky', with their 'secret understanding', sending out little signals to each other like candles in the surrounding darkness. All who are still fresh and eager, unsubdued and undismayed by the world, they are ready to defend. Mr. Forster is a novelist of ideas, and his books are at the same time a criticism of life; and it was pursuit of the implications of both the ideas and the criticism in the novels that eventually forced him to step out of their covers and enter a world about which Forrest Reid knew and cared nothing—a world increasingly public, and—though in the best

---

[1] They are 'The Story of a Panic', 'Other Kingdom', 'The Curate's Friend', and 'The Road from Colonus'. All of them were reprinted in *The Celestial Omnibus and Other Stories* (1911).

[2] First published in 1902.

And Instantly his fear was gone —
He half laughed half cried in the sudden
upsurge of relief, as when stepped across
the threshold, the most lovely creature
he had ever beheld. It was a little deer —
still harmless — with dark soft shy eyes
and smooth dappled coat. And those four
small delicate hooves
had made the knocking on the wooden
floors, which had so frightened
him. Here it was, actually in the room,
bringing with it a kind of wild fragrance of
the woods. It had come to him, this little
messenger without a message — But
perhaps it had a message, for as he
put his arms round it and began to
stroke it, it turned and they walked
together down the small passage
the darker stairs and to a door
which stood slightly ajar.

He opened the door: but the
were gone.
the winter and the night? Gone like
a dream — gone — and, before he had
taken two steps forgotten. The old
man was forgotten, the room forgotten,
the house forgotten. There was nothing —
nothing but a world of gleaming
sunshine — a world of leaves and running
water . . . . —

Tom sat, opened his eyes sleepily in the darkness.

open slowly and inevitably, as to the Hand of Glory.

That last dreadful summons on the door itself would be worst of all. ~~Knowing~~ Better to avert it, better to go to meet it, and he sprang across the room and flung the door wide.

Instantly his fear was gone. He half laughed, half cried, in the sudden wonderful uprush of relief, as there stepped across the threshold no hideous phantom, but the loveliest little creature he had ever beheld. It was a ~~little~~ deer——still far to young to have horns—— with dark soft ~~shy~~ eyes and smooth dappled coat. And those four small delicate hoofs ~~hooves~~ it must have been that had made the knocking ~~on the wooden floors~~ which had so frightened him. ~~Now~~ It had sought him out, was actually in the room, bringing with it a kind of wild ~~spring~~ fragrance of the woods. It had come to look for him, this little messenger without a message, for as he put his arm round it and began to stroke it, it turned and they walked together down the dark passage and the darker stairs, and along another passage leading to a side door which stood ~~slightly~~ ajar.

The boy pushed open the door; but the winter and the night were gone. Gone like a dream——gone, and, almost before he had taken two steps, forgotten. The old man was forgotten, the room forgotten, the house forgotten. There was nothing——nothing but a world of gleaming sunshine——a world of cool green leaves and running water....

2 lines blank

* * *

sense—political. Forrest Reid was neither a novelist of ideas nor a critic of life, he was solely a creative artist; but the link—the feeling for the *spirit* of youth—is there none the less, in spite of all the differences of temper and range.

It is to be feared, indeed, that one whole side of Forrest Reid's interests must have gone by the board where E. M. Forster was concerned. 'E. M.', he remarked when he was describing their first meeting in *Private Road*, was 'not metaphysical'—which was a pity, for problems like these always had an interest for Forrest Reid. Not that he was a subscriber to any recognizable metaphysical system; nor was passionate belief an attitude of mind that came easily to him. He had no organized system of opinions and his views on these matters have to be sought scattered in the pages of the books. Formal creeds left him coldly hostile, yet he could 'believe' in religion, in so far as it was 'the symbol of an ideal'. But he did not make the mistake of equating his kind of belief with others': 'Dreams, aspirations, ideals—these may result in faith; but faith is not knowledge, and one can have a passionate faith in an illusion.' His whole attitude, in fact, was nearer to pantheism than to theism or orthodox agnosticism: the 'spirit I searched for was a spirit of nature—a god, but not God.' The qualities *he* admired were the human qualities of innocence and faithfulness.

> *I love the fond,*
> *The faithful, and the true.*

Clare's lines epitomized his own creed.

But some of his friends were quick to point out what appeared to them to be the dangers of this position: A.E., Basil de Selincourt, François Mauriac, and André Raffalovich. Mauriac in particular spoke in the plainest terms, finding in his spiritual and mental attitude 'le vide effroyable que creuse dans les êtres l'absence de Dieu'; and de Selincourt, in a lengthy correspondence, hinted that in his treatment of 'the element of the supernatural so prominent in all your books' Forrest Reid seemed to consider 'the question of what the ultimate and encompassing spiritual reality is as of less importance than the obtaining in the novel under your hand of a particular artistic effect. . .', in support of which opinion he might, the following year, have quoted Richard's 'conversion' in the last pages of *At the Door of the Gate*, which is depressingly unreal and far less credible than the moon story in *The Bracknels* which was the actual occasion of the criticism; for whereas the moon story was frankly *spiritualistic*, the action which Richard is made to take shows a lamentable lack of insight into the real nature of the workings of the 'encompassing *spiritual* reality', of which de Selincourt had spoken. But in face of these several admonitions Forrest Reid remained obstinately unconvinced. 'Both A. E. and de Selincourt knew exactly what they believed, had reached a position they could justify to themselves intellectually, whereas I—much less fortunate—could evolve no creed, nor even an approximation to one.' (*Private Road*, pp. 168–70.) Nevertheless, for all the lightness with which he handled the issue when writing about it in *Private Road* it is, I think, obvious to anyone who reads the books carefully that at some earlier time religious problems had been real ones to him; and that they had left, as such struggles do, their mark. That mark, in the earlier novels, took the form of a preoccupation with sin which itself turns on an antecedent sense of religious guilt. Mr. Forster, in his essay, first noticed this tendency. He felt that Forrest Reid made 'too much fuss' over sin. 'He is never puritanical', he added, 'but he is always a puritan.' This is to be hardly fair. Forrest Reid himself had to break away from surroundings which were in essence doubtless not dissimilar to those he described in many of his books. That is a hard thing to do, and it is harder still to preserve a mental and emotional equilibrium afterwards. Instincts and ideas transmitted by heredity and acquired in earliest childhood can be covered over but never completely eradicated. Some residue of former feeling will sooner or later declare itself. But that is not all. If the attitude towards sin which E. M. Forster deprecates is regarded as the obverse side of a medal whose face portrays something brighter and very different, the point of view will not perhaps appear so strange. It is only natural, after all, that the intense feeling for the loveliness of youth should be accompanied by a dread of anything which would tarnish or smirch that image.

Nevertheless, there *is* something in E. M. Forster's criticism: sin does bulk large in the early novels, although after *Apostate* this theme melts away under the rays of the sun which, as he once humorously remarked, was 'nearly always shining' in his later books. The treatment is, of course, always oblique; there is nothing personal or didactic. George McAllister in *Following Darkness*, with his mysterious bundle of obscene photographs, is symbolical of Forrest Reid's distaste for this aspect of evil. And Peter's own father, with his gloomy, narrow, uncompromising beliefs is, in a different way, symbolical too. But his portrait is symbolical of revolt from, not of sympathy for, conventional religious ideas.

Temperamentally antagonistic to formal Christianity as he was, 'to its doctrines, its theory of life, the shadow it cast across the earth', this did not of course mean that he was spiritually insensitive or incurious. There was the interest in dreams and in the whole world of the supernatural. The entire original plot of one of the novels, *Uncle Stephen*, came to him in sleep, while he was dreaming—its original title had been '*My* Uncle's a Magician'—and some of the actual writing, though not the product of dreaming, has a curious dream quality—the passage, for instance, in *The Gentle Lover*, describing Allingham's walk in the Bois de Boulogne, where the scene 'took on a strangely poetic quality, a quality as of something re-enacted in the spirit, that had happened long ago'. And in the books many of the boys themselves dream dreams which Forrest Reid probably himself experienced. There is Grif's dream in the country churchyard and Tom's dream about the Garden of Eden, or his terrifying nightmare after reading Granny's book with its Chinese pictures, or, rather similar, Peter's 'staircase' dream in *Following Darkness*. And, of course, there are his own beautiful childhood dreams—if dreams they can be called, for they seem more visionary than dreamlike—which he wrote about in *Apostate*.

But more often than not dreams don't lend themselves to the

purposes of story-telling. They are too irrational, too oddly constructed. The 'dream collaborator is . . . not really an artist, for
it is just where the artist would be most meticulous that *he* is most
careless.'

Here, however, is the rather beautiful beginning of one of the
dreams which he describes in *Private Road*:

'It seemed to me [he writes] that it was morning and that it was
time to get up. . . When I had finished dressing I went downstairs and out into the open air, but not into the familiar scene of
Ormiston Crescent. . . . With the closing of the door it had vanished. . . . I was in the midst of a park-like country, green and
fresh and bathed in sunlight. I walked on over the dewy grass,
and there was a sound of water, of running water, as from a
hidden stream. Then, floating in the air about five feet above the
ground, I saw a little boy. He could not have been more than
seven or eight, and he was asleep, lying in the air horizontally,
poised there like a small angel on a cloud . . . in fact he was in the
position of being carried, and, accepting this suggestion, I placed
my arms beneath him. . . . I noticed now that he was suspended
in the air by a thin, nearly invisible cord. This cord, moreover,
was being gently drawn in, like a fishing line, and following the
direction of the pull I crossed the grass to the steps of a tower.
The pull was very feeble, but it was now upward, and after climb-
ing a few steps I stopped, and began myself to pull in the contrary direction. Immediately there was a commotion above, and I
heard angry voices, and one voice in particular crying out, "He'll
drown the princess: the princess will be drowned."

'Simultaneously I perceived that I and the sleeping boy and the
country we were in were all at the bottom of a lake, through
whose clear waters the tower rose into an upper world.'

(*Private Road*, pp. 220–2.)

Now it is obvious that dreams such as this (whatever their
alleged significance in terms of the theories spun by Freud and
his successors) cannot be turned into material for a story. Where
they do perhaps succeed is in communicating a peculiar emotional

experience which can, subsequently, act as some sort of stimulus to creative activity. This particular dream seems to have been a very happy and moving one: 'The actual beauty of the opening scene—the morning and the green landscape, the bright air and the floating boy—was extraordinary. It was like the fantastic opening of some tale in *The Arabian Nights*, but with nothing of the exotic Arabian colouring.'

It was really innate pantheism, not a detached interest in problems of metaphysics or the fascination of the dream-world, that took for him the place of religion. 'It may be,' he remarked in *Apostate*, 'that the religious emotion is universal, finding an outlet, if not in this way, then in that; and it may be there was something of its rapture in my apprehension of nature.'

In its mixture of sensuousness and objectivity Forrest Reid's feeling for nature was thoroughly Greek. Greece represented for him all he most admired and everything on which he had most set his heart, and when he *did* discover it, the revelation enriched his whole life. There was relief, and joy too, in finding that so much he had thought unique or unusual in himself had been shared by this Mediterranean people thousands of years before— the love of nature, the worship of youth, the 'sense of fellowship with every scaled and furred and feathered creature'; the vivacity of intellect, the frankness of response, and, above all, the mythopoeic sense of wonder—'O Solon, Solon, you Hellenes are never anything but children'.

Long afterwards he put all this feeling into *Demophon*, the book he embroidered around the ancient story of Metanira and Demeter, which, in differing forms, appears in so many of the collections of Greek mythology; and later still, into the beautiful set of translations which he made from the Greek Anthology.

Scarcely a page of direct description in *Demophon*: yet with the very first words of the story we are transported into the clear sharp air of Attica:

'Beyond the grove of laurels sacred to Artemis lay a blue, crinkled sea. It glittered dazzlingly in the hot sunshine; and far out in the bay where water and sky met, the dark rocks of Salamis rose like a dream-island, because a God had dropped a haze about them.

'High overhead an eagle passed, bearing some small white woolly beast in his talons; and before he had disappeared there emerged on to the rough dusty track that wound up from the shore through the hillside fields a man, a little girl, and two goats. The man climbed slowly and laboriously, having a heavy wine-skin upon his shoulders; the little girl carried a basket of figs; the goats, with the perversity of their kind, strayed to this side or to that.

'The man walked without lifting his gaze from the stony path before him. His name was Keleos. He was on the threshold of old age, his beard was grizzled, his skin tanned like leather, and the sweat ran in beads from the roots of his matted hair to his bushy eyebrows. The little girl was hot too, but she was almost naked, and her slenderness made her cool to look at. Her body was thin as a boy's; her limbs were burnt by the sun to a golden brown. She had a very dirty face, because she had rubbed a dirty hand across it more than once; nevertheless, she was beautiful. Her father had promised to rest when they reached a suitable resting place, but the suitable resting place seemed always a little farther on. For the third time, in the shrill monotonous voice of child-hood, she called out, "Daddy, is this a good place?"'

(Demophon, pp. 13–14.)

What a perfect beginning is this to the 'traveller's tale'! We can feel straightway the silent heat of noon, the harsh vertical rays of the sun as they pour down on our heads; can feel around us too the warm rocks, the still, yellow cornfields and the vines, the dusty wayside temples and, in the distance, the blue mountain ranges with their crown of snow. And this effect is achieved by very much more than mere surface decoration; the feeling has soaked through into the texture of the story, so that in all Demophon's marvellous adventures we never forget that it is in a sun-baked southern land—the Greece of fable and myth—that they take place, and not among the soft green fields of his creator's native island.

Yet this feeling was there long before, as a very young man, he discovered the Greek attitude. He arrived at his own pantheistic beliefs independently of outside influences. 'In wood and river and plant and animal and bird and insect it had seemed to me there was a spirit which was the same as my spirit. . . . There were hours when I could pass *into* nature, and feel the grass growing, and float with the clouds through the transparent air; when I could hear the low breathing of the earth, when the colour and smell of it were so close to me that I seemed to lose consciousness of any separate existence. Then, one single emotion animated all things, one heart beat throughout the universe, and the mother and all her children were united.' (*Apostate* [1926], pp. 207–8.)

This mystical awareness of the natural world made him correspondingly sensitive to the whole range of ordinary natural impressions. He distilled the emotions created by nature and entwined those emotions with the emotions in his books. Peter's love for Katherine in *Following Darkness* is blended with the lovely Ulster scenery whose beauty runs through the book like a golden thread. The beauty of high summer in *The Spring Song* and *The Retreat*, the other beauty, of the winter woods at Derryaghy in *Following Darkness*, of Bruges or Florence in *The Gentle Lover*, sketched so lightly, like some drawing in soft grey chalk—are all evidence of this same gift.

And it was not only beauty of landscape that he captured. Surroundings that were devoid of all the usual elements of beauty he could infuse with a strange, unexpected, almost perverse beauty of their own—the damp, dismal squalor of Belfast with its mean streets and narrow lives, the Bracknels and the Seawrights and the rest.

His power of describing natural scenery developed with his own skill in writing. The later books are happier, and the landscapes more accurately and freshly drawn. The gloomy images of Belfast life, which hung like dark clouds over so many of the earlier books, fade away altogether in the sunshine which from start to finish fills *The Retreat*. The description of Tom's picnic with his friend Pascoe is a perfect evocation of happiness, for shore and sky and children are bathed alike in the same atmosphere of innocent loveliness. It was the same atmosphere that he captured many years earlier in *The Spring Song*; the description there was more direct, simpler and with less of art perhaps, but it was the same world still, the world we can read about in the pages of Traherne and Vaughan, that lies along the 'ancient track' which none of us can tread more than once:

'Morning lay in splendour over the world. The sun was high in the heavens, and the trees threw dark shadows on the mossy ground. On the other side of the river was a sea of waving cornfields . . . and in the river itself the sky and the clouds were reflected, and the green banks that stood high above the surface. A waterfowl swam into a leafy clump of willows . . . a wagtail pruned his feathers as he stood perched on an old stump; and a rat, sitting up on his hind legs, nibbled delicately at the stems of the grasses . . . as he stooped above the river, like a little river god, hugging his knees, Grif saw a dragon-fly floating on the surface. Its green and yellow body flashed in the sunlight, but its gauzy wings had become wet and useless, so that it could not rise. . . .

'When he had rescued the dragon-fly he put it on a dock-leaf in the sun, where its wings would dry quickly. He lay watching it, for it was indeed an extraordinary beast, with great eyes and mouth, and splendid, mailed coat, green and yellow, barred with black lines. It lay still for a while as if exhausted, but presently its silvery transparent wings unfolded, and next moment it had sprung into the air.'

(The Spring Song, pp. 170–1.)

This is beautiful in its simplicity, and full of natural observation naturally expressed, but in beauty of colour and maturity of expression the other piece I am going to instance will fully bear comparison with it. It occurs in *The Retreat*; Tom is staying on holiday at Greencastle with his mother and father, and the passage describes a sunset on that lovely stretch of Donegal coast:

'The tide was full or nearly full, and Tom scrambled out as far as he could over the lichened barnacled rocks, till the water was lapping at his feet. The thickly crusted rocks were the colour of tarnished silver, and up the numerous channels between them the water swelled and sucked backward with a hollow melancholy sound.

'The sun had vanished nearly an hour ago . . . but it was still reflected in the clouds, and the reflection was mirrored in a crimson track, almost the colour of blood, across the tumbling sea. On the opposite shore, soft as a pastel drawing, the hills were outlined in dark slate-blue against a paler sky.

'The light was fading fast.

'The Manor House, large and square and white, had become like a phantom house glimmering against the black background of the wood. . . . Up the faint blue sky there rose a heavy column of cloud, like a genie escaping from a jar. Cloud upon cloud, the sky was strewn with them, loose and floating, those underneath tinged to gold, those nearer earth grey or faint mauve, with deep translucent wells between them of pale pea-green and silver-blue. But on the farther shore darkness was descending like a curtain, blotting out the pattern of the hills; and a peculiar mystical happiness had descended upon Tom—dreamily peaceful—almost ecstatic—for it was only remotely related to this world.'

(The Retreat, pp. 171–2.)

The secret of this kind of writing lies in the combination of two qualities: concreteness of description with sensuousness of conception. The subject—whether it be a dragon-fly or a sunset or a drowned boy—is never lost sight of. It is described, and its beauty becomes apparent in the description.

'It was a boy of twelve or thirteen. The water was still oozing from his stained and ragged clothing, and spreading out in a dark patch on the soil. The hands were clenched: the face was uncovered. The blue eyes were wide open; the corners of the mouth drooped; and there was a frown on the forehead which gave a strange expression of sternness, almost of anger, to the whole countenance. The fixed and sightless eyes stared up at the sky as if with an implacable enmity. A strip of green water-weed was mixed into the dark hair close above the ear.'

(*Retrospective Adventures*: 'An Ending', p. 258.)

Here is an incident whose inherent ugliness is turned unexpectedly into a strange cool beauty. This is what Keats meant when he declared that beauty *was* truth; that directness of observation, 'the innocent eye', was itself the pledge of redemption from all unloveliness.

The method is simple. There are no loose ends, no strainings after beauty, no laborious effects—the feeling springs unbidden from the accuracy of the observation, where careless observation could only have led to dishonest feeling.

Here is another scene, from *Apostate*. It is different, but the same spirit—or so it seems to me—informs this description too. It is a picture of the docks at Belfast on a winter's morning:

'In the still, grey water the boats, looking strangely naked and black, were reflected as in a glass. Gulls wheeled restlessly about the masts and funnels; the wintry sun shone on frozen ropes and slippery decks; the ground rang with a hard metallic sound. Crates and bales, boxes and sacks were being piled on the wharves; iron trucks were busy, for the dock-labourers were working hard to keep themselves warm, their faces, ears, and hands scarlet, their breath turning to vapour the moment it passed their lips.'

(*Apostate* [1926], p. 230.)

It is like nothing so much as painting, the whole thing touched in—even to the dashes of colour—like a carefully worked miniature: a detail from a Dutch seascape perhaps, or, maybe, a Bonington. And again the beauty is in the description itself, its sober precision and delicacy.

These same qualities of precision and delicacy are what make memorable the etched description of the countryside surrounding

Mrs. Carroll's house at Derryaghy, the woods bare in all the austereness of winter, and

'beautiful with the strange and delicate beauty of naked trees.
. . . Dark slender branches traced fantastic arabesques against the grey sky above my head. The black- and silver-stemmed birches gave the note that was carried out through all the colouring. Only the fir-trees, laurels, and an occasional holly-tree, were green. I loved the woods in winter . . . the wind whistled so hollowly in the leafless trees, and the darting birds were so black against the sky, and all was so silent and solitary, with a sort of frozen loveliness, that I could conceive of nothing more beautiful even in the green pomp and splendour of summer. . . . The leaves of the laurels and holly were coated with frost; the dead fronds of the bracken were a dull brown; here and there the sombre colouring was splashed with the red leaves of brambles. There was a hint of approaching snow in the air, there was almost a silence of snow, and I seemed to feel it drawing closer to me through the cold, remote sky. The ground was hard as iron. Sometimes a single leaf, pallid and faded, trembled still at the end of a twig . . . .'

(*Following Darkness*, pp. 190–1.)

The response to natural beauty of the characters in the books is a frankly pagan one, an attitude of mystical worship. Nature, Forrest Reid seemed to feel, was not merely a passive backcloth to human activities; it had a life of its own, and an atmosphere alive with infinite suggestion, or omen. There is enchantment, but with the enchantment, behind it, there lurks something else, a something certainly not benevolent, but dangerous, unknown, and strangely unsettling. As often as not, disaster attends on the character who is granted a glimpse of that other world: on Denis, who hangs himself, and on Grif, who falls into the clutches of Dr. Bradley. Both of these fail in their struggle with the supernatural, and pay the penalty. Often, however, the impact of the unseen world is less destructive, produces only a sweet disturbance of the senses, a feeling of enchantment, of mystery. Grif, listening to the

flute by the river-side, knew that enchantment and that mystery,
so did Tom Barber in the strange house near his home or while
dreaming on the shore at Greencastle, and so had Denis too known
it, or the anonymous hero of 'The Truant'.[1] More often than not
it is at night that the strange forces of nature reveal themselves
most potently: to Ricky, for instance, alone on the mountainside
of Slieve Donard. Passing out of the wood into moonlight, he

'stepped into a magical world for which he was hardly prepared
—a world remade, a world bathed in an amazing white fire,
a world of mysterious shadows, where nothing was solid. Climb-
ing a little higher, he turned and looked below him. The black
wood stretched down, like an immense, crouching beast sleeping
upon the radiant mountain side. And the sea, black, glittering,
secret, touched with silver fire—that also was ancient, a god, the
dwelling-place of gods.'

(At the Door of the Gate, p. 107.)

In an essay on W. H. Hudson, Forrest Reid speaks of the beauty
in his descriptions of natural things, those pieces of writing which
are, he says, 'more than descriptions'. Forrest Reid shared the
same gift, and he, like Hudson, is the creator of such another
'lovely, innocent, passionate world wherein we "walk by flowery
places . . . or at some late hour by moonlight . . . with the delight,
the sense of wonder in all life, which is akin to, if not one with,
the mythical faculty, and if experienced in a high degree is a sense
of the supernatural in all natural things"'. (Quoted in Retrospective Adventures, p. 119.)

---

[1] In Retrospective Adventures.

V

The Criticism

> *Poesy subsisteth by herself, and after one demeanour and con-*
> *tinuance her beauty appeareth to all ages. In vain have some men of*
> *late, transformers of everything, consulted upon her reformation,*
> *and endeavoured to abstract her to metaphysical and scholastic*
> *quiddities, denuding her of her own habits, and those ornaments*
> *with which she hath amused the world some thousand years.*
> *Poesy is not a thing that is yet in the finding and search, or*
> *which may be otherwise found out.*
>
> DRUMMOND OF HAWTHORNDEN

Forrest Reid's position as a critic was almost as unique as
the place he made for himself by his novels.

It was not such an important position, but its implications
are quite as interesting. His standpoint was one very rarely met
with today, because he subjected everything he read to the test
of his own personal sensibility. For the schools of 'applied' literary
criticism so fashionable today he had little use; an approach to
literature that ignored the flame of beauty which must burn at
the heart of all genuinely imaginative writing was of no interest or
significance for him; he passed it by. 'As I am always preaching,
the mind behind the work is what really matters, what makes that
work sympathetic or just the opposite. Cleverness in itself is nothing.' Nor was mere truth to life enough; to be memorable the
writer's work had to be infused with something deeper than accuracy of observation, important though this was, and with something more sustained than technical virtuosity. 'If fiction is to be
an art I think it must be more than mere realistic reporting, must
be a source of inspiration, emotion, vision. . . . Nobody, I dare
say, found beauty in the monotonous dripping of rain till Verlaine
wrote his poem about it, nobody found beauty in fogs until

Whistler painted them.' An imaginative work, he believed, 'if it is to be first-rate, must possess three qualities—beauty of subject, beauty of treatment, beauty of writing.'

Beauty there had to be; otherwise there could be no art. To care for art for its own sake was, after all, only to care for the beauty which that art enshrined. Art for art's sake—abused in practice as the phrase had become—meant art for beauty's sake, no more and no less; and the pursuit of poetry for its own sake was 'the pursuit both of truth and of goodness', for, in Andrew Bradley's words, 'wherever the imagination is satisfied, there, if we had a knowledge we have not, we should discover no idle fancy but the image of a truth'[1].

Such a view of literature must have its limitations, but the limitations it imposes are self-limitations, and what is lost in breadth has its compensations in deeper insight and sympathy. This he recognized himself, for after all, as he pointed out, 'the personal appeal in poetry is everything, because without it, for the particular reader concerned, there *is* no poetry.' (*The Milk of Paradise*, p. 7). Here for him was the crux of the whole matter: the critic was only qualified to judge a work of art—as a work of art —if he could feel it on his pulses. That was the final test.

I said 'work of art' where Forrest Reid spoke of poetry alone, and this needs a word of explanation at the outset. Poetry was at the same time something much wider and also much more confined in scope than mere metrical composition. Pope wrote in regular stanzas, and so did Milton; but one would no more call Pope a poet than describe Milton as a versifier; unless one were to take the risk, in Housman's apt phrase, 'of calling in ambiguity of language to promote confusion of thought'. Hardy was a poet; but he would be a rash person who would confine that poetry to *Wessex Poems*, *Satires of Circumstance*, and the rest. Indeed, a case can be made out—and this I think Forrest Reid conclusively demonstrates—for some of the prose reaching greater heights than much of the strict poetry. Certainly to anyone at all sensitive to prose rhythm the portrait, in *Jude*, of little Father Time in the rail-

[1] A. C. Bradley, *Oxford Lectures on Poetry*: 'Poetry for Poetry's Sake.'

way carriage, on his solitary journey to Aldbrickham, is at least as moving as 'Midnight on the Great Western', which is one of the best-known things in *Moments of Vision*. But—so the canons of literary judgement have determined—one is 'poetry', while the other is not.

Against this view Forrest Reid resolutely set his face. *Any* literature that evoked emotion *was* poetry. Poetry was a response on the part of the reader, not a definition which could be imposed by pedants from their lecture-rooms: 'it is exactly upon the presence in it of what is essentially poetic that the value of not only verse but of every form of imaginative literature depends.' (*W. B. Yeats*, pp. 55–6.)

The dangers in such an outlook are obvious; unless sensibility is accompanied and controlled by self-discipline the critic's discrimination will turn to capriciousness, or worse. It is an attitude which places an immense burden of responsibility on the shoulders of the critic. He must be acutely aware of his limitations, recognize what he can criticize with integrity, and recognize also the kind of writing to which he cannot bring the gift of discriminating sympathy which is his chief asset. He must be able to winnow emotional prejudice from aesthetic judgements, the immediately attractive from the permanently important.

No one was more aware of the necessity for all this than Forrest Reid himself. His practice as a critic exactly matched his own convictions. It was not enough, he believed, merely to analyse the contents of a book; like Yeats, he saw that criticism must be *re-creation* as well. And such was his anxiety to do himself—and his subject—justice that he was scrupulous in the care he took to avoid writing about those authors with whom he was not in sympathy, or with whom he had imperfect acquaintance. Himself a careful reader,[1] accustomed (as he acknowledged) to articulating the words noiselessly with his lips rather than skimming over the pages with his eyes, he took his literary pleasures with

[1] J. N. Hart remembers *Uncle Stephen* being read to him from the MS. 'He was', says Mr. Hart, 'an excellent reader, acting the parts of each character.'

discrimination, unhurriedly savouring the bouquet of his chosen
author.

His two chief critical books are his studies of W. B. Yeats and
Walter de la Mare. In addition, he published what has become
the standard work on the wood-engravings of the 'Sixties, two
volumes of miscellaneous critical studies on subjects ranging from
Emily Brontë to Henry James, and a long essay, of some importance, on the appreciation of poetry. Besides this, there was some
reviewing for the *Manchester Guardian* in the twenties and later he
reviewed novels in the *Spectator* twice a month in the years immediately preceding the war. Mr. Knox Cunningham has extracted
the *Spectator* notices and they are now collected in a single, and
probably unique, volume, in which is provided evidence of some
of his most valuable critical qualities. This was journeyman work,
but there was never anything of the 'dust-wrapper' critic about
him. Often it meant thankless drudgery—which involved reading
perhaps three or four novels, of widely differing merit, each week
—yet he was always fresh, always candid, and always scrupulously
fair. He never indulged in those displays of smartness or malice
which were steadily becoming a recognized part of fashionable
reviewing. He made no secret of his prejudices, and he did not dog-
matize, but he contrived nevertheless to drop a number of critical
dicta by the way. His critical position was consistent, and based
on a definite view of literature: and he managed to convey to his
readers as the weeks passed some indication of what that view
was.

From the body of his critical work it is possible to trace a clear-
cut attitude emerging. It is a very personal attitude, and a very uncompromising one. Forrest Reid 'knew'—very definitely knew
—'what he liked'; but he was not content only to tell you what he
liked; he told you why he liked it, and in so doing produced in his
reader that feeling of stimulation, that immediate desire to go to
the original which is, after all, the real touchstone of effective
criticism.

Lying behind all his judgements, and forming the basis of his
outlook, was a very acute sense of moral values: 'Forrest', wrote

one of his friends, 'was above all an enthusiast, who had little time for the intellectual who balances each question with exact precision. A favourite saying of his was that intelligence is a moral quality. His whole attitude to life was moral rather than intellectual.' And so faults of style or syntax were more easily forgivable than lapses in taste. These, for in many ways he had the susceptibilities of a Victorian, made him merely depressed or indignant. 'The most difficult thing in the world is to make people realize that the essence of good taste is simplicity' (this was apropos of a difficulty that had arisen with the printers over one of his books). 'It's much easier to deal with those who have no taste at all than with those who have heaps but all of it bad.' Ever since he had written his article on George Moore in 1905 this had been a preoccupation. 'If one sets this bustling, selfish, sensual world of people'—the world, that is, in which we live when we are reading *Mike Fletcher* or *Spring Days*—'beside the world that Tourgenieff created, how vulgar, how third-rate they instantly become, what shoddy specimens of humanity!' In that article the moral distaste had been almost *too* evident, had indeed affected rather unfairly his estimate of Moore's position as an artist; but that the prejudice was still very much alive thirty years later is evidenced by his icy notice of a book which passed under his eye towards the end of his time on the *Spectator*. As a little masterpiece of its kind it is perhaps worth quoting in full, though as the luckless author is still alive his identity must be concealed:

'Of Mr. ——'s *Judas* perhaps the least said the better. It is the story of the betrayal of Christ, who figures as one of the characters. His words are quoted from the Bible, but the conversation of Mary Magdalene and others is Mr. ——'s invention and enlivened with plenty of "Why the hells" and "Bloody bastards". Anatole France once suggested that that mysterious sin against the Holy Ghost might be bad taste. Mr. ——'s vulgar little novel inclines me to accept this theory.'

(*Spectator*, 7th April 1939.)

The reference to Anatole France is characteristic: the quality of

186

sanity was what he shared with the French writer. Sanity, and a charitableness which arose from the possession of a sense of humour and a sense of proportion. Like Anatole, he could see no virtue in the contemporary cult of obscurity:

'I have a deep-rooted dislike for obscurity whether in prose or verse; I obstinately maintain that the subtlest shades of thought and feeling can be expressed so that they may without difficulty be understood. The effort to extract a meaning is not inducive to a state of mind favourable to aesthetic receptivity.' (1920.)

'Simplicity and lucidity', he wrote to J. N. Hart, 'are very important qualities in style—to my own mind you can't have a good style without them.' What mattered, 'as I am always preaching', was the mind behind the work. Too many people, he lamented, had only a 'stop-press' interest in literature and this warped their verdicts on writers of their own times, and on earlier writers as well. This is not to say that he demanded the establishment of any rigid standards, and the setting up of a French Academy to codify these. His criticism hadn't the splendid assurance, the air of certainty and finality worn by Johnson or Macaulay. It was opinionated, but never arrogant, and it was characteristic of him that he should have wanted to gather one of his critical collections under the modest title *Personal Remarks*. No one could have been more convinced of the ultimately subjective nature of all except purely textual criticism:

' . . . in questions of aesthetics, we can only record our individual impressions, the uncertainty of which becomes apparent when we recollect how frequently the same work even for ourselves has had a very different value at different periods of our lives . . . but . . . Are the books we grow out of always and necessarily inferior to those we grow into? Is there any absolute standard of excellence to which we can appeal?'

One of the things he *did* grow out of was the essay on Ernest Dowson[1] which was his first published criticism. In this stiff

[1] See Bibliography, 1905.

187

little piece the Pater influence was still dominant, and although he faithfully recorded his individual impression it didn't somehow ring with much conviction: the effect of the poems he compared, quaintly, to that of 'a child, entering at dusk a great empty silent room' and caressing 'very softly and timidly, the notes of a piano he found there'. The essay, though touching in the way earliest work usually is, was imitative, mannered, 'aesthetic'; and he was careful that it should never be reprinted. He was as discriminating a critic of his own work as he was of others'; and to look at his surving unpublished and uncollected papers (which are very few) is to have confirmed the impression created by a reading of *Private Road*. Anything he wrote which dissatisfied him he usually destroyed; once a complete novel was burnt. One of his 'literary daydreams' which never materialized was a life of Porson, the Greek scholar, by whom he was fascinated. He did write a brief sketch, but wisely didn't print it: in its present form it lacks shape and animation.

But although he had his own very definite prejudices, this did not prevent him being continually surprised by the prejudices of others:

'I have been skimming through a Life of Thomas Hardy [he writes to Knox Cunningham]. It is written by his widow and is stodgy in the extreme. There is a marked lack of affection for Henry James "who has a ponderously warm manner of saying nothing in infinite sentences" (H's own words), "a writer who has no grain of poetry, or humour, or spontaneity in his productions." But listen to H. J. writing to Stevenson: "Oh, yes, dear Louis: *Tess of the d'Urbervilles* is vile. The pretence of sexuality is only equalled by the absence of it, and the abomination of the language by the author's reputation for style."

'Such things are hardly credible, coming from such men. How could anybody with the faintest sense of humour accuse Henry of lacking that quality? and how could anybody with a sense of beauty think *Tess* vile and its style abominable? In both cases the accusations are so grotesque that they recoil on their makers' own heads. As the opinions of Brown, Jones, or Robinson one would dismiss them as merely stupid, but here they are depressing.'

The two chief qualities he brought to his critical books were sense, and sensibility. It is easy to forget the sense for the sensibility; but it was there, as his essays on Rimbaud or Andrew Lang show. 'In all literature there is no more enigmatic figure than that of Arthur Rimbaud'—so begins his essay on that astonishing youth; but—he continues—'I feel inclined to add, none less agreeable.' As trenchant is his judgement on the Verlaine affair: to be told that 'his' —Rimbaud's—'conduct from first to last was precisely that of the "young delinquent", without a moral sense, without a conscience, without scruples, and without affection. . . one thing at least seems certain, that he never cared a straw for Verlaine', is a refreshingly sensible breath of criticism after much that has been written on this subject.

There are some equally sane judgements in the essay—which, to our inestimable loss, was all he ever wrote—on Henry James. So much has been written about 'The Master' of recent years that he is rapidly joining that select company, the critical literature on whom far exceeds in bulk their own published productions. Much of that literature is highly esoteric; what we miss in it is precisely the firm judgement that cuts through the web of minutiæ, the judgement that both illuminates and, by providing an external point of reference, suggests more than a shelf-ful of painstaking but parochial theses can supply; '. . . place *Wuthering Heights* beside that mature and masterly performance, *The Wings of the Dove*, and note what happens. It is not the work of the beginner, the amateur, that suffers. Viewed side by side, *The Wings of the Dove* seems an elaborate work of art fashioned in a studio by the cunning hand of man, but *Wuthering Heights* is a radiant thing that has been breathed into wild and imperishable life by the breath of the Divine Spirit.' (*Retrospective Adventures*: 'Henry James', p. 88.)

Something of the discounting of intellectualism and theory which is implicit here is much more clearly visible in his sharp criticism of the Symbolists. Intricacy in art—*Mallarméism* as he called it here—when it was needless, for so it seemed to him to be in their books, made him impatient. A poem ought to turn 'much more upon the natural, though of course cultivated, sensitiveness of the reader than upon his scientific knowledge'. Poetry 'depends upon what never *can* quite be said' and that is why such a poem as Yeats' 'He bids his Beloved be at Peace'[1] is a failure, because to 'have to turn to a note, whether we turn to it before or after reading the poem, is fatal, keeps us firmly attached to a world of ink and paper. Our magician has failed, and we watch him coldly and sceptically, as Elijah watched the too sanguine priests of Baal.'[2]

But alongside these more considered judgements there were struck out chance remarks which opened unexpected vistas:

'The essential difference between realism and romanticism in fiction is easier to feel than to define. It is less a matter of detail than of atmosphere. The method of *Pickwick*, for instance, might seem to promise realism, yet Pickwick strikes us as a romance. There is behind it a guiding purpose and intelligence kinder than life, the author shows partiality, distinguishes between the just and the unjust, bestows rewards and punishments, cannot bear to leave Mr. Jingle unrepentant, Mr. Stiggins unchastised, or Mr. Pickwick to a lonely old age.'

Towards the end of his life, in *The Milk of Paradise* (the little book whose earliest title had been *The Child's Guide to Poetry*) he concluded a brief chapter about Wordsworth's poetry with such an

[1] In *The Wind Among the Reeds*.

[2] In this connexion a remark of Mr. John Sparrow, in his little book *Sense and Poetry*, may not be without interest: 'It is precisely this desire to interpret instead of to feel, to look for a meaning which is not there, that leads the critics to call symbolist poetry obscure. To ask what Mr. Pound or Mr. Eliot meant by writing the poems that have been quoted ['Concava Vallis', 'Rhapsody on a Windy Night'] is as misguided as to ask what Mr. Yeats meant [in 'The Cap and Bells'] by dreaming of a red garment and a blue. To neither question is there any answer: the only difference is that Mr. Yeats' dream has an intelligible structure, while Mr. Eliot's reflections on a windy night have not: in the first case we look for two meanings where we should be content with one, in the second for one meaning where we should be content with none at all.' (*Sense and Poetry*, pp. 87–8.)

illuminating comment. Discussing *The Prelude* he puts forward a novel and suggestive theory to explain the comparative failure of the poem. 'Possibly the subject—a spiritual autobiography—demanded the freedom and variety of prose, together with a technique which would have eliminated the numerous and tedious digressions. For though he clung tenaciously to verse, one can see in Wordsworth not only an autobiographer, but a potential novelist.' (*The Milk of Paradise*, p. 50.) And we experience the same mild yet pleasant shock of surprise when he speaks of the village clowns in *A Midsummer Night's Dream*—Snug, Quince, Bottom, and the rest—as resembling the peasants in an early Hardy novel; or of Norman Douglas's achievement in developing and transforming 'the Peacockian novel'. Perceptive as these remarks showed him to be, he was also enough of a realist to be able to strike a shrewd blow when he thought it was needed; and his demolishment of whatever pretensions the Celtic Druids may have had to a philosophy is a memorable piece of ironical, yet deflationary, writing. And when occasion demanded he could be stern without ever sacrificing fairness or generosity. 'There is nothing in his books', he comments when writing about Firbank, 'that is not in *The Importance of Being Earnest* and *South Wind*'; and the essay in which he examines the work of the American novelist W. D. Howells is a model of this kind. Firmly, but in a manner perfectly gentle, Howells is 'placed'. The 'place' is not, as it happens, a particularly high one, but nobody, least of all Howells himself, can have felt wounded at the estimate: which is, in point of fact, a singularly gracious one.

But underlying comments and verdicts such as these there was the continual response to beauty. A particular kind of beauty usually, full of delicacy and sadness—the beauty evoked by 'dreams and desires and sombre songs and sweet'. It was most often in poetry, in the poetry of Rossetti or Yeats, or, perhaps, Edgar Allan Poe, that he found the quality for which he was searching, that 'divine homesickness', that 'longing for an Eden from which each one of us is exiled'; but it was visible in certain kinds of prose as well. He was as sensitive to prose as to poetry, finding in its subtler, less obtrusive rhythms an equally valid beauty. He would, he tells us, always read any serious work of prose literature aloud, though under his breath, because only when the words themselves were articulated could the hidden music be apprehended. On this point his views were firm: 'It seems to me', he wrote in his book on Yeats, 'that the vocal test is the final test for all style, whether prose or poetic. . . . Every misplaced accent, every rhyme that is but a rhyme for the printed page, and which the speaking voice cannot rest upon, is a blot, a fault in technique.' (*W. B. Yeats*, p. 90.)

Sheer beauty of sound—which was what he found so pre-eminently in the poetry of Yeats himself—was, then, a touch-stone of beauty in writing. In his own critical work he found this beauty in widely differing places: in Emily Brontë—prose as well as poetry—in W. H. Hudson, Seumas O'Kelly, de la Mare, of course, or William Morris.

As a critic he quoted what he liked; and often, starting out from quite personal recollections and impressions, he would feel a way into his subject from that end. In the essay on Stella Benson, after describing their only meeting, which occurred shortly before that talented artist's death, he immediately proceeds to quote. At that meeting their conversation had been entirely about animals; and so it is almost natural that the quotation should be about an elephant race:

'At the sound of the pistol shot, they moved forward with serene dignity, not even the babel of shrieks and curses from the amateurs on their backs could induce them to fall out of line. In a perfect row they started; in a perfect row they proceeded very slowly along the track, pensively waving their trunks to keep one another in step; in a perfect row they breasted the tape at the other end. And then they all sighed happily, satisfied to feel that they had done their duty. It was the most impressive race I ever saw.'

This was exactly the sort of thing Forrest Reid liked, the neat-ness of the writing and the humour of the observation. What he liked was, of course, always interestingly unusual and often very beautiful. And if this penchant often made him appear, in his estimates, to present a foreshortened view of his subjects, to make them a little too much resemble each other, this was easily overlooked: because his critical sympathies were, considering his chosen point of view, wide, surprisingly wide; and they were far from conventional. His instinct was for the little known, the insufficiently appreciated; indeed he was, he admitted, 'like Coleridge, of whom Hazlitt grumbled that he "somehow always contrived to prefer the *unknown* to the *known.*"' (*Private Road*, p. 67.)

He was never happier than when doing belated justice to forgotten books and authors: Anstey's fantasies perhaps, or *Mehalah*, that strange tale of Baring-Gould's. This preference for the neglected was never a forced one, never led to those tiresome exhumations of poetasters and tedious belletrists with which we have become so familiar. What he dug up was always worth resurrecting, because his instinct for beauty was a sure one. Surprising discoveries he made—the poetry of Arthur Lyon Raile[1] for instance, gnarled, gnomic, and yet full of a 'remarkable constancy of spirit and of faith', unflinchingly honest; or the forgotten tales of Seumas O'Kelly (writing in the tradition of the Turgenev of *A Sportsman's Sketches*), or certain nineteenth-century poets, Allingham perhaps, or the inexplicably overlooked Sydney Dobell, author of 'Orphan's Song' and that unforgettably poignant little masterpiece 'Return'.

But fondness for the out-of-the-way or unfashionable never led him to lose his sense of proportion and always he recognized great art for what it was; and whether or not great artists are, as Swinburne thought them to be, 'bad, or mad, or sick', they are, he knew, always essentially *lonely* men, standing apart from move-

[1] It is not generally known that the pseudonym Arthur Lyon Raile concealed the identity of Edward Perry Warren (1860–1928), the American classical scholar and connoisseur. See Osbert Burdett and E. H. Goddard's *Edward Perry Warren: the Biography of a Connoisseur* (London: Christophers, 1941). For this information I am indebted to Mr. John Gere.

ments and coteries and fashions, the shifts and turns forced upon their less gifted brethren. Perhaps his best essays are those which deal with work by writers of established fame—Henry James, Emily Brontë, Jane Austen, the three essays on Shakespeare. The last are particularly successful. Not, it is true, because they tell us anything original to add to that enormous literature. But their charm would surely compensate—for all but the most unbending savants—their failure to produce any grain of novelty to cast on the pile. Or rather, perhaps one of them does contribute a single grain. And also, personally, the 'Note on Caliban' is my favourite. 'It is', the author tells us, 'a note of remonstrance.' Poor Caliban! Traduced by that long line of commentators and actors—often, as he shows, with little or no textual authority—reduced for the pleasure of our latter-day groundlings to the status of a 'gibbering, slobbering ape'. Forrest Reid comes to his rescue; coarse the creature may have been, half-beast that he undeniably was, yet at times 'his words have an untutored dignity and pathos, reminding us of Taine's admirable judgment: "Au fond toutes les bêtes sont nobles. Ce sont des enfants qui ont gardé la simplicité, l'indépendance et la beauté du premier âge."' The simplicity and loyalty, the rough kindness of the artless brute make an instant appeal to Forrest Reid's nature, and the essay Caliban inspired is quite one of its author's most delightful and characteristic things.

All the Shakespeare notes are on the lyrical and romantic plays, the ones in most affinity with Forrest Reid's own outlook, compact as they are of 'youth and moonshine, of love and music, of a mellow wisdom', of, above all, that 'complete surrender to the spirit of beauty'.

Beauty equally lyrical, though wilder, stranger altogether than any that we associate with the innocent witchery of the woods and fields of Illyria or Arden, he found in *Wuthering Heights*. The essay on Emily Brontë is a judicious summing-up of that unquiet spirit's work, and it shows admirably his method of trying to blend sympathy with criticism, one illuminating the other:

'The beauty of *Wuthering Heights* is created by sheer intensity of feeling, by a fire of the creative imagination that sets all ablaze in its own flaming ecstasy. Actually it is a naked book, without ornament. It contains no elaborate descriptions of nature, none of that detailed noting of the colour and mood of a landscape which we find in the work of Thomas Hardy. A line suffices; and it is by a magic of suggestion that the moorland scenery is kept so constantly before us—in rain and storm, in sunshine and frost and snow. For we never appear to be reading of these things; certainly they are never insisted on. On the other hand, the two chief characters are more perfectly in harmony with, more closely woven into, their surroundings than any characters in any tale by Hardy. They are themselves a part of a great pagan hymn to earth; their lives, their minds, their passions, have been moulded by the winds that sweep across the bleak dark moors; we cannot even imagine them in another setting.'

(*Retrospective Adventures*: 'Emily Brontë', p. 36.)

There is nothing pretentious or obscure about this criticism. There has been no attempt to grapple—as many critics have mistakenly attempted—with the ineffable or the esoteric, no needless mystification; and hence everything that is said here seems lucid, illuminating, and just.

It was subjects like these which it most suited his taste to explore; but once or twice he ventured rather beyond his self-imposed range. The most notable instance of this which comes to mind is in the little collection of essays entitled *Notes and Impressions*. I am thinking of the reprinted review of Virginia Woolf's early novel *Jacob's Room*. It is interesting to notice the manner in which Forrest Reid undertakes this task. He is writing, we must remember, when Virginia Woolf was comparatively little-known, when almost nothing had been written about her, and when her name was rarely heard outside those circles in Cambridge and Bloomsbury in which she herself moved. Confronted with an entirely new development in the art of the novel, he frankly acknowledges his bewilderment, without ever losing his head. He sees what it is that she is after, even if he cannot follow her more than a little of the way. 'I looked', he said, 'for a story and was disappointed, because there *is* no story.' But that did not make him wish to throw the book aside in impatience, as many less temperate critics would have done (and did); he is determined that, so far as he can give it, Virginia Woolf shall have her due: the 'plain fact is,' he declares, 'that to enjoy *Jacob's Room* it is better not to read it as a novel, but as a series of detached scenes and impressions.' There is, of course, a story of sorts, and characters, but what are they except 'means to an end', the end being 'simply the expression of Mrs. Woolf's own reaction to life'? This essay, slight enough as it seems on the surface, is in reality a remarkable proof of Forrest Reid's percipience as a critic. The sense—and the sensibility—which I mentioned earlier enabled him to form, unguided, an estimate of Virginia Woolf's aims that was undoubtedly the correct one. To have done that at the time he did was an achievement.[1]

The sensibility which helped him to detect the quality in *Jacob's Room* was usually, however, put to less pioneer use. It is significant that Yeats and de la Mare—the two chief objects of his critical attention—were both writers whose prose was nearly as accomplished as their poetry. In this respect Forrest Reid's two chief critical themes could not have been more happily selected. Both were to him intensely sympathetic writers, for whose work he felt an affection which, in one case, was deepened by the added intimacy of friendship. Both pitched their tents in that uneasy twilit territory lying between fantasy and reality, both sought after that 'beauty no mortal life could e'er fulfil', which lies beyond time and the world's cares.

The book on Yeats is the more successful. It was a subject after

[1] Possibly it may not be fanciful to suggest that Forrest Reid went even further: and that when he came to write his own later books something of Virginia Woolf's indirect method—whether consciously or unconsciously—found its way into his own tales. At least it can be claimed that Tom's thoughts and day-dreams constitute a 'stream of consciousness' of their own.

Forrest Reid's own heart. There was music in everything, or almost everything, that Yeats wrote, and to this music the critic gave instant response. It is indeed a possible weakness of the book that it is so very largely concerned with the poetry. But we must remember that his study appeared only a few months before the first instalment of Yeats's own beautifully written autobiography, and this may account for the thinness of the biographical information in Forrest Reid's book. We know a great deal more about Yeats now than we did in 1915. In particular a recent book[1] has revealed the full story of his desolatingly unhappy love-affair with Maud Gonne, has shown too how its long-drawn-out anguish was directly responsible for some of Yeats's loveliest poetry. It is at least as possible though, that his concentration on the poetic approach was deliberate. Yeats's prose tales were very beautiful— beautiful, that is, until Lady Gregory muffled their cadences and dressed them up in Kiltartan; but it is as a poet that Yeats will surely be remembered; not as a dramatist or a story-teller, but for the 'slow, trailing splendour', the 'wonderful, faltering rhythms' of his verse.

There is another defect which was also inevitable.

The book appeared in 1915, and this of necessity made it an interim one. It is the early and early-middle Yeats that are considered here, not the Yeats of *The Tower*, still less the Yeats of *Last Poems*, or *On the Boiler*. All the poet's later dabblings in astrology are perforce unconsidered; perhaps, one reflects, they would never have been considered in any case; for the sections which attempt an analysis of Yeats's philosophy are the weakest in the book. Indeed, if we take these chapters at their face value, there seems to have been remarkably little philosophy to analyse, unless we dignify by the name of philosophy the doctrines of symbolism, and of 'the great memory of nature', with which we are presented. There is, certainly, a 'traceable sequence of ideas', as Forrest Reid himself admitted; and it is possible to see in the writings 'the application of a philosophy which a careless reader might be inclined to dismiss as vague and obscure, were it not that

[1] R. Ellmann, *Yeats: the Man and the Masks* (Macmillan, 1949).

in certain of his prose writings we find it stated with complete lucidity, and reduced to a more or less ordered system.' The pity of it is that although we learn a great deal about 'blue robes', 'Eternal realities', and Villiers de l'Isle Adam, we never hear any more of the 'ordered system'; whose 'complete lucidity' indeed is not made more apparent by an arbitrary division of the subject into two sections, headed 'Life' and 'Aesthetic' respectively.

In all this Forrest Reid—and possibly Yeats too—was out of his depth; but the book's other gaps and omissions, however unavoidable, must obviously lessen the value of the work as a comprehensive study. Perhaps, however, its chief value lies all along in something quite different—in the application of a theory of poetry to a particular poet. Most of Yeats's poetry which is here considered is today regarded, at best, as distinctly old-fashioned. Thus, Mr. MacNeice, a recent critic of the poet, briefly dismisses the early work, written in what is characterized as a 'languid, self-pitying, late-Victorian manner', for so much Pre-Raphaelitism.

Against this view Forrest Reid always set himself. He applied the 'vocal test' and the result of his test could not be other than self-evident to him. It is thus a double pity that his book was written in 1915, and not a score of years later; much of Yeats's best later poetry could then have been assessed. As it was, he remarked justly on the falling off which is noticeable in *The Green Helmet* (1910), noted the recovery in *Responsibilities* (1914) and, while giving this book its full due, foresaw in the poetry to come a 'declination from the highest beauty'—the beauty of 'The Stolen Child', 'The Land of Heart's Desire', 'Cradle Song'—to 'a lower beauty' (p. 243); the replacement of the 'vision and the faculty divine' by the 'hard intellectual quality' of the later lyrics. Forrest Reid was, I think it will be generally agreed now, mistaken in this view. Yeats's genius was undergoing a transformation, certainly; and he came in time to reject his old singing, contemptuously dismissing it as

> . . . *a coat*
> *Covered with embroideries*
> *Out of old mythologies*

but the change was one which he himself was aware of and approved—witness the 'look of tortured irritation' noted by Lady Dorothy Wellesley,[1] a friend of Yeats's later life, when any of his early poems were mentioned, 'Innisfree' most of all—but that the 'walking naked' represented a falling off from his previous achievements is not, I think, a view that can be convincingly sustained.

Forrest Reid's study was, from this point of view, written at an awkward time, a time of transition in Yeats's development. He can hardly be blamed for failing to see into the future, for failing to realize that the future work, besides being 'principally dramatic and narrative, with now and then a song' would also contain such imperishable poems as 'Sailing to Byzantium', 'The Wild Swans at Coole', or 'The Circus Animals' Desertion'; and that the style 'now as austere as any style could well be', would, in spite of his later political and metaphysical preoccupations, and his sexual torments, produce a new, even starker simplicity of effect in some of the last songs of all. But in such things as, for instance, 'Those Images', or 'Three Things'; or (in *Words for Music Perhaps*) the poem called 'Those Dancing Days are gone', with its lovely refrain:

> *I carry the sun in a golden cup,*
> *The moon in a silver bag.*

—he did find the equivalent, in a more contemporary diction, of the 'pure poetry' of his youth, to which he at last returned. These songs, it is true, never again attained that effortless simplicity which was, as A.E. said, the despair of lesser poets.

> *Though you are in your shining days,*
> *Voices among the crowd*
> *And new friends busy with your praise,*
> *Be not unkind or proud,*
> *But think about old friends the most:*
> *Time's bitter flood will rise,*
> *Your beauty perish and be lost*
> *For all eyes but these eyes.*

[1] W. B. Yeats: *Letters on Poetry . . . to Dorothy Wellesley* (Oxford, 1940).

That had the inevitability of great poetry, and only came once. To Forrest Reid he seemed never again to reach that early perfection. 'There's something human lacking—' he wrote of the poet's later years, 'kindness, geniality, sympathy, humour, and when it comes to the casting of horoscopes even intelligence.' And he also deplored the 'senile florescence of sex'.

The fact is that the early Yeats and the later Yeats both have their separate beauties, and it is only natural that one should differ from the other. After all, Yeats's poems were written over a space of half a century; it is a far cry from the Yeats of *The Rose* to the angry poet who accused himself of having 'invented a patter'; and if he had not undergone development during that long span of time he would not be the very great poet he is now acknowledged on all sides to be.

All this, however, is irrelevant to Forrest Reid's book. Its value does not lie in its speculations about the future but rather in its appreciation of all that Yeats had up to that time produced. It is incomparably the best thing that has yet been written on this period of Yeats's career, a study full of sympathy and sensitive criticism. Forrest Reid never lost sight of his subject, never wandered off into irrelevancies; for one of the most striking features of the book is the skill with which Yeats is detached from the Irish literary movement, of which he had become regarded as the leader, and is considered purely on his merits as an artist. For the Irish Renaissance indeed Forrest Reid entertained little enthusiasm. 'Bad art is good art's worst enemy, and a spirit of patriotism, upon which all Irish criticism that is not based upon personal friendship or politics seems to be based, is but a blind guide in questions of aesthetics.' (*W. B. Yeats*, p. 234.) The neglect of Forrest Reid's study can only coincide with the neglect of the early Yeats himself, and the temporary ascendancy of new schools of criticism; when the wheel turns full circle the book will without doubt receive its due.

I said that the book exemplified a theory of poetry; and it is this which gives it value as criticism. But it is at the same time a possible source of weakness. Joubert, in his *Pensées*, drew a distinction

between the poetry of images and the poetry of ideas. Forrest
Reid's response to the pure beauty of verbal music, his determination that a work of art should be judged *as* a work of art, and not
as an improving tract or an academic thesis, often tempted him
to take a somewhat one-sided view of poetic achievement. There
was sound—but there was also sense. Actually, this weakness did
not greatly matter because, at the time he wrote his study, the
intellectual content in Yeats's poetry was still small; but it does
prompt the suspicion that his lack of sympathy for the later work
may have been more on account of its intellectual difficulty than
because of any falling off, or change of emphasis, in its beauty of
effect. But what he *did* admire in Yeats's poetry, his 'wonderful
uniformity of spirit', is the same quality which we feel in this
criticism. An even, steady light pervades the book, making it
singularly pleasant to read. This is not to accuse the work of
idolatry. Forrest Reid stakes high claims for his subject: 'If
Shelley is a great poet, if Keats and Coleridge and Rossetti are
great poets, then Mr. Yeats is a great poet also, greater, I think,
than any of these' (p. 249)—high praise indeed—but strictures,
where necessary, are never withheld; only they are not the strictures of someone who is determined that his subject shall con-
form to his own conception, but rather the careful comments of
a fellow-artist and craftsman. His comments are always relevant,
always fair, and never merely clever or dogmatic. Forrest Reid
is never concerned to show himself off, but rather to show off his
subject. When he remarks that, in considering Yeats's work as a
whole, 'it is only gradually that one becomes aware of something
that is lacking in it . . . In all these high passions one misses just
the one thing upon which the whole *quality* of our spiritual vision
depends . . . the highest spiritual beauty of all . . . a kind of moral
fragrance' (pp. 217–8)—we recognize at once the truth and pro-
fundity of the criticism expressed.

He held, as few hold today, that all criticism has to be subjective, the recording of quite personal impressions. This gives
to his critical work a quality of intimacy, a personal flavour, which
lifts the criticism to the level of art, makes it itself a thing of beauty.

It is, in fact, that most difficult of achievements, *creative* criticism. Its essential prerequisite is that an uncommon spiritual sympathy should exist between writer and subject; which is in itself likely to mean that this kind of writing will always be rare. This identification Forrest Reid succeeded in making when he came to put down his thoughts about W. B. Yeats.

A quality less tangible than literary admiration or congruity of ideas went to this work. Yeats meant to him, it is easy to see, more than either of these. His philosophy, he eloquently declared:

'. . . has something in it of Platonism; his poetry is a setting free of the soul by means of mortal and changing things that it may gaze upon immortal and unchanging things. That is exactly what the Platonic Socrates sought to do by dialectic, and what he actually does do when poetry has not been overshadowed by dialectic. Both ancient philosopher and modern poet throw their net among the stars, and capture a strange and wandering loveliness that will always seem unearthly and illusive to those who, consciously or unconsciously, have accepted materialism, and to those upon whose souls the practical cares of life have closed down like a coffin-lid.'

(P. 60.)

Something of the same deep spiritual tie is implicit in the study of Walter de la Mare, which he wrote fifteen years later. In fact, the affinity here is even closer. But it is an affinity, not an absolute identity. Both writers have interested themselves in the same periods of life—the earliest. But Mr. de la Mare's is an interest which, primarily, is almost scientific—a questing, probing, analytic inquiry, directed into uncovering the workings, the impulses and the subject-matter of a child's mind. Now this is precisely what we miss in Forrest Reid's own books. Where Walter de la Mare uses a microscope for his observations, Forrest Reid relies upon the naked eye. He is less curious to discover what is going on inside a child's head than eager to be moved by that child's aspect, or manner. The note of intellectual inquiry is absent.

There is another difference. Youth is a subject not often dealt with in Mr. de la Mare's books, his sympathies or emotions are

not strongly engaged. His eye, through the microscope, is trained
upon a child, and for him the wonder and the magic of childhood
cease as soon as the prison-house shades begin to gather. It was
just this spectacle of the 'distress of boyhood changing into man'
(Yeats's phrase) which so deeply stirred Forrest Reid's com-
passion; and this is the point at which the two friends' writings
diverge.

And yet in spite of the shift in emphasis, at the deepest level
their aims are similar ones. That lack of 'moral fragrance', which
he noticed in Yeats, was to become in much of that poet's subsequent work almost embarrassingly absent, but it is a quality
Walter de la Mare's writing has never lacked. His poems, beyond
and above the ravishment of their music, diffuse a gentle humanity that can only rarely be detected in the Irish poet's work, which
veers easily towards the poles of Shelleyan idealism or political
and metaphysical astringency.

De la Mare had always been a deep influence in Forrest Reid's
life ever since the day, many years before, when they first met.
They shared the same vision of life, wrote so often about similar
situations, read each other's proofs, even, as de la Mare said in
the preface to one of his later books,[1] 'shared the same inkpot.'
And it is pleasant to remember that it was largely due to de la
Mare's efforts that Forrest Reid, but for his death, was to have
become the recipient of a Civil List Pension. But this profound
sympathy could really be said to have been born still earlier, before they met in the flesh, born on 'a winter afternoon many
years ago, in the University Library at Cambridge, when I was
prowling round the shelves upstairs and took down by the

---

[1] *Pleasures and Speculations*; and in Forrest Reid's inscribed copy of de la
Mare's *The Lord Fish* the author wrote the following lines:

To F.R. from W.J.

> *Once were two Friends whose livelong wish*
> *was in a sea of Ink to fish:*
> *Though oft of even Hope forsook*
> > *By hook and crook—*
> > *By crook and hook,*
> *They, now and then, hauled up—a Book.*
> *See! here's another: look!*

merest chance a thin pale-blue volume called *Songs of Childhood*, by Walter Ramal. I had never heard of Walter Ramal, and . . . it was as if in the silence and fading light of that deserted library, I had, like some adventurer in the Middle Ages, sailed all unexpectedly into sight of an unknown and lovely shore.'

There is a little sketch which Forrest Reid wrote in 1914, entitled 'A Garden by the Sea'. Later he incorporated it, with modifications, into his novel *The Spring Song*. It is a slight enough little thing, only a few pages, but in atmosphere and characters it tells its own story. The tale is simple. A man, now in middle age, revisits a house dear to him in his childhood. It was a place he had discovered quite by accident, but, sitting down in the neglected unkempt garden, he recalls in memory that distant day when first he had pushed open the green door which led into that enchanted country. He remembers those who had been so gentle and kind to him there: the Captain, 'an odd-looking old gentleman with a red face and white hair and the queerest of clothes', long retired from the sea, and Miss Caroline, his sister, with her 'thin hair, the colour of old silver . . . parted in the middle and smoothed closely down on either side of her forehead' and 'a cap of soft white lace with a lilac ribbon in it'; remembers too the scents and sounds of that summer garden of long ago, when the 'hours passed lightly as a dream' and all was innocence and tranquillity. 'The moon had come out from behind the clouds as I sat smoking a second and a third pipe, listening to these echoes from the past. A cat glided stealthily through the grass, disappearing in the shadow of the wall. The moonlight grew brighter and the shadows blacker. The place, the hour, my own state of mind— all were singularly appropriate to ghosts, but no ghosts came. The Captain, Miss Caroline—and with them everything they represented of leisure and graciousness and quiet—had retreated too far to return, and even my memory of them was tinged with legend. Yet long ago beauty lingered here—lingered like the grey moths now hovering among the tangled currant-bushes—lingered for a space before taking flight.' Here is a prose as full of poetry as Shelley's or Yeats's or Hardy's—or Mr. de la Mare's.

Captain Batt and his sister, indeed, are pure de la Mare creations, Miss Caroline reminding us a little, even, of the immortal Miss Duveen.

And yet this is no piece of plagiarism or pastiche. It is an instance, rare enough though it may be, of a joint possession of the title-deeds to a peculiar and almost unanalysable gift. Why this gift should appear, in two writers, at the same time and place in history, is something of a mystery; but there it is, and all we can do is to be grateful for the strange coincidence.[1]

It seemed necessary to make this point—in illustration of de la Mare's phrase about the inkpot—as a necessary perspective to Forrest Reid's book. For it is, I think, a failure. Something, somewhere, has gone wrong. That it should be so may seem strange. The almost telepathic literary sympathy which existed between Walter de la Mare and Forrest Reid ought, we might think, to have been in itself the guarantee of a book of more than ordinary value. And there, perhaps, if we reflect for a moment, we may find a part at least of the reason for the disappointment which the thing produces in us. Paradoxically, too great a degree of sympathy often results in weakness of communication. And that is what has happened here, surely. Projection of feeling rather than identification often leads to the best results in these cases. Forrest Reid knew his subject *too* well, sympathized *too* closely. He was, also, a close personal friend, with all that must imply in unconscious distortion and unwitting lack of critical detachment. He stood too near the picture to be able to give us a really comprehensive and detached account of what the artist was about. Some of Mr. de la Mare's best poetry had yet to be written or

[1] Mr. Roger Senhouse has most kindly shown me the three highly interesting versions he possesses of Mr. de la Mare's story 'An Ideal Craftsman'. They show that this tale went through no less than six stages between its inception in 1905 and the appearance of the finally revised version in *On the Edge* in 1930. (1) The initial appearance in the *Monthly Review* for June 1905. (2) Forrest Reid's numerous corrections and revisions on the proofs of the above, after publication. (3) A version by Forrest Reid, prepared from this corrected copy with (4) further manuscript alterations and corrections in Forrest Reid's hand. (5) Another version by de la Mare, prepared from (3) above, and later (6) heavily revised by himself, with many passages completely rewritten. Only at this point (one imagines) did *these* craftsmen allow exhaustion to supervene.

published: *Memory*, *The Fleeting*; the anthologies, themselves works of art; some marvellous late lyrics, in *The Burning-Glass*; the philosophical poem *The Traveller*. This last is, in a sense, the counterpart in poetry of *The Three Mulla-Mulgars*. That tale had been written in such a way that the reader 'can if he likes view in it his own earthly pilgrimage.' It was not an allegory, and about Thumb, Thimble and Nod there is nothing allegorical—whereas *The Traveller* quite definitely *is*—but in spite of this the two very different books do, in a way, hang together.

It is, moreover, a fault of the study of de la Mare that what we are offered in place of criticism is often something dangerously resembling chat. This accounts for the atmosphere of thinness which clings to the book, the over-readiness to embark on discursive side-issues. The chronological plan of the book is not a good one, and itself makes for aimlessness; and if at times we find ourselves wondering whether Forrest Reid ever did sit down and think out exactly *what* it was that he wanted to say—this is because it is, I think, obvious to a careful reader that he himself would have owned the justice of the criticism. He knew the difficulties with which he was faced, was 'conscious that it is difficult to praise quite freely the genius of a living writer, at least when that writer is a friend of many years', and would have been ready to admit the irresoluteness of the book.

Perhaps indeed it is mistaking the point to judge it as criticism proper; ought not the book rather to be looked upon as a semi-private tribute, in the form of Lemaître's *impressions toutes personnelles*, from one friend to another? The author himself claims for his book no more than the value of 'notes', a commentary.

'The landscape'—the setting, that is, of Mr. de la Mare's prose and verse—'is always spiritualized, becomes a changeless, eternal landscape of the soul. There are old churchyards,[1] and old gardens,

---

[1] A fondness for which he shares with his critic. Cf. *Following Darkness*, pp. 82–5; the 'little country churchyard near Ballinderry' in *Apostate*, pp. 198–9; *Brian Westby*, pp. 187–92; and, of course, Tom's adventure at the end of *The Retreat*. All these passages breathe a speculative, dreamy, half-formulated Platonism—or alternatively an agnosticism brushed by the wings of faith—which at all times formed a latent ingredient in Forrest Reid's thinking.

with green sunken walks and trees spreading mossy and lichened boughs above them. There are dark old houses, with the wind sighing through their key-holes, and perhaps, from an upper casement, a face looking "out of sorcery". There are the burning fires of frost and stars, and black ice-bound winter pools, and frozen snow marked by the rabbit's "tell-tale footprints". There are birds hovering within vision, yet singing out of a molten glory of Paradise.'

(Pp. 246-7.)

This is not criticism, but that it is something more valuable than the mere easy-handed applause which passes for much criticism today no one can deny. What it is *not*, however, is the 'Critical Study' that the title-page has promised us. But perhaps we should be grateful none the less.

His examination of the verse was almost uniformly a favourable one, but that was because he believed that criticism must illuminate rather than censure, where that was possible; and in truth there is little at which we can cavil in this wonderful poetry. Working through the output in more or less chronological order, we are taken from those earliest things in *Songs of Childhood*:

> *O for a heart like almond boughs!*
> *O for sweet thoughts like rain!*
> *O for first-love like fields of grey*
> *Shut April-buds at break of day!*
> *O for a sleep like music!*
> *Dreams still as rain!*

which are 'hardly more than strains of music', right up to the latest poetry he had then written:

> *Think! in Time's smallest clock's minutest beat*
> *Might there not rest be found for wandering feet?* . . .
>
> *No, no. Nor earth, nor air, nor fire, nor deep*
> *Could lull poor mortal longingness asleep.*
> *Somewhere there Nothing is; and there lost Man*
> *Shall win what changeless vague of peace he can.*

207

—the poems which are shadowed with doubt, a doubt which only 'at rare moments passes into tremulous faith', and are filled with the longing for that 'lost Paradise from which each one of us is exiled', such a longing as might have come over

'some unrecorded child of Adam wandering near the impenetrable hedges of Eden. . . . While out of the tree, the snake, his father's enemy, watches him with bright unblinking eyes.'

The pages where he examines the poetry are the most successful parts of Forrest Reid's study, and a consideration of what he has to say on this topic may serve as an introduction to his views on the whole subject.

'A poem', Forrest Reid declares, 'is a collaboration between the poet and his reader.' There are two kinds of poetry; there is, firstly, the 'kind in relation to which "liking" expresses accurately enough the quality of our responsiveness.' This is the verse of sentiment or humour or occasion, and its countless exponents produce the great bulk of what we loosely call poetry. But above and beyond all this, there is another level, the level where poetry is 'either a passion or . . . nothing'. Poetry of this kind is 'a kind of magic, the poet a kind of magician, working by means of symbols, and by the weaving of a spell.' By the earlier type of verse we are charmed, amused, excited even; but poetry of this second kind evokes a deeper response, because it strikes at the roots of our whole emotional life. This is the poetry, and the only poetry, with which Forrest Reid was concerned. His attitude on this point was, said Mr. Forster in a reminiscence, 'childish but firm. A poem was a person, you either liked it or you didn't.' Either, that is, 'Annabel Lee' or 'Summer Dawn' sent a shiver down your spine or it did not. If it didn't you were an object of commiseration, never of reproach. This is not to say that Forrest Reid ever identified himself with the acrobatics of the egregious Abbé Brémond; his poetic faith—it wasn't really a theory—stood or fell by its application to particular poems, and never by a rigid doctrine of *poésie pure*.

This is what gives interest to his own anthology. *The Milk of Paradise* is not criticism. Nor does it resemble 'that large and by no means exclusive anthology' *The Oxford Book of English Verse*, whose pages shelter 'quite a number of writers who are not, in any sense of the word, poets at all.' It is a florilegium, the very personal choice of one very personal person, and the golden thread that binds it all together, the one virtue every poem in the book shares, is the ability to arouse, in the ears of one listener at least, that authentic 'thrill', so easy to recognize and so difficult to describe, and which for Housman was more a physical than an intellectual experience. Forrest Reid would have held, with Poe, that a long poem was 'a flat contradiction in terms', and from this it follows that the poetry he quotes in *The Milk of Paradise* is almost entirely lyric poetry.

But Forrest Reid went even further than Housman. For he widened the whole scope of poetry. To think of it as 'exclusively the property of literature' was a pedant's error. 'The sound of the waves on the sea-shore, a landscape seen in a certain lighting, a group of children gathered in the street at dusk round the glowing brazier of a night-watchman' (p. 12)—all of these were equally 'poetic' in the emotion they transmitted to the sensitive observer. Poetry proper, in fact, was no more than a specific instance of a general phenomenon, as old as the human race and as young as the latest child to be thrilled by the ancient magic of the words of the familiar nursery rhyme:

> *How many miles to Babylon?*
> *Three score and ten.*
> *Can I get there by candlelight?—*
> *Yes, and back again :*

—calling up its picture of 'an old fantastic town of towers and turrets, lit by waving candles, and with windows all ablaze in dark old houses'. (*Following Darkness*, p. 15.)

There is, however, a weakness in this view, a weakness of which Forrest Reid was not perhaps sufficiently aware. We have seen how Joubert used to speak of two kinds of poetry, the poetry of images and the poetry of ideas. A poem, to be beautiful, need possess only excellence of image; but if poetry aspires to *greatness* it must be rich also in excellence of ideas; must show traces of Pater's 'severe intellectual meditation', or that 'fundamental brain-work', which Rossetti postulated as a necessity in the composition of lasting work. This is what Forrest Reid was sometimes tempted to miss; to miss, that is, the highest beauty for the most musical. *Paradise Lost* was favourite reading and the grave, slowly unfolding magnificence of many lines and passages never failed to move him; but to the intellectual power and organization behind the poem, its massive architecture, he showed himself (at least in his writings about poetry) perhaps less sensitive. It is not a fault, but it *is* a limitation, a limitation all the more to be regretted for being, as I emphasized, an unconscious one.

An example of what I mean by 'greatness' in poetry is, of course, the *Paradiso* (and, for that matter, *Paradise Lost*); or, to come a little lower down the scale, the metaphysical poets of the seventeenth century, Donne especially. Donne was able, time and time again, to clothe the most subtle, involuted thoughts in resonant words of a music unforgettable. I am thinking of such wonderful things as 'The Anniversarie', 'Aire and Angels', or 'The Extasie'. Here thought and feeling are one, and the feeling slips over the thought like a well-fitting glove. Here—or so it seems to me—lies the ultimate achievement in poetry, sound and sense alike at the flood.

Forrest Reid assigned to meaning a very subordinate share in poetry, even on occasion denying its necessity. For poetry as the 'quarrel with ourselves' he never had much sympathy. He quotes Coleridge in support of the assertion that many poems are made more, not less powerful, by an obscurity of intention; as in those magic lines:

> *The bailey beareth the bell away*
> *The lily, the lily, the rose I lay,*

which sink into the mind like a charm and whose music is the more haunting for being in part unintelligible to us; like a crystal into whose heart we gaze and gaze without ever quite capturing the fugitive picture it holds in its depths. Yet, even so, this is hardly a fair comparison. In this poem the mystery, the concealed meaning, is deliberate; and that is a very different thing from an absence of any meaning at all.

> *The wan moon is setting ayont the white wave,*
> *And Time is setting with me, O!*

Burns's lines, by whose melancholy crepuscular beauty Yeats was so haunted, *do* mean something, and very beautiful and affecting they are, but they are not 'great' poetry. Puck's music too is incomparable, but its limitation of content does not justify us in calling what he sings 'great' poetry. His songs, like Burns's, lacking 'moral fragrance', leave one side of our nature unmoved.

I spoke earlier of that impulse felt by Forrest Reid for exploring the unknown rather than the familiar. Whether it was the mechanical effusions of Master Romney Robinson, that youthful poetic prodigy of eighteenth-century Belfast, or the then undeservedly neglected fantasies of Edward Garnett, the novels of W. D. Howells, or *Le Baiser au Lépreux, Longman's Magazine*, or a remarkable and little-known modern novel, *The Young Desire It* —the same adventurous and independent judgement was at work. It was this itch for the neglected and the little considered which may perhaps have contributed as much as anything to the growth of his enthusiasm for the wood-engravers' work of the last century. This, and the fact that these lovely pictures succeeded in doing what he later achieved in his own writing; that is, they 'accepted life as it was and turned it into beauty'. He has left (in *Apostate*) a vivid description of his first stumbling on what was to become a life-long interest; of how, when he was about fifteen, exploring in the lumber-room at home and accidentally dislodging a pile of dusty magazines, he noticed that

'one of them lay open, showing a woodcut that caught my attention. The paper was toned to an ivory yellow; the design showed a little harbour with a woman and a child walking by the water's edge, and a man standing on the wharf, holding a bag on a truck. In the background were the black naked ropes and masts and spars of the boats, and the whole thing seemed to me charming.'

(Apostate [1926], p. 173.)

It was the beginning of a passion which found fruit, many years later, in the compilation of the monumental and authoritative Illustrators of the Sixties.

'There and then, under the sunless pallor of the skylight, I sat down and looked for other drawings. There were plenty, for there were heaps of these old magazines—Good Words, Cornhills, Quivers, Argosys, Once a Weeks. To me they were treasure trove.'

Illustrators of the Sixties is a difficult book for a layman in these matters to write about, but even to the untrained and inexpert eye it soon becomes clear that here, despite its author's over-modest claim that it represents no more than the 'chronicle of a hobby'— is the definitive work on one phase, albeit a minor one, of nineteenth-century English art. I say 'art' deliberately; because even a casual inspection of these liberally illustrated pages can leave one in no doubt as to their aesthetic value. Cuts like 'The Maids of Elfen-Mere', or Pinwell's illustrations to Jean Ingelow's poems, 'The Trial Sermon' (by Whistler), Millais's 'St. Agnes' Eve', drawn for Tennyson's poem, or Sandys's 'The Sailor's Bride' have a strange boding power, an impassioned imaginative vigour which make them, quite unmistakably and uniquely, works of art. What emerges most strongly from a study of this book—after we have noted the skill, the economy with which Forrest Reid has marshalled and made attractive such a mass of detail—is the same quality that runs through the novels: that is, unfailing taste in treatment of a subject where sentiment, sentimentality, and downright sloppiness all meet and, often, commingle. There are very few illustrations, in this book, where sentimentality has been allowed to do service for sentiment; and, needless to say, there is no sloppiness. Indeed, some of the most lovely and successful illustrations that Forrest Reid has chosen are precisely those which come from that obscure borderland that fringes, but never touches, sentimentality. Just how successful some of these can be we have only to turn to 'Rung into Heaven' (on p. 53) to see for ourselves. Lawless has, as Forrest Reid points out, escaped sentimentality 'by a dangerously narrow margin', but that the picture does escape it is, he thinks, 'one of its triumphs'.

Lawless was, in his way, among the happiest of the 'Sixties artists; but if we seek for a real master in his own genre we must, I think, acknowledge it in Arthur Hughes. Hughes is an artist who has never received his due, or anything like it, at the hands of posterity. A few of his delicate, wistful paintings—full of the spirit of youth, and the fragility of its beauty—are well known from their presence in the galleries: The *April Love*, for instance, in London, or *Home from Sea*, or the lesser-known *King's Orchard* at Cambridge. But his retiring nature, coupled with an avoidance of all publicity, and the fact that he led a happy but singularly un-eventful life, all conspired to make his name quickly forgotten. With Forrest Reid's book before us, there is now no risk of his work in one direction at least—as a woodcut artist—not receiving its proper attention when his full achievement comes to be measured.

The world in which Arthur Hughes dwelt was very similar in its emotional climate to the one made familiar to us by Forrest Reid—the world of innocence and childhood. Everything he did breathed this atmosphere of youthful comeliness. The drawings which he made for *At the Back of the North Wind*, *The Princess and the Goblin* and the rest, are fairy drawings, 'conceived in a mys-terious world, out of space, out of time', in a past in which 'every-thing is created anew after the dreamer's desire', where all is 'sweet, gentle, innocent'. And yet the small human beings he portrays for us there, 'somehow *are* human—his little boys and girls—in spite of their half angelic sexlessness and strange air of dreamy gravity'; and as we follow the adventures of North Wind and Diamond, the coachman's son, in George MacDonald's tale, the drawings, with their beauty 'at once so strange and so homely' seem 'to bring into one world the cat purring on the hearth, and the wildest gleams of fantasy'. Technically, Hughes's work often leaves much to be desired, and that is a fault, but he knew 'those

white designs which children drive',[1] he breathed the same air as
Vaughan and Blake and Traherne, and because of this his short-
comings are redeemed.

Hughes's work is perhaps the outstanding discovery for Forrest
Reid enthusiasts; but the whole book is full of good things. There
is, for instance, the work of that neglected artist John Dawson
Watson. One of his drawings reproduced here is 'The Aspen',
which appeared in *Good Words* for 1863. There is nothing at
first in this sombre study to catch the eye. All we can see are two
figures, their backs turned to us, wandering at dusk beneath some
gloomy trees which overhang a black, still river. And yet the
whole sketch is one 'positively steeped in poetry'. The air is heavy
with all the 'sadness and decay' of autumn, and the young mother
bending over her child whose arm clings, as if for protection,
around her waist, seems in the act of reconciling that neat, dark-
clad and (although his—or her—back is all we can see) oddly
attractive little creature to the traverse of that misty twilight
which lies before them. It is a most affecting thing; not only
because of the atmosphere it so powerfully conveys, but in the
very placing and attitudes of the two forms who occupy the foreground, their spiritual interdependence and physical proximity.

> *O dreamy, gloomy, friendly Trees,*
> *I came along your narrow track*
> *To bring my gifts unto your knees*
> *And gifts did you give back;*
> *For when I brought this heart that burns—*
> *These thoughts that bitterly repine—*
> *And laid them here among the ferns*
> *And the hum of boughs divine,*
> *Ye, vastest breathers of the air,*
> *Shook down with slow and mighty poise*
> *Your coolness on the human care,*
> *Your wonder on its toys,*
> *Your greenness on the heart's despair,*
> *Your darkness on its noise.*[2]

[1] Vaughan, 'Childe-hood', in *Sacred Poems*.
[2] Herbert Trench, 'O Dreamy, Gloomy, Friendly Trees'.

But it is barely possible to give an idea of the riches stored within the covers of this book; it is only when we pause and reflect that, besides the artists referred to above, the work of Simeon Solomon, Fred Walker, Arthur Boyd Houghton, J. W. North, D. G. Rossetti—not to mention that strangely powerful illustrator Frederick Sandys, or du Maurier, or the immortal Charles Keene—are all illustrated and commented upon, that we begin to realize the full extent and variety of these artists' achievements, and the copious documentation they have been afforded. Forrest Reid's capacity to fire enthusiasm was never put to better purpose than here. For all its comprehensiveness it is essentially the story of one collector's discoveries. Within its necessary limits the book is a model of what this kind of study should be—packed with information and yet unhampered by any trace of pedantry, fastidious yet personal and warmly human. In its pages the critic comes close and, standing at our shoulder, speaks directly to us.

VI

The Dream

I am certain of nothing but of the holiness of the heart's affections,
and the truth of Imagination.
                    Keats, Letter to Bailey, 22nd November 1817

> *All I love*
> *In beauty cries to me,*
> *'We but vain shadows*
> *And reflections be.'*
>   Walter de la Mare

The time has come to draw together the threads of this brief study. Perhaps its pages should be thought of as an anthology, or garland, rather than as an attempt at a more formal view of its subject. For the author has become increasingly conscious, while putting together these disconnected notes, that his role is little else than that of a commentator on the passages he has selected. This has been deliberate; indeed it was unavoidable. In the pages of *Apostate* and (although it wasn't so much a work of art) in the equally interesting *Private Road*, Forrest Reid left behind him two singularly complete records of his personality. Explicitly, or by implication, whatever he conceived essential to an understanding of the circumstances of his life was presented in these books. But this wasn't all: *Apostate* and *Private Road* are in one sense a selective chronicle of external events, but at a deeper level they can (especially *Apostate*) also be looked on as in some sort a chronicle of the emotions as well. They didn't, that is, only attempt to recount past events, they re-created past atmosphere too. And it was because the atmosphere in Forrest Reid's books was carefully worked up in long stretches of writing that its unique character could be effectively conveyed only by reproducing lengthy passages. Scene and character are interwoven, and create one total impression. No understanding of his genius could be complete which did not emphasize the extraordinary faculty for wrapping these impressions about his reader, of transporting him to an entirely different world, insulating him from any but those emotions he wished to evoke. The full power of the rarely occurring climaxes, even the significance of some of the quite everyday incidents, only sink into the imagination when we look at these events in the books as tangible objects, preserved and enhanced in a magic fluid, floating in solution (as it were) in this emotional circumambience.

What does Forrest Reid's work, looked at as a single imaginative whole, amount to? Has the vision that shines through book after book any value, and assuming it has, is it a value that can be expressed in words at all?

What he was trying to do was either supremely important or it was nothing. He was, that is, certain either of bringing off a unique achievement or else of failing completely. His art, by virtue of its integrity and its craftsmanship alone, is assured of a permanent place in English writing. That place will not be among, nor even a little way below, the great household names; he was content with his own 'half-inch of ivory' and very little that he wrote can be judged, by the conventional critical standards, to be of any wide significance. His work will always appeal chiefly to a minority, but a minority whose standards are more firmly based than those of most majorities. 'If I had a thousand readers,' Landor once remarked, 'I should be quite out of conceit with myself', and making due allowance for this patricianly low estimate Forrest Reid might have said much the same about his own writing. His books didn't have spectacular sales. 'I never had much success myself,' he remarked, speaking of his American career: 'but that means nothing, since I have none of the qualities that go to make a successful writer either at home or abroad.'

Topicality is one of these qualities; and there is nothing topical about Forrest Reid's writing. He was once asked, by a literary paper, to define the relevance of his art to existing conditions; a question to which he gave the following memorable reply:

'It has no more and no less relevance to them than the Odyssey has to the "existing conditions" of the age of Homer, or than *A Midsummer Night's Dream* has to those of the Elizabethan age.'

Holding this belief, he was able to view the reception of his books by the public in a manner at once philosophical and completely objective. 'He had an amazingly good press,' he wrote to J. N. Hart when *Peter Waring* was published in England, 'but most of my books have that and it seems to make very little difference.' And writing to the same friend a few years later about his novels, 'I shall be surprised', he remarked with his humorous, deprecating irony, 'if they bring me a reward even in the next world.' Norman Douglas, who told him 'you seem to have *just the right* admixture of Celtic elements in your composition', proffered unusual words of encouragement. He had been reading *Demophon*. 'It stands to reason', he wrote, 'that a delicate thing like that will not appeal to the general public. Why should it? Thank God it doesn't!' Yet behind Douglas's robust and cheerful comments there did lie a truth. The books explored certain seams of experience and passed by others, richer but more exploited, without a word. 'My range' (he admitted) 'is very narrow, and the moment I try to pass beyond it, as I have done on several occasions in the past, the result is deplorable.' Yet in spite of the restriction of range there is never any trace of the self-consciousness or quarrelsomeness that usually betrays the writer who deliberately seeks a small audience from motives of self-distrust and a mutual vanity. He never made the 'big spectacular splash in the promiscuous pond of fiction'; neither had he any 'contribution to make to the modern novel'. The suggestion that he had something to bequeath to that amorphous profusion he would have found a sober, if scarcely reassuring thought.

Such phrase-making meant nothing to him. His chosen corner was a small one—deliberately small; but the illumination he cast into its shadows revealed much that is not often made visible. He worked always on a small scale; scarcely an event in the novels—unless it be the letter Owen Gill receives from Tolstoy—that would have caused the least stir outside their covers. He concentrated his regard, said E. M. Forster, 'upon a single point, a point which, when rightly focussed, may perhaps make all the surrounding landscape intelligible.'[1]

Of his corner, his world—and to him it was always the only world that mattered—he is the undisputed master. It is probably safe to say that no other writer has made a comparable exploration of the world of youth. There could be no room for hatred or bitterness in the artist's outlook. People are *persons*, not bundles of ideas, and it is what they are, not the labels stuck on them, that really matters. He agreed with Anatole France: 'les choses humaines', Anatole had said in *La Vie Littéraire*, 'n'inspirent que deux sentiments aux esprits bien faits: l'admiration ou la pitié.' Towards all living things in that world, in their springtime of life, Forrest Reid's admiration and pity went out in abundance. He knew youth through and through—knew the beauty and ugliness, the intensity of its small excitements and its strange little sadnesses, the breathless aspirations and the black, all-enveloping disappointments—with an imaginative intensity that penetrated deep into the heart and mind of childhood and adolescence.

'There is a sense', he wrote, 'in which it would be true to say that Denis and Grif and Peter are mere pretexts for the author to live again through the years of his boyhood, to live those years, as it were, more consciously, if less happily.' The books are, in fact, written from the inside, in a way that books about the young have never quite been written before or since. That is, while he was writing them he lived within this world he was creating.

'I used to think', Stella Benson once confessed, 'that growing up was like walking from one end of the meadow to the other; I thought that the meadow would remain, and one had only to turn one's head to see it all again. But now I know that growing up is like going through a door into a little room: and the door

[1] E. M. Forster, *Abinger Harvest*, p. 80.

shuts behind one.'[1] Forrest Reid knew that 'little room'; but the door never shut behind *him*, the meadow was always close at hand, and when he wrote his novels his eyes were resting on its slopes and he could feel the sunshine on his face and hands.

For that reason there are no types, no dummies, because every character was conceived in the round, with an exactness of touch which is, in sum, extraordinary. Nearly everyone—certainly all the youngsters—*live*. They are real boys, real children, we could meet them, have met them ourselves.

And nothing is more remarkable than the way in which the atmosphere of mingled beauty and strangeness in which the stories are bathed is never achieved at the expense of a necessary realism. It is, rather, achieved *through* realism. But the everyday, almost commonplace settings of the novels form only a part of the whole. Behind beauty, as behind ugliness, there lurks mystery. Just what exactly this mystery *is* we are never told; but its presence is all the more surely felt for it never being precisely defined. Lying just beyond our reach, over the horizon, sometimes casting up its shadows along the earth and threatening all the landscape, blotting out the sun like a dark cloud, is an impalpable, ambiguous, phantasmic country; the country Fournier called the 'lost domain', his *pays sans nom*. Nearly all the novels of Forrest Reid enact themselves in this equivocal territory, half-real, half-visionary, where the commonplace imperceptibly slides into the marvellous, and the world we know fades away to reveal, shining through its familiar everyday dress, another world of which

by starlight and by candlelight and dream light

we catch only glimpses.

The expression of emotion in definite terms is a difficult feat; it is, as one modern critic has perceived, 'the central problem of literary art'.[2] That problem, after some false starts, Forrest Reid

[1] Quoted in R. Ellis Roberts's *Portrait of Stella Benson* (Macmillan, 1939), p. 45.

[2] Herbert Read, *English Prose Style*, p. 164.

eventually solved. That he solved it, this 'central problem', with in his own framework of realistic treatment, and that he went on to combine the two things, the realism and the romanticism, is proof indeed of mastery.

The solution did not come easily. It was a long time before he resolved to treat his subject squarely. If we leave aside *Following Darkness* as being in some respects an unusual book, it was not really until *Demophon* in 1927 that he found his true subject: the imaginative development of a single boy, observed at his own level and through his own eyes. After that discovery he never faltered; what had stood in the way of success in the earlier stories—the introduction of family complications (as in *The Bracknels* or *At the Door*) or melodrama (Flamel in *The Gentle Lover*, Dr. Bradley in *The Spring Song*)—was cut away, no longer allowed to obscure the central theme. In *Demophon* and its successors nothing stood between the author and his subject, and that is what makes the Tom Barber novels a masterpiece. It is also what makes them almost impossible to write about. In these stories there are no plots, no moral lessons, and hardly ever a grown-up. What *is* there (beside much else in darker strain) is the constant evocation of happiness—Tom's happiness—a happiness which fills the books and irradiates the natural beauty of fields and flowers and woods, the wild creatures that inhabit them and the blue sky above them. For Tom, a 'solitary child', is, we feel, as much part of nature as they are, and his feelings and instincts as natural as those of the befriended animals with whom he 'finds pastime'.

About the emotion which permeates the books it is difficult to speak without seeming crude or halting. 'No matter how objective, how impersonal I tried to be,' (he recollected) 'this subconscious lyrical emotion before long crept in. . . . Such an emotion runs all through the moon-story in *The Bracknels*, all through Grif's story in *The Spring Song*, and through much of Peter's in *Following Darkness*: more, it . . . constitutes the very atmosphere of these tales. . . .'

Other people's poetry, too, kept floating into the novels: Tom's mother singing Jean Ingelow's lovely song—her voice softly floating up to Tom's bedroom through the warm summer night; Tom himself, fascinated by the alternate beat and *rallentando* of 'The Bells' as he stands day-dreaming in the empty belfry of the church at home; Denis, alone in the firelight with Hubert Rusk, breathing 'Tears, idle tears' as the light closes on a dark winter's evening; or Allingham at Pisa sitting with his bitter thoughts in the deserted Campo Santo, and repeating to himself those lines of Shelley's:

> *The sun is set; the swallows are asleep;*
> *The bats are flitting fast in the gray air;*
> *The slow, soft toads out of damp corners creep—*

In such situations, where the least shade of meaning counts for so much more than the bare terms of direct statement, criticism loses significance. Forrest Reid was no mystic, and had little sympathy with the mystical temperament, but, lying beyond expressive capacity of words or speech, which were no more than 'of ultimate things unuttered the frail screen', was something in his writing that can only, I think, be called transcendental.

For him the world of dreams was the real, the more satisfying world, the one which he most vividly apprehended. But it was, this world of dreams, an ideal world as well. And in the convex mirror which it held up to his imagination he saw reflected and gathered together all his own longings and desires. He saw, most clearly of all, the beauty of youth, in nature and in art, its sadness and its cruel ephemerality:

> *Youth, and prime, and life, and time,*
> *For ever, ever fled away.*

These mirrored images he came in due course, though not without struggle, to recognize for mirages, ever beckoning forward the dusty traveller to an oasis gleaming and shimmering at the horizon's edge. And so, sharing the common experience of humanity, of 'hope constantly renewed and constantly sinking into disillusionment', he turned aside to art; and there, stretching the delicate threads of an ideal world, he spun the fabric of his writings. And this is perhaps the most apposite place to mention a project which at one time was never far absent from his mind, the project of a realistic novel. It is difficult to speak about *The Green Avenue* (for that was to have been its title) without knowledge of the plot; because although in Forrest Reid's mind the book was much more than a mere literary day-dream, more precisely formulated, nothing was ever put down on paper.[1] But enough is known to make it clear that the novel would have stood apart from all the published work, would have made a very different effect on his readers. *The Green Avenue* (if it had been written) *might* have shocked. Certainly the theme dealt with a moral and emotional problem which requires, even today, great courage to handle; or perhaps it was fear of ridicule, or worse, misunderstanding, which held him back; but whatever his motive may have been, his closest friends realized that until the ideas behind this unwritten book had been given some expression, Forrest Reid's work was, however seemingly complete, in a private sense always unfinished.

So in the books, 'real' life came to be a transcript of the life he led in dreams, and in this shadow-land the boys in the novels live. 'They that are awake have one world in common, but of the sleeping each turns aside into a world of his own.' The words of old Herakleitos were very real ones for Forrest Reid. Young Tom scarcely knew whether the angel who appeared to him in broad sunshine that day at Glenagivney was a real angel or a dream angel, and for us it really does not greatly matter; for Gamelyn, with his fishing-rod and his cress-lined basket of trout, his beauty that 'seemed to shine through his rags', is only, after all, a physical symbol of that imaginative world which, though unseen by mor-

[1] Stephen Gilbert writes: 'I'm not sure in what period Forrest Reid thought about *The Green Avenue*. I would imagine the late twenties and early thirties. By the time *Young Tom* came along it had been given up. Probably it was abandoned at some time between the publication of *Brian Westby* and *The Retreat*.'

tal eyes, was always the 'real' world to Forrest Reid, and the one to which he so readily 'turned aside'. The little boy in 'The Truant', lost in reverie on the river bank, can drift as easily into the dreaming as into the waking world:

' . . . he let his mind slip away into a magical world. . . . The hot sunshine was lovely; he could feel it even where he was lying in the broken, dappled shadow of the beech: it was like a warm sea in which he floated. He loved it; he loved all the beautiful things around him; he loved the earth, and the river, and the trees, and the sky. . . .

'He repeated a poem he had learned at school—about a Lady of Shalott. . . . The pictures swam up to him as through a deep green water, then sank away again and were lost. He opened his eyes wider. A bright light lay over everything, and an imaginary scene took the place of the actual scene before him. He saw a countryside rich with green grass and wild flowers. He saw red sleepy poppies and blue cornflowers, and ripe fields of bending barley. He saw the beauty of the earth—of silver streams and green woods . . . and somehow he knew that from all these things the strength of his life had been drawn; and he worshipped the spirit of the earth—worshipped with an unconscious adoration and a conscious delight—as he surrendered his mind and soul to the joy of the passing hour. . . .

'With his penknife he cut off a lock of his crisp brown hair and threw it to the river—a gift, or a sacrifice . . . he sat on the bank watching his brown lock of hair floating on and on, borne by a swift current, in and out, past little islands from which water-rats peeped out with bright eyes, past old grey crumbling bridges, past mossy stones and scarlet-and-blue weirs, past smooth lawns and ripening cornfields, and meadows, and woods—on and on, down and down.'

The truant, tranced with the beauty of the summer scene, sinks deeper and deeper into his reverie, a reverie which slides, imperceptibly, into a dream. And because that dream is surely one of the loveliest things Forrest Reid ever wrote, I am going to repro-

duce it here as my final illustration of his art. It is really a miniature fairy-story, but so diaphanous is it, so slight in its beauty, that
it seems to the reader to be no more than a mirage conjured up by
the warmth and the richness of that perfect day, brief as the
flicker of a butterfly's wings or the rainbow flash of a kingfisher
against a green shady stream:

' . . . the river at last widened out into a shallow pool, and in
this pool some young girls were bathing; and one of them was a
princess and the others were her maidens. The lock of hair reached
the pool and was floating away when the princess saw it. She lifted
it out of the water and hid it from the others, while they, laughing
and calling, continued to splash the bright glittering water to the
sky.

'The princess hurried to the bank, and ran up the wide marble
stairs to the palace, and hurried to her own room. Then, when she
had dressed herself, she put the hair in her bosom, and all day
long till nightfall it lay upon her warm breast like a bird brooding
on its own happiness. But in the night, when she was alone, and
not a sound disturbed the stillness, she took the hair from its secret
hiding-place, and laid it upon her pillow where the moonlight
touched it. And the princess knew that it was a boy's hair. She
looked at it as it lay so brown on her white pillow, and from its
beauty she created this boy's beauty, and as she kissed it the hair
began to sing.

'It sang a love song: it called her out into the woods, and she
obeyed its call. She took one thread of the hair, and it gave her
light, and guided her through the palace. The locked doors
opened of themselves when she laid the single thread of hair
against them. They swung back noiselessly on their heavy hinges
and closed noiselessly behind her. The boat into which she
stepped unmoored itself from the bank as she laid the thread of
hair upon it, and glided swiftly upstream to the enchanted forest.
And he—he watched it all, and was waiting in the moonlight
beside the river when the boat drew in to the bank and the princess stepped ashore. He saw her childish beauty and the love in her

eyes. He opened his arms and she came to him; and they stood like that, cheek by cheek. . . .'

(*Retrospective Adventures*: 'The Truant', pp. 266–8.)

In this parable, as one reader interprets it, lies the clue to the whole matter. The books are the pursuit of reality conceived in terms of illusion; of art for life's sake. For what gives beauty its chief, its sharpest value, is just our knowledge that, behind everything else, our passionate response to it is but 'a protest of the personality against the realization of its final extinction'. For 'in contemplating the light come and go upon the façade of a building, the moon setting behind St. Mary's spire outside my window . . . or seeing the blue sky through the apple-blossom of my childhood, in that very moment it seemed that time stood still, that for a moment time was held up and one saw experience as through a rift across the flow of it, a shaft into the universe.'[1] Differently expressed, this was very much Forrest Reid's own position.

And that, perhaps, is as far as any of us can get. 'Heart-mysteries' here, no doubt; 'and yet'—Forrest Reid could say with Yeats—

> . . . and yet when all is said
> It was the dream itself enchanted me:
> Character isolated by a deed
> To engross the present and dominate memory.[2]

From this point understanding can go forward; but here criticism must halt.

In the pages of Forrest Reid's books art has arrested the hand of time and illusion has cheated reality. Or, rather, 'players and painted stage' of Yeats's poem are themselves 'reality'; because Tom Barber, and Denis Bracknel, and Grif and Peter Waring and the rest will continue to live in that familiar world for which they were created, a world full of sunlight and earth's loveliness, yet ever haunted by mystery and fringed with dream.

[1] A. L. Rowse, *A Cornish Childhood* (1942), pp. 17–18.
[2] 'The Circus Animals' Desertion' (*Last Poems and Plays*).

Appendix

A BIBLIOGRAPHY OF THE WRITINGS
OF FORREST REID

Among the papers left by Forrest Reid at his death was
a checklist of his published writings—novels, criticism,
contributions to periodicals, and miscellaneous publications. These characteristically methodical notes, together with a
few items he evidently overlooked, form the basis of the present
bibliography. While I think the list is almost complete so far as
work published in this country and in Ireland is concerned, it is
possible that certain foreign (chiefly American) reprints and
articles in periodicals may have eluded me. They must, however,
be very few. But to avoid any misunderstanding, it should be
emphasized that this bibliography is not a formal one; my only
object has been to assemble in the most convenient form all the
available information about Forrest Reid's work which is likely
to be of interest or value to his readers. A good deal of material
which would have had perforce to figure in a list drawn up in
strict form, has therefore been omitted.

Perhaps a word should be added with regard to the dedications.
It is not the normal practice for these to be included in a bibliography; but here it seemed justified because the dedications of
Forrest Reid's books were usually the expression of real spiritual
debts. They were never formal. Often the recipient played some
part, directly or indirectly, actively or passively, in the shaping or
the background of the book; so becoming involved with its
development in a very intimate fashion.

BOOKS BY FORREST REID

1. THE KINGDOM OF TWILIGHT   1904

London: T. Fisher Unwin. *The First Novel Library.* MCMIV
(Printed at Edinburgh.)

Cr. 8vo. 7¾ × 5. pp. [x +] 306.

Volume IX in Fisher Unwin's series.

Dedication: FOR/ANDREW RUTHERFORD

Published in April, price six shillings.

The correct binding, a square one, is in pale green cloth, 'but
some copies were bound in brown cloth [this binding is a
better one] for Smith's and Mudie's'.

The front cover of the former is lettered in dark green, thus:
THE/KINGDOM OF/TWILIGHT/FORREST REID//
[decorative design 2¾ × 1¾, *enclosing*] The/First/Novel/
Library//

There is also a decorative publisher's device, 3¼ × 1¾, in the
centre of the back cover.

The spine-lettering (also in green) reads: THE FIRST/NOVEL/
LIBRARY/THE/KINGDOM/OF/TWILIGHT/FOR-
REST REID// T. FISHER/UNWIN

Part of the half-title, title-page, etc., are printed in green.

2. THE GARDEN GOD. *A Tale of Two Boys*   1905

London: David Nutt. (Printed at Edinburgh.)

4to. 8¾ × 7. pp. [xiv +] 103.

Dedication: TO/HENRY JAMES/THIS SLIGHT TOKEN/ OF
RESPECT/AND ADMIRATION

Published in November, price fifteen shillings. Second impression, April 1906, price six shillings.

The first impression is in limp white parchment covers, t.e.g., and
sometimes has a white silk book-marker. At top of front
cover, in gilt: THE . GARDEN . GOD [half-row of five

ornamental devices] At foot: [row of nine ornamental devices] FORREST REID

Gilt spine-lettering, reading: [ornamental device] THE [ornamental device]/GARDEN/[ornamental device] GOD [ornamental device]/FORREST/[Another ornamental device] REID [the same ornamental device]//NUTT

3. THE BRACKNELS. *A family chronicle*   1911

London: Edward Arnold.

Cr. 8vo. 7½ × 5. pp. [iv +] 304 + 8 pp. adverts.

Published in October, price six shillings.

Bound in pale grey cloth, with ornamental black lettering on front cover: The/Bracknels//Forrest Reid—and also on spine, thus: The/Bracknels/ Forrest/Reid//Arnold

4. FOLLOWING DARKNESS   1912

London: Edward Arnold.

Cr. 8vo. 7¾ × 5. pp. [iv +] 320 + 8 pp. adverts.

Dedication: To E. M. F[orster].

Published in October, price six shillings.

Bound in pale grey cloth with, at top of front cover, in black lettering: FOLLOWING/DARKNESS/ } [ornamental design]. And on spine: FOLLOWING/DARKNESS/ FORREST/REID//ARNOLD

5. THE GENTLE LOVER. *A comedy of middle age*   1913

London: Edward Arnold.

Cr. 8vo. 7½ × 5. pp. [viii +] 319.

Dedication: To MAC [John McBurney.]

Published in October, price six shillings.

Bound in buff-coloured cloth, with ornamental designs blind-stamped on front cover and spine, and with decorative black lettering on front cover: *The Gentle/Lover//Forrest*

Reid—and also on spine, thus: *The/Gentle/Lover/Forrest/Reid//*Arnold

6. W. B. YEATS. *A critical study* 1915

London: Martin Secker MCMXV *and* New York: Dodd, Mead and Co., 1915.

Demy 8vo. 9 × 5¾. pp. [11 –] 258 + [ii] + 16 pp. adverts. [None in American edition.] (English and American editions printed at Plymouth.)

Dedication: TO/BASIL DE SELINCOURT

With a frontispiece photograph of Yeats, and a bibliography.

Published in October, price seven shillings and sixpence.

Bound in black cloth, t.e.g., with, at top of front cover: W. B. YEATS/A . CRITICAL . STUDY . BY/FORREST . REID/[triangular ornamental design]; the whole in gilt lettering and surrounded by two gilt rules ¼ inch from edges of front cover. Gilt lettering on spine thus: [double rule] /W. B/YEATS/./FORREST/REID// MARTIN SECKER/ [double rule]

7. AT THE DOOR OF THE GATE 1915

London: Edward Arnold *and* Boston and New York: Houghton Mifflin Co., 1916. (English edition printed at Guildford; American edition printed at The Riverside Press, Cambridge.)

Cr. 8vo. 7¾ × 5. (American edition 7½ × 5.) pp. viii + [2 –] 332 + [i +] 8 pp. adverts. [None in American edition.]

Dedication: TO/WALTER DE LA MARE

Published in September, price six shillings.

Bound in dark blue cloth (American edition in dark green cloth) with, in gilt lettering on front cover, at top left corner: At the/Door of/the/Gate/Forrest/Reid—the whole enclosed in a square of gilt rules. On spine: At the/Door of/the/Gate/Forrest/Reid [similarly enclosed in a square of gilt rules]//ARNOLD ['Arnold' enclosed in a rectangle of gilt rules.]

8. THE SPRING SONG — 1916

London: Edward Arnold *and* Boston and New York: Houghton
Mifflin Co., 1917. (American edition printed at The River-
side Press, Cambridge.)

Cr. 8vo. 7½ × 5. pp. viii + 312.

Published in October, price six shillings.

Bound in bright green (sometimes ribbed) cloth with, in bold
black lettering on front cover: THE SPRING SONG/FOR-
REST REID The same on spine, thus: THE/SPRING/
SONG/FORREST/REID//ARNOLD

American edition bound in coffee-coloured cloth, with ornate
rectangular device (6 × 3¾) on front cover containing lettering, thus: THE/SPRING SONG/*By*/*Forrest Reid* Small
flower device on spine between title and author's name.

9. A GARDEN BY THE SEA. *Stories and Sketches* — 1918

Dublin: The Talbot Press Ltd.; London: T. Fisher Unwin Ltd.
(Printed at Dublin.)

Cr. 8vo. 7¼ × 4¾. pp. viii + 152.

Dedication: TO/KENNETH HAMILTON

Published in January 1919, price three shillings and sixpence.

Bound in stout sage-green boards, gilt lettering on front cover:
A GARDEN/BY THE SEA—and, at the foot, Forrest
Reid's signature in facsimile, also gilt. Unpolished oatmeal-
coloured cloth spine, with white paper label reading:
[double rule]/ A / GAR / DEN / BY / THE / SEA/[rule]/
REID/[double rule]—black lettering.

Contains:

In Memoriam [a poem; dedicated to S. J. Ireland]	1916
A Garden by the Sea	1914
Courage	1914
The Truant	1918
Kenneth	1918

* The Reconciliation
  The Accomplice
  An Ulster Farm   1913
  The Special Messenger   1914
* A Boy and His Dog   1918
  Costello's Story
  An Ending   1914
* A Trial of Witches   1911
  Autumn [a poem]   1911
             1916

   * Not reprinted in the later *Retrospective Adventures.*

10. PIRATES OF THE SPRING   1919

Dublin: The Talbot Press Ltd.; London: T. Fisher Unwin Ltd. *and* Boston and New York: Houghton Mifflin Co., 1920. (English edition printed at Edinburgh.)

Cr. 8vo. 7¼ × 4¾. (American edition 7½ × 5.) pp. [iv +]356.

Dedication: TO/R. J. WRIGHT

Published in March 1920, price seven shillings.

Bound in blue cloth (American edition in light green cloth), blind-stamped on front cover: PIRATES OF THE SPRING// FORREST REID Gilt spine-lettering, thus: PIRATES/OF THE / SPRING / FORREST / REID // THE TALBOT / PRESS LTD Front cover of American edition has title and author stamped in gilt in a shield device (2 × 4½) at top of cover, thus: PIRATES OF/THE SPRING/BY FORREST REID/

There also appears to be an edition with the imprint: Dublin/The Phoenix Publishing/Company, Limited/[n.d.] This has identical pagination with the normal edition, but has 'The Library of Modern Irish Fiction' imprinted on the front cover. There is a frontispiece, 'Palmer stirred the fire', by K. Maigment. *A Garden by the Sea* is also bound into the volume, the title-page bearing a publisher's imprint similar to the one quoted above. The pagination here is also identical with that in the separate edition.

11. PENDER AMONG THE RESIDENTS   1922

London: W. Collins Sons & Co. Ltd. *and* Boston and New York: Houghton Mifflin Co., 1923. (Printed at Glasgow.)

Cr. 8vo. 7½ × 5. pp. [vi +] 278 + iv pp. adverts. [None in American edition.]

Dedication: To/Mrs. Frank Workman

Published in November, price seven shillings and sixpence. The date of this book is given on the verso of the title-page, thus: Copyright 1922.

Bound in dark blue cloth (American edition in coffee-coloured cloth), with red lettering on front cover reading: PENDER AMONG/THE RESIDENTS/FORREST REID There is also a publisher's device in the bottom right corner; the whole being enclosed by a double red rule ¼ inch from edges of front cover.

Spine-lettering also in red, thus: [double rule]/PENDER/ AMONG THE/RESIDENTS/[small device]/FORREST/ REID//[publisher's device]/COLLINS/[double rule]

12. APOSTATE   1926

London: Constable & Co Ltd *and* Boston and New York: Houghton Mifflin Co., 1926.

Demy 8vo. 9× 5¾. pp. [iv+] [3 –] 235.

Published in June, price ten shillings and sixpence.

There is also a special signed edition, bound in white cloth, t.e.g., of which fifty copies were printed. This limited edition was issued in April at a price of forty-two shillings. *Apostate* was reprinted as No. 3 of Constable's *Miscellany* in July 1928.

The book is dated as being written between November 1923 and April 1925.

Ordinary edition bound in brown cloth, t.e.g., with gilt spine-lettering: APOSTATE/ . /FORREST/REID//

12a. APOSTATE

1947

London: Faber and Faber. (Printed at Edinburgh.)

Demy 8vo. 8¾ × 5½. pp. [7 –] 177.

A reissue, without alteration, of the 1926 edition. There are eight
wood engravings, seven in the form of vignetted chapter-
headings, by Reynolds Stone. The text has been reset.

Published in February, price ten shillings and sixpence.

Bound in light grey cloth, t.e. blue, with gilt lettering, reading
from top to bottom of spine: APOSTATE FORREST
REID * FABER—'APOSTATE' is printed on a thin
rectangle of blue cloth, which has a gilt surround.

13. DEMOPHON. *A traveller's tale*

1927

[London:] W. Collins Sons & Co. Ltd. MCM XXVII

Post 8vo. 8 × 5½. pp. [13 –] 270.

Dedication: *To/J. S. R*[utherford]./*In Affectionate Token of a/Long
Friendship*

Published in September, price seven shillings and sixpence.

Dated as being written between September 1925 and November
1926.

Bound in brown buckram, with gilt spine-lettering, thus: DEMO-
PHON/ ○ ○ /FORREST/REID//COLLINS The design
facing the title-page is reproduced from an amphora in the
British Museum.

14. ILLUSTRATORS OF THE SIXTIES

1928

London: Faber & Gwyer Limited.

Cr. 4to. 10¼ × 7¾. pp. xv + 295.

Published in October, price sixty-three shillings.

With index, etc., and ninety-one illustrations, mostly full-page.
The quality of reproduction is high.

There are two bindings: one in light green buckram, the other in dark green cloth, both t.e.g. There is a small Arthur Hughes design stamped in gold at the top of the front cover. Gilt spine-lettering, reading: ILLUSTRATORS / OF THE / SIXTIES/[star]/FORREST/REID//FABER & FABER

15. WALTER DE LA MARE. *A critical study*   1929

London: Faber & Faber Limited *and* New York: Henry Holt and
     Co., n.d. [1929]

Post 8vo. 8¼ × 5½. pp. [11 –] 256.

Dedication: TO/J. N. HART

With a frontispiece photograph of de la Mare; and an index.

Published in May, price ten shillings and sixpence.

Dated as being written between September 1928 and January
     1929.

There appear to be two formats of this book. One is bound in
     yellow cloth with a paper spine-label, printed in black:
     Walter/de la Mare/A Critical/Study/*/Forrest/Reid/*Faber
     & Faber*—the whole enclosed in a rectangular three-ruled
     surround. The other edition is bound in green cloth with gilt
     spine-lettering: WALTER/DE LA/MARE/A CRITICAL/
     STUDY / [asterisk] / FORREST / REED [sic] / / FABER
     AND/FABER

The American edition is in grey boards with a brown cloth spine.

16. UNCLE STEPHEN   1931

London: Faber & Faber Limited.

Cr. 8vo. 7¾ × 5. pp. [7 –] 340.

Dedication: TO/ARTHUR GREEVES

Published in October, price seven shillings and sixpence. A Cheap
     Edition was brought out in 1935, and the book was (after
     some revision) reissued in 1945. The new edition was a book
     of 256 pp.

Dated as being written between August 1929 and April 1931.

Bound in dark red cloth (top edge also red), with gilt spine-lettering: Uncle/Stephen/*by*/Forrest/Reid// Faber &/Faber

There is a German edition, *Onkel Stephen*, translated by Hans R. Dufour. (Braunschweig: Löwen-Verlag GmbH. 1947. 385 pp.)

17. BRIAN WESTBY   1934

London: Faber & Faber Limited *and* Toronto: Ryerson Press, 1934.[1] (Printed at Cambridge.)

Cr. 8vo. $7\frac{3}{4} \times 5$. pp. [11 –] 298.

Dedication: TO/STEPHEN GILBERT

Published in February, price seven shillings and sixpence.

Dated as being written between January 1932 and September 1933.

Bound in light green cloth, with red spine-lettering, thus: *Brian/ Westby/by/Forrest/Reid//Faber and/Faber*

18. THE RETREAT; *or*, *The Machinations of Henry*   1936

London: Faber and Faber *and* Toronto: Ryerson Press, 1936. (Printed at Plymouth.)

Cr. 8vo. $7\frac{3}{4} \times 5$. pp. [9 –] 299.

Dedication: To/KNOX [S. Knox Cunningham.]

Published in March, price seven shillings and sixpence. Reissued in England in 1946. The new edition was a book of 208 pp.

Dated as being written between January 1934 and October 1935.

Bound in dark red cloth, with gilt spine-lettering, thus: The/ Retreat/*by*/Forrest/Reid//Faber and/Faber

19. PETER WARING   1937

London: Faber and Faber Limited *and* Toronto: Ryerson Press, 1937. (Printed at Plymouth.)

[1] The Ryerson Press acted as representatives in Canada of Messrs. Faber & Faber; the edition was not an independent reprint and the books did not appear under their imprint. The same applies to Nos. 18-21.

Cr. 8vo. 7¾ × 5. pp. [11 –] 374.

Dedication: To/E. M. FORSTER/now as then

Published in September, price seven shillings and sixpence.

This is a revised and largely rewritten version of the novel *Following Darkness*, first published in 1912. Forrest Reid wished it 'to be regarded as a new book'.

Peter Waring has been three times reprinted: by the Albatross (Volume 378 of the Modern Continental Library; pp. 279) in 1938; by the Reader's Union (London—in conjunction with Messrs. Faber & Faber) in 1939; and by Penguin Books Ltd., of Harmondsworth, Middlesex (No. 551; pp. [9 –] 253 + 3 pp. adverts.) in November 1946, price one shilling. Of this latter edition approximately one hundred thousand copies were printed.

The original edition was bound in dark red cloth, with gilt spine-lettering, thus: PETER/WARING/[small design]/Forrest/Reid//Faber and/Faber

20. PRIVATE ROAD   1940

London: Faber and Faber Ltd *and* Toronto: Ryerson Press, 1940. (Printed at Glasgow.)

Demy 8vo. 8¾ × 5¾. pp. [11 –] 243.

A book of autobiographical reminiscence, in some sort a continuation of the earlier *Apostate*.

Published in May, price ten shillings and sixpence.

Dated as being written from 'January–December, 1939'.

Bound in brown cloth, with gilt spine-lettering: PRIVATE/ROAD/ . /FORREST/REID//FABER AND/FABER

21. RETROSPECTIVE ADVENTURES   1941

London: Faber and Faber Limited *and* Toronto: Ryerson Press, 1941. (Printed at Plymouth.)

Demy 8vo. 8¾ × 5½. pp. [15 –] 286.

Published in June, price twelve shillings and sixpence.

Bound in brown cloth, with gilt spine-lettering thus: [two gilt
rules]/RETRO-/SPECTIVE/ADVEN-/TURES/[two gilt
rules]/FORREST/REID/[two gilt rules]//FABER AND/
FABER

Most of the articles in *Retrospective Adventures* had been first published elsewhere; all were revised before this appearance in
book form, and occasionally two or three articles were re-
fashioned into one.

Contains:

* In Memoriam [a poem]   1916

BOOKS AND WRITERS

Andrew Lang and '*Longman's Magazine*'	1938
Master Romney Robinson	1924
Emily Brontë	1920
Minor Fiction in the Eighteen-Eighties	1930

Originally published in *The Eighteen-Eighties*:
essays by Fellows of The Royal Society of
Literature. (Cambridge: The University Press, 1930.)

Some Reflections on '*A Midsummer Night's Dream*'	1924
Henry James	1914–20
W. D. Howells	1919
Hugh Lofting and the Nursery Shelf	1923–27
W. H. Hudson	1918–24
The Poet's Bestiary	1928

A review of Norman Douglas's *Birds and Beasts
of the Greek Anthology*.

Arthur Rimbaud	1924
Persuasion	1930

An introduction to the World's Classics edition
of Jane Austen's novel.

Stella Benson	1924–40
The Host of the Air	1920

A review of Lady Gregory's *Visions and Beliefs
in the West of Ireland*.

The Letters of Katherine Mansfield	1928
Richard Garnett	1925
Arthur Lyon Raile	1928
Seumas O'Kelly	1920

MISCELLANEOUS ESSAYS

* A Garden by the Sea	1914
Stephen Gooden: an iconographical note	1930
Bruges	1915
* Kenneth	1918

TALES

* The Special Messenger	1918
* The Accomplice	1913
Breeze	1927
* Courage	1914
The White Kitten	1924
* An Ending	1911
* The Truant	1918
* An Ulster Farm	1914
* Costello's Story	1914
* Autumn [a poem]	1916

* Reprinted from *A Garden by the Sea* (1918).

22. NOTES AND IMPRESSIONS   1942

Newcastle, Co. Down: The Mourne Press. MCMXLII

Slim Cr. 8vo. $7\frac{1}{2} \times 5$. pp. [11 –] 62.

Price four shillings.

Bound in thin, light green boards with semi-decorative black
lettering on front cover, reading: NOTES AND/IMPRES-
SIONS/FORREST REID Same lettering on spine, reading
from bottom to top: NOTES and IMPRESSIONS [small
scroll design] FORREST REID

All the six essays comprising this book had appeared previously
in one or other of the following periodicals: *The Irish Statesman, The Nation and the Athenaeum, The New Statesman, The
Spectator.*

Contains:

Shakespeare's Lyrical Plays
A Note on Caliban   1924
The Owl of Minerva   1920
Arthur Machen   1922
Phil May   1932
Notes on Novels [Reprinted reviews.]

23. POEMS FROM THE GREEK ANTHOLOGY *translated by Forrest Reid*   1943

London: Faber and Faber Ltd. (Printed at Glasgow.)

Post 8vo. 8¼ × 5¼. pp. [7 –] 72.

Published in November, price five shillings.

Bound in light blue cloth, with gilt spine-lettering reading from
top to bottom of spine: *Poems from the Greek Anthology.
Forrest Reid Faber*

24. YOUNG TOM; *or, Very Mixed Company*   1944

London: Faber and Faber Ltd. (Printed at Bristol.)

Cr. 8vo. 7½ × 5. pp. [5 –] 169.

Published in May, price seven shillings and sixpence. It was
reissued in England in a cheaper edition in 1950.

Dated as being written between November 1942 and October
1943.

Bound in dark red cloth, with gilt lettering reading from top to
bottom of spine: YOUNG TOM FORREST REID
FABER In the cheaper edition a picture wrapper replaces
the plain candy-pink one used for the first issue; otherwise
the format is identical.

There is a German edition, *Der Kleine Tom, oder, Sehr Gemischte
Gesellschaft*, translated by Friedrich Wall. (Braunschweig:
Löwen-Verlag GmbH. 1947. 256 pp.) There are seven illus-
trations by Ilse Meister-Zeyen.

25. THE MILK OF PARADISE. *Some thoughts
    on Poetry*   1946

London: Faber and Faber Ltd. (Printed at Glasgow.)

Post 8vo. 8¼ × 5. pp. [7 –] 80.

Published in August, price six shillings.

Bound in blue cloth, with gilt lettering reading from top to
    bottom of spine: THE MILK OF PARADISE FORREST
    REID F & F By an error, the book's title was printed on
    the dust-wrapper as 'Milk of Paradise'.

26. DENIS BRACKNEL   1947

London: Faber and Faber Ltd.

Cr. 8vo. 7½ × 5. pp. [9 –] 253.

Dedication: To/DOREEN SHERIDAN

Published in September, price nine shillings and sixpence.

A rewritten version of the novel *The Bracknels*, first published in
    1911. 'The theme remains, but from first to last it has been
    so completely rewritten that the result is practically a new
    book.' The book appeared posthumously.

Bound in blue cloth, with decorative gilt spine-lettering: Denis/
    Bracknel/ Forrest/Reid//Faber

ARTICLES IN PERIODICALS, ETC.

1905

The Exhibition of Pictures at the Royal Hibernian Academy,
    Dublin [The Lane Collection], *Ulad*. Volume 1, No. 2. Feb-
    ruary, pp. 20–23. Not reprinted.

Pan's Pupil, *Ulad*. Volume 1, No. 3. May, pp. 17–19. A short
    story, perhaps in subject showing the influence of E. M.
    Forster. Not reprinted.

Ernest Dowson, *Monthly Review*. June, pp. 107–13. Not
    reprinted.

1906

Emily Brontë, *Northern Whig* (Belfast). 2 June. Not reprinted.

1908

Prose Studies, *Christ's College Magazine* [Cambridge]. Volume XXII, No. 66 (Lent Term, 1908), pp. 71–6. (Printed at Cambridge Univ. Press.) Contains: The Old Barge (reprinted in *Private Road*), After Nicias and After Plato (reprinted in *Poems from the Greek Anthology*), Hyde Park and In Westminster Abbey and Edgar Poe and Tapestries in the Cluny Museum (not reprinted).

1909

The Novels of George Moore, *Westminster Review*. August, pp. 200–8. Not reprinted.

1911

Sir Thomas Browne and a Trial of Witches, *Westminster Review*. February, pp. 197–202. Reprinted in *A Garden by the Sea*.

The Exhibition of Pictures in the Free Library, Belfast, *Northern Whig*. 4 August. Not reprinted.

An Ending, *English Review*. April, pp. 60–6. Reprinted in *A Garden by the Sea* and *Retrospective Adventures*.

Modern Picture Galleries: a lecture, *Evening Telegraph* (Belfast). 27 November and 29 November. Not reprinted.

1912

The Early Work of Mr. W. B. Yeats, *Irish Review*. January (Volume 1, No. 11), pp. 529–36. Partly reprinted in *W. B. Yeats: A Critical Study* (1915).

The Boy in Fiction, *Morning Post*. 29 October. Not reprinted.

1913

The Accomplice, *Morning Post*. 9 September, p. 5. Reprinted in *A Garden by the Sea* and *Retrospective Adventures*.

1915

Bruges, *Irish Monthly*. May. Reprinted in *Retrospective Adventures*.

1916

Costello's Story, *in* The Thistle Souvenir Book in aid of Scottish Women's Hospitals for Foreign Service, pp. 76–8. Printed and published by John Horn Limited, Glasgow [1916]. Forrest Reid stated in *A Garden by the Sea* that this story was also published in *The Irishman* and *The New Weekly*. The latter (edited by R. A. Scott-James) was suspended in August 1914 after twenty-three weekly issues. *The Irishman* was published from 1916 to 1919. 'Costello's Story' does not appear in either of these. Probably Forrest Reid's article was due to appear in one or other of them at a date subsequent to the suspension of publication. In *Retrospective Adventures* the story is dated 1914. Reprinted there and in *A Garden by the Sea*.

By the Nursery Fire [A poem], *The Irishman*. 15 January.

Henry James, *Northern Whig*. 4 March. Not reprinted.

Henry James, *The Irishman*. 5 March. Not reprinted.
Two articles written on the occasion of Henry James's death.

Courage, *Country Life*. 27 May. Reprinted in *A Garden by the Sea* and *Retrospective Adventures*. In Forrest Reid's checklist this story is placed under 1914. I cannot find any earlier appearance than the *Country Life* article. Forrest Reid's date may refer to the year it was written.

In Memoriam [A poem], *Northern Whig*.[1] Reprinted in *A Garden by the Sea* and *Retrospective Adventures*.

Kenneth, *Saturday Westminster Gazette*. 1 June. Reprinted in *A Garden by the Sea* and *Retrospective Adventures*.

An Ulster Farm, *English Review*. June, pp. 487–91. Reprinted in *A Garden by the Sea* and *Retrospective Adventures*. Forrest Reid dates this story to 1914, but this is the earliest record I have been able to trace of its appearance in print.

A Naturalist's Boyhood, *Saturday Westminster Gazette*. 26 October. Reprinted as 'W. H. Hudson' in *Retrospective Adventures*.

---

[1] This is the reference given in Forrest Reid's checklist. I have not, however, been able to trace the poem in the *Northern Whig* for that year.

1917

A Garden by the Sea, *in* The Thistle Souvenir Book (No. 2). In aid of N.U.W.S.S. [National Union of Women's Suffrage Societies] Scottish Women's Hospitals for Foreign Service, pp. 51–3. [Printed and published by John Horn Ltd., Glasgow and London.] [1917.] Reprinted in *A Garden by the Sea* and *Retrospective Adventures*. Part of this story was used in a chapter of *The Spring Song* (1916).

1919

W. D. Howells, *Irish Statesman*. 27 September and 4 October. Reprinted in *Retrospective Adventures*.

The Visitors, *Irish Statesman*. 25 October. *Living Age* (Boston). 6 December, pp. 604–7. A short story; not reprinted.

Seumas O'Kelly, *Irish Statesman*. 6 December. Reprinted in *Retrospective Adventures*.

1920

The Poet as Naturalist, *Irish Statesman*. 17 January. Reprinted as 'W. H. Hudson' in *Retrospective Adventures*.

Emily Brontë, *Irish Statesman*. 21 February and 28 February. Reprinted in *Retrospective Adventures*.

Poems Pleasant and Unpleasant, *Irish Statesman*. 6 March. Not reprinted; reviews of two recently published books of poetry.

Of Groves and Twilight and the Court of Mab, *Irish Statesman*. 27 March. Reprinted as 'Seumas O'Kelly' in *Retrospective Adventures*.

The Owl of Minerva, *Irish Statesman*. 17 April. Reprinted in *Notes and Impressions*.

The Letters of Henry James, *Daily Herald*. 28 April. Reprinted in *Retrospective Adventures*.

The Letters of Henry James, *Irish Statesman*. 15 May. Reprinted in *Retrospective Adventures*.

British Literature, *Times of Brazil*. 5 June. Printed in English with a translation into Spanish; not reprinted

University Literature, *Nation and Athenaeum*. 13 August. Not reprinted.

The Host of the Air, *Nation and Athenaeum*. 22 October. Reprinted in *Retrospective Adventures*.

1921

Orange Peel, *Nation and Athenaeum*. 30 April, pp. 168–9. A short story; not reprinted. Against the entry in Forrest Reid's checklist is the comment: 'Proof went astray and the text full of mistakes.'

In the Dark, *Saturday Westminster Gazette*. 8 October. Reprinted in *Apostate*.

The Perfect Novel, *Nation and Athenaeum*. 11 November. Reprinted in *Notes and Impressions*.

Arthur Machen, *Nation and Athenaeum*. 11 November. Reprinted in *Notes and Impressions*.

The Nursery Shelf, *Weekly Westminster Gazette*. 2 December. Not reprinted; but some of the material was used in the article 'Hugh Lofting and the Nursery Shelf', in *Retrospective Adventures*.

Ulster Players, *The Times*. 5 December. Not reprinted.

Ulster Painters, *The Times*. 5 December. Not reprinted.

1923

Retrospective Adventures, *Irish Statesman*. 27 October. Partly reprinted in *Apostate*.

Modern Irish Prose: The Novel, in *The Voice of Ireland*. A survey of the race and nation from all angles, by the foremost leaders at home and abroad. Edited by William G. Fitz-Gerald. John Heywood Ltd., Dublin, Manchester, London, and Blackburn. [Corrected edition: 1924.] Pp. 481–4. Not reprinted.

1924

Midsummer Night's Dream, *Irish Statesman*. 23 February. Reprinted in *Retrospective Adventures*.

W. H. Hudson, *Freeman's Journal*. 8 March. Reprinted in *Retrospective Adventures*.

Master Romney Robinson, *Irish Statesman.* 5 April. Reprinted in *Retrospective Adventures.*

Arthur Rimbaud, *Irish Statesman.* 9 August. Reprinted in *Retrospective Adventures.*

The White Kitten, *Nation and Athenaeum.* 11 October, pp. 51–2. This short story also appeared in a New Zealand journal, whose name has vanished; it was reprinted, with a tailpiece by S. R. Bolton, on pp. 10–12 of *An Ulster Garland* (Belfast: M'Caw, Stevenson & Orr, Ltd., 1928), and in *Retrospective Adventures.*

A Note on Caliban, *Ulster Review.* December. Reprinted in *Notes and Impressions.*

1925

Hopes for Ulster Literature, *Ulster Review.* January. Not reprinted.

The Sage and the Necromancer, *Irish Statesman.* 17 January. Reprinted as 'Richard Garnett' in *Retrospective Adventures.*

Apostate, *Irish Statesman.* 7 March. Reprinted in *Apostate.*

Belfast, *Ulster Review.* May. Reprinted in *Apostate.*

1926

W. B. Yeats, *Harmsworth's Encyclopaedia,* pp. 1851–6.

1928

Pagan Poetry, *Irish Statesman.* 14 April. Reprinted as 'Arthur Lyon Raile' in *Retrospective Adventures.*

The Poet's Bestiary [Norman Douglas's *Birds and Beasts of the Greek Anthology*], *Irish Statesman.* 5 May. Reprinted in *Retrospective Adventures.*

The Letters of Katherine Mansfield, *Irish Statesman.* 8 December. Reprinted in *Retrospective Adventures.*

1929

The Poetry of the Rose, *The Rose Annual* (National Rose Society), pp. 124–7. Not reprinted; a brief account of the symbolism of the rose in literature.

1930

Charles Keene, Illustrator, *Print Collector's Quarterly*. January, pp. 23–47. Illustrated. Not reprinted.

Persuasion [An introduction to the World's Classics Edition of Jane Austen's novel]. Reprinted in *Retrospective Adventures*.

Minor Fiction in the 'Eighties. In *The Eighteen-Eighties*: essays by Fellows of The Royal Society of Literature. Cambridge University Press. This essay was also reprinted in the *London Mercury* for October (pp. 515–29), and the New York *Bookman* for August (pp. 491–502). A separate offset limited to six copies was taken for the author.

1931

Breeze, *Saturday Review*. 23 May, pp. 754–5. A short story; reprinted in *Retrospective Adventures*, where the date (probably the date of composition) is given as 1927.

1932

The Line Engravings of Stephen Gooden, *Print Collector's Quarterly*. January, pp. 51–73. With twelve full-page reproductions of Stephen Gooden's work. The text reprinted in *Retrospective Adventures*, where the date is given as 1930.

Criticism and Reviewing, *Current Literature*. February. Not reprinted.

Phil May, *New Statesman*. 12 November. Reprinted in *Notes and Impressions*.

1934

The Artist and The World Today, *Bookman* (London). May, p. 93. Consists of his brief answers to three questions on this topic. Forrest Reid was asked to contribute along with a number of other contemporaries. There is a small photograph.

1935

Childhood and Children, *The Listener*. 8 May. Not reprinted; a review of Walter de la Mare's anthology *Early One Morning*.

1937

Wizard of Fonthill, *The Listener*. 10 March. Not reprinted; a review of Guy Chapman's *Beckford*.

Fiction [Fortnightly reviews of current fiction], *Spectator*. Forrest Reid's reviews appeared in the issues of 28 May; 11 and 25 June; 9 and 23 July; 6 and 20 August; 3 and 17 September; 1, 15, and 29 October; 12 and 26 November; and 10 December. Not reprinted.

1938

Andrew Lang and Longman's [Magazine], *London Mercury*. March, pp. 502–8. Reprinted in *Retrospective Adventures*.

Fiction [Fortnightly reviews of current fiction], *Spectator*. Forrest Reid's reviews appeared in the issues of 7 and 21 January; 4 and 18 February; 4, 18, and 25 March; 1, 15, and 29 April; 13 and 27 May; 10 June; 8 and 22 July; 5 and 19 August; 2, 16, and 30 September; 14 and 28 October; 11 and 25 November; and 9 and 23 December. Not reprinted.

1939

Fiction [Fortnightly reviews of current fiction], *Spectator*. Forrest Reid's reviews appeared in the issues of 13 and 27 January; 10 and 24 February; 10 and 24 March; 7 April; 5 and 19 May; 9 and 30 June; 14 and 28 July; 11 and 25 August; and 8 September. The articles stopped on the outbreak of war owing to the difficulty in getting books posted to Ireland. Not reprinted.

1942

Poems from the Greek Anthology [A selection], translated by Forrest Reid, *The Bell* (Dublin). Volume 4, No. 4. July, pp. 266–9.

In addition, the following unpublished pieces in typescript, among Forrest Reid's papers, are worth mentioning:

The Great Mr. Porson (dated 11 May 1942), 46 pp.

Furnished Apartments [see *Private Road*, p. 34].

Lewis Carroll and Tenniel, 33 pp.

Criticism, 8 pp.

BOOKS AND ARTICLES ABOUT FORREST REID

Forrest Reid. By E. M. Forster (1919). Reprinted in *Abinger Harvest* (Edward Arnold, 1936), pp. 75–80.

Forrest Reid. By S. M. Ellis. *The Bookman* (London). May 1920 (Volume LVIII, No. 344), pp. 65–6. With a (probably contemporary) photograph. Reprinted (without the photograph) in the author's *Mainly Victorian* (Hutchinson, 1924), pp. 343–6.

Pipes of Pan in Belfast. By Ernest Boyd. *New York Sunday Tribune*. Weekly Review of the Arts. 11 June 1922, p. 4.

The Achievement of Forrest Reid. By John Boyd. *Dublin Magazine*, 1945. July–September issue, pp. 18–24.

Forrest Reid: 1876–1947. By E. M. Forster. *The Listener* (London), 16 January 1947. An appreciation written on his death. Accompanied by a photograph of Forrest Reid with E. M. Forster. Reprinted (without the photograph) in the author's *Two Cheers for Democracy* (Arnold, 1951), under the title 'Forrest Reid', pp. 277–9.

Forrest Reid. By F. M. Godfrey. *Time and Tide* (London), 18 January 1947. A brief critical estimate.

Forrest Reid: An Introduction to His Work. By John Boyd. *Irish Writing*. The Magazine of Contemporary Irish Literature. Edited by David Marcus and Terence Smith. No. 4 (Cork, April 1948), pp. 72–7.

The Arts in Ulster. A symposium edited by Sam Hanna Bell, *etc.* (Harrap & Co., Ltd., 1951). The chapter 'Ulster Prose', by John Boyd, contains an estimate of Forrest Reid's work on pp. 111–16.

NOTES

Forrest Reid. A Critical Study. By John Boyd. 174 pp. There is a copy of this study among Forrest Reid's papers. It is in typescript, was written about 1945, and has never been published.

An obituary notice of Forrest Reid appeared in *The Times* on 7 January 1947: this was accompanied by a short appreciation from the hand of G[eorge]. H. P. B[uchanan]. There was a further brief tribute in the issue of 11 January by J. N. B[ryson].

The broadcast given by Mr. John Sparrow on 1 February 1947, a few weeks after Forrest Reid's death, has not been reprinted.

A five-minute talk to Northern Ireland listeners was given by Mr. Stephen Gilbert on 26 January 1947. This was printed as 'Forrest Reid—The Man', along with a short appreciation by Robert Lynd, in the Royal Belfast Academical Institution *School News* for Easter, 1947 (Vol. 55, no. CLXXV), pp. 54–8.

Forrest Reid. A critical appreciation of his work. By George Buchanan. A talk given on the Northern Ireland Home Service on 7 January 1948. No. 12 in the series *Writing in Ulster*. The text of this broadcast was largely composed of extracts from a special memorial talk given to the Belfast P.E.N. in 1947.

A Portrait of Forrest Reid. A broadcast discussion in which eleven of Forrest Reid's friends took part. Given on the Northern Ireland Home Service on 3 February 1952.

Forrest Reid was made an Honorary Doctor of Literature of the Queen's University, Belfast, in 1933; and was a member of the Irish Academy of Letters. *Young Tom* was awarded the James Tait Black Memorial Prize for the best work of fiction published during 1944.

There are two portraits of Forrest Reid: by Arthur Greeves (in the possession of the Royal Academical Institution, Belfast); and by J. S. Sleator, P.R.H.A. (in the Belfast Museum and Art Gallery). The latter painting is reproduced in *The Arts in Ulster* (see above).

INDEX

Note.—*This index does not include (save in one instance) references to characters in Forrest Reid's novels, or real persons, etc., referred to in the quotations made from Forrest Reid's books.*